# THE
# TOYOTA
# WAY
## *to* LEAN
# LEADERSHIP

# THE
# TOYOTA
# WAY
## *to* LEAN
# LEADERSHIP

### ACHIEVING AND SUSTAINING
### EXCELLENCE THROUGH
### LEADERSHIP DEVELOPMENT

## JEFFREY K. LIKER
## GARY L. CONVIS

New York  Chicago  San Francisco  Lisbon
London  Madrid  Mexico City  Milan  New Delhi
San Juan  Seoul  Singapore  Sydney  Toronto

1 2 3 4 5 6 7 8 9 0   DOC/DOC   1 6 5 4 3 2 1

ISBN 978-0-07-178078-0
MHID 0-07-178078-5

e-ISBN 978-0-07-178079-7
e-MHID 0-07-178079-3

McGraw-Hill books are available at special quantity discounts to use as premiums and sales promotions or for use in corporate training programs. To contact a representative, please e-mail us at bulksales@mcgraw-hill.com.

This book is printed on acid-free paper.

To my son Jesse, whose deep insight and sage advice shaped the entire theme of this book.
—Jeff Liker

To my wife, Deborah, who has been my strongest supporter throughout our wonderful life journey together.
—Gary Convis

# Contents

# Foreword

It is a bit difficult for outsiders to understand how precious the Toyota Way is within our company and the challenges of growing leaders who live our values. It is a constant journey to find new and better ways to develop Toyota leaders. For this reason I am pleased that Gary Convis and Dr. Jeffrey Liker chose to write this book. I knew Gary well when he was a great leader at NUMMI, and I had the opportunity to work with him. This was a period of intense learning for Toyota about how to teach our culture to others brought in from the outside. Dr. Liker has devoted himself to deeply understanding our way from the outside. I am really very impressed when I read his books by how well he explains the way we think.

In a speech I made shortly after becoming president in 2009 I vowed to be closest to the *gemba*. Whenever there are real objects there is a *gemba*. When customers drive our cars the *gemba* is how they are using our products and what works for them and what causes them difficulties. As the current leader of the company I must model the behavior I expect from others. Going to the *gemba* means observing firsthand how our products are being designed, built, used, and what problems we have. There are always problems because we are never perfect. The only way we can really understand the problems is at the *gemba*.

This takes me to the role of leadership at Toyota, the subject of this book. At Toyota we have always invested heavily in developing leaders who understand and live the principles and values of the company. We want our DNA to be encoded in every leader and every team member at every level of the company. We expect greatness from all of our people. We expect them to accept and conquer challenges that may seem overwhelming at first glance. The greatness in people comes out only when they are led by great leaders. We are all growing and learning, and we all need teachers and coaches to help guide us. We say at Toyota that every leader is a teacher developing the next generation of leaders. This is their most important job.

A real irony is that respect for people requires that people feel the pain of critical feedback. When team members share with us the results of their improvement activities we always say "show us the bad news first. What is it you still have problems with?" If we do not give people accurate feedback based on real behavior they are not growing and we are not respecting them. The job of a leader is not to put them in positions to fail, but to put them in challenging positions where they must work hard to succeed and still see how they could have been even better. Our goal is for *every* Toyota team member from the worker on the production floor to our most senior executives to be working to continuously improve themselves. We all need *sensei* who will guide us to the next level of achievement. I personally still have many *sensei* teaching me.

The explanation that Gary and Dr. Liker give of how we develop leaders is yet another opportunity for us in Toyota to reflect and learn. I hope their book gives you some ideas of value for you personally and your company.

Akio Toyoda
President, Toyota Motor Corporation

# Prologue

## Toyota as a Model in Light of a Period of Intense Challenges

This book is about making lean leaders, and it unabashedly uses Toyota as the model *par excellence* for lean leadership. We believe that the biggest gap in capabilities in the lean movement, and the root cause of the failure of many lean programs, is in leadership. As you'll see through the course of the book, lean leadership is quite different from the typical leadership models and managerial styles of Western companies (American or European)—or, for that matter, of most Japanese companies.

When we started writing this book in early 2008, looking at Toyota as a shining example of consistently excellent leadership would have been entirely uncontroversial. The company had been profitable for more than 50 consecutive years and had risen from obscurity to be the largest motor vehicle manufacturer in the world. Moreover, for many organizations, the Toyota Way had become a blueprint and a guide to excellence. As 2009 ended, however, an outside observer couldn't be blamed for wondering whether we should be looking at Toyota as a case study of failed leadership, not as a model to follow. As we were preparing this book for publication at the end of 2011, Toyota was still recovering from a third major blow in less than five years—

the Japanese earthquake and tsunami—and had not recovered the "invincible" aura it had enjoyed back in 2007.

Indeed, the news about Toyota, particularly early in 2010, would have led most people to conclude that Toyota had lost its way. Millions of cars recalled, claims of runaway vehicles, persistent rumors of serious defects being hidden or denied, admissions of failure and apologies from senior executives—all pointed to a company that was better suited to be a cautionary tale than an inspiration.

Given the existence of this book, you may not be surprised to hear that we think that Toyota is indeed still an inspiration today. That being said, we also think that there were some serious failures of leadership and leadership development at Toyota. In fact, we think that some departments of Toyota simply failed to live up to the Toyota Way in some of their actions and behaviors as the recall crisis unfolded. Those failures do not mean, though, that we can't learn important lessons from Toyota on how to make lean leaders. In fact, they mean that there is all the more to be learned. The conclusion of Toyota's efforts to reflect and learn from the various crises, efforts led by Akio Toyoda, was not that there were flaws in the Toyota Way, but rather that there were failures in following the Toyota Way. The recommended solution to these problems wasn't fundamental change but increased attention to fundamentals. In other words, the company needed (as always) to return to the basics of the Toyota Way.

As the Toyota Way teaches, there is much to be learned from failures—but only if the true failures and their root causes are identified and understood. And based on our combined more than 50 years of history working for or studying Toyota, our extensive contacts within the company, and other research that we've pursued, we've found that the real problems that Toyota encountered in the triple crises from 2007 to 2011 were quite different from the general perceptions of those problems in the media. A clear-eyed view of the problems and Toyota's ultimate responses to the crises that challenged admiration of the Toyota Way led us to believe that Toyota is as good a model for lean leadership as it ever has been, and perhaps better.

So before we launch into the book itself, let's take that clear-eyed view.[1]

# The Great Recession

The recession hit the automobile industry earlier than most other industries. Leading up to 2008, raw material prices, particularly steel, were skyrocketing. Then, early in the summer of 2008, oil prices shot up, reaching the highest levels they had ever been. It was enough of a shock to send sales of popular pickup trucks and large sport utility vehicles (SUVs) that consumed a lot of suddenly very expensive gasoline into a nose dive. Losing 40 percent or more of sales was common in the industry, and Toyota was no exception.

Dealing with a crisis caused by broad economic forces was not new to Toyota. In fact, the Toyota Production System (TPS) became famous in Japan during the 1973 oil crisis, when Japanese internal sales and exports plummeted, yet Toyota recovered to profitability much faster than other Japanese companies. Why? Toyota's efforts to eliminate overproduction and inventory via just-in-time production throughout the supply chain meant that it could quickly adapt as demand for fuel-efficient Toyotas increased in the United States. This dramatic success led to a movement to teach TPS throughout Japanese industry and eventually throughout the world.

The 2008 recession was different. For several years, Toyota's large trucks and SUVs had been selling more rapidly than they could be produced. The company had allowed inventories of these vehicles to creep up to meet the strong demand; it had even added significant new capacity for building trucks in the form of a new plant in San Antonio, Texas, dedicated to building Tundras. When the oil price spike caused demand to plummet, the problems of excess inventory and overcapacity became frighteningly apparent. Toyota made the difficult decision to stop all U.S. production of the Tundra and Sequoia SUVs for three months to allow inventory levels to adjust.

While overproduction leading to this shutdown revealed some weaknesses in following the Toyota Way, in the response to the recession, the company showed that it had not abandoned Toyota Way principles. Even though the plants were shut down for three months, team members were not laid off during the downtime.[2] Rather, the company invested in developing its people via training and *kaizen* activities. The great need for this training revealed that during the years of breakneck growth, the company had not been investing enough in developing team members. The training and *kaizen* in Toyota continued for many more months throughout the world as the global recession kicked in and demand plummeted for all vehicles.

Toyota's ability to invest in team members rather than laying off massive numbers of workers, as every other global automotive firm did during the recession, was based on another Toyota Way principle: self-reliance. Anticipating a phase of rapid growth after World War II, Toyota had allowed itself to become deeply indebted to finance investments. When growth was not as fast as planned, the company nearly went bankrupt. As a result the founder, Kiichiro Toyoda, was forced by the lenders to lay off workers, and then he resigned. The danger of relying on others for financing could not have been clearer. Since that time, the company has hoarded cash by being frugal even in the best of times so that it can be independent in the worst of times. That's what happened during the Great Recession. The company had huge cash reserves and very little debt. As a result, it could invest in team members and absorb large short-term losses. It could continue to build for the future while most other companies were focused simply on surviving the present. That doesn't mean that there wasn't cost-cutting. But the cost-cutting was distinctly different from the common stories during the recession. Executives cut their own compensation first—salary as well as bonuses—and reduced their own perks before asking workers to share the pain. Ultimately, there were no involuntary lay-offs in wholly owned Toyota Engineering and Manufacturing, though overtime, bonuses, and temporary labor were eliminated.

As a result of these forward-looking actions, the company survived the recession exceedingly well, returning to profitability quickly, with plants operating at even higher levels of quality, productivity, and safety than before the recession started. But then the recall crisis hit.

## The Recall Crisis

The natural place to begin the story is with the horrific crash of a Lexus driven by an off-duty California Highway Patrol officer in San

Diego in August 2009. Unlike the vast majority of crashes, what happened during this tragic accident, which cost four people their lives, was recorded via a telephone call to a 911 operator. The car in question was a loaner from a Lexus dealer (the family had dropped off its car for routine maintenance). While driving down a suburban highway, the driver lost control of the speed of the vehicle. The car would not slow down, but instead accelerated until it topped 110 miles per hour no matter what the driver tried to do. A passenger in the car called 911 seeking help as the car sped along out of control. Before a solution that would stop the vehicle could be found, it collided with a sports utility vehicle, shot over an embankment, and crashed, killing all four passengers and catching fire. Rampant speculation then began in the media that this was caused by electromagnetic interference that made the car's computer controls go haywire and accelerate the car out of control.

This set off investigations by newspapers, the National Highway Traffic Safety Administration (NHTSA, the government body that regulates highway safety), the U.S. Congress, and eventually NASA, which was contracted by NHTSA. The *Los Angeles Times* set up a special investigative team (presumably aiming for a Pulitzer Prize) to focus on Toyota and expose serious electronic problems leading to sudden unintended acceleration (SUA) by Toyota vehicles, problems that Toyota was purportedly covering up. The situation illustrates how facts can be confused, leading to snowballing rumors and even vicious attacks to satisfy the interests of individuals and organizations.

By now at least a few people have read the San Diego police report, or summaries of the report, which was completed in October 2009 and posted on the Internet, two months after the accident and three months before the crisis reached its most fevered pitch, but which did not get a great deal of media attention until much later. The thorough police investigation demonstrated beyond doubt that the real cause was human error in the dealership that loaned out the car. The dealership put the wrong all-weather floor mat, a too large one from an SUV that barely fit into the driver compartment of the loaner passenger car, and failed to secure it to the clips designed to hold the mat in place—completely violating clear standard operating procedures. The result, predictably, was an entrapped accelerator pedal. There was no defect in the original vehicle; instead, a defect was created by the dealer who prepared the car. NHTSA, Toyota, and Toyota contractor Exponent ultimately investigated case after case of purported SUA, and none had been the result of electronics problems; in almost all cases, the cause was human error—the driver pushing down on the accelerator pedal when he or she thought that it was the brake pedal. To prove to a doubting Congress that this was true, NHTSA even contracted NASA to do an independent investigation, the results of which were reported one year after the most heated period of the crisis. In February 2011, one year after the frenzy, Secretary of Transportation Ray LaHood summarized the results of the investigation in a press conference: "The verdict is in. There is no electronic-based cause for unintended high-speed acceleration in Toyotas. Period."

So everyone can walk away, go home, and forget that this misinformed attack on Toyota ever happened, right? Certainly Toyota could not do that. Errors made by Toyota were revealed; for example, a sticky pedal that was slow to return on a small number of cars (12 confirmed cases in the United States, out of more than 2 million sold); Prius brakes with software adjusted so that the ABS system kicked in at unusual times, creating a strange sensation and possibly leading the driver to apply too little pressure; and a Lexus SUV's traction control not being sensitive enough for a *Consumer Reports* test of driving into a sharp turn at 60 mph and suddenly taking your foot off the accelerator without applying the brakes. Fortunately, none of these issues caused any known accidents, but they were errors nonetheless.

Recall after recall made Toyota appear to be suffering from sudden quality and safety issues galore. Most of this was caused by Toyota's reaction. After it became clear how deep the crisis was, Toyota began recalling anything and everything, often before it had the time to investigate. For example, the Lexus that was criticized by *Consumer Reports* was recalled the same day the *CR* article came out. A closer look showed that this epidemic of recalls occurred only in the United States, and that all other auto companies caught the disease in 2010, when 600 separate recalls and service campaigns were reported by NHTSA, the most since 2004.[3] Toyota was a small percentage of those in terms of the number of different recalls, although it was a large percentage in terms of the number of vehicles recalled, mainly because of the 2.3 million vehicles using the particular accelerator pedal that in rare circumstances could get sticky.

Arguably, Toyota did not have an unusual number of actual technical problems leading to these massive recalls, but got caught in a political tsunami caused by a multiplicity of interests: congressional representatives pursuing reelection, the media desperate to reverse shrinking revenue during the Great Recession, trial lawyers whose American targets were at or near bankruptcy, and "expert" witnesses paid by trial lawyers. Yet, with all these speculations about rising quality problems as a result of focusing too much on growth and profitability over the decade from 2000 to 2010, in the fall of 2009, Toyota had won more quality and safety awards than any other automaker. The quality surveys dipped significantly in the spring of 2010, when Toyota was in the news nonstop for recalls, then suddenly, by the fall of 2010, when the media had calmed down, Toyota had the leading vehicles in 10 of 17 *Consumer Reports* categories and led all automakers in J.D. Power awards for three-year durability and for vehicles lasting more than 200,000 miles. Toyota topped all automakers in awards, including those from Polk, Kiplinger's, the Insurance Institute for Highway Safety, and Motorist Choice. By halfway through 2010, it had regained its lead as number one in the United States in retail sales, with the Camry once again being the bestselling passenger car. Obviously, if its cars got diseased, the recovery was remarkable—a matter of months. This success was somewhat short-lived when the worst earthquake in Japanese history, followed by a tsunami, virtually halted parts shipments from the hard-hit north of Japan, stopping or slowing most Toyota production for months.

# The Great East Japan Earthquake and Tsunami

Just as Toyota's sales and profitability were returning and the company was again on the road to regaining its elite position, the Japanese earthquake and tsunami of 2011 struck. It was the worst disaster in the recorded history of Japan.

Toyota and its direct suppliers were relatively unaffected, since the bulk of its operations are near Nagoya, inland in central Japan. They did have one new plant up north producing Yaris, a compact vehicle sold around the world, but the damage was minor and the plant was back on line quickly. Another northern plant producing batteries for hybrid vehicles was also affected, but it too came back on line quickly. Toyota engineers made quick work of realigning and revalidating equipment; production of hybrids resumed within two weeks of the disaster.

Yet, as Toyota quickly found, many of the basic raw materials its suppliers depended on came from the northeast of Japan, near the epicenter of the disaster. Most disturbing to Toyota, it discovered they knew little about the affected companies that were suppliers to suppliers and thus not directly managed by Toyota. Toyota worked with its suppliers, made some direct visits, and put together a map of all the suppliers affected by the disaster. It found there were 500 parts that it was not able to procure just after the March 11 quake.

Toyota immediately sent teams of its engineers, along with equipment vendors, to the north to solve the problems of suppliers one by one. This meant removing debris, realigning machines, repairing them—whatever it took. By April, the list of unavailable parts had been cut to 150. By early May, it was down to 30 parts that Toyota could not procure.

In addition, Toyota provided a great deal of relief to the affected areas—for instance, by bringing in tanker cars of water and many supplies. American Toyota employees, dealers, and suppliers collectively donated more than $7 million to support the tsunami victims in Japan.

After the recession, the recall crisis, and now this natural disaster, one might think Toyota's coffers were empty and it would need to turn to the old Western recipe of layoffs. But with Toyota's deep pockets, it continued to bring regular team members to work, even at plants that did not have the parts to make any cars, and continued the intensive *kaizen* and training, all while investing in one of the biggest overhauls of its product lineup ever through intensive R&D. In addition, team members at Toyota's U.S. plants also used paid production downtime that resulted from the disaster in Japan to help support communities across America. Team members at the engine factory in Alabama, for example, devoted more than 10,000 volunteer hours to support relief efforts in communities that were devastated by recent tornadoes, volunteering for 73 projects across eight Alabama counties. Then Japanese team members returned the favor, contributing over $300,000 to the U.S. tornado relief effort.

With the disciplined and heroic efforts of Toyota and its dedicated suppliers, the company was able to get most cars back to full production by early June, and full production was back by September—in about half the time of the original forecasts. With a spate of new models (about 80 percent of all models would be renewed in the next few years), it was preparing to roll again. The renewed financial crisis in August 2011 did not help the cause, but it seemed inevitable that in the next few years, the economy would recover enough to support a sales level sufficient to return Toyota to significant profitability and refill the coffers.

## Were There Leadership Failures?

In many ways, we can view these three crises as demonstrations of the incredible resilience of Toyota and an affirmation of the strength of the Toyota Way. But the Toyota Way itself dictates seeing any problems as opportunities to reflect and strengthen the company. There were deep reflections and an enormous amount of *kaizen* in the company.

In the case of the Great Recession, Toyota was unhappy with the amount of inventory it had built up—overproduction, the most fundamental of what Toyota defiend as the seven wastes in processes. It had seen signs of oil prices increasing and believed that it should have recognized that sales of large vehicles were threatened. But it kept building until the crisis hit, and it was left holding far too much inventory and capacity.

The recall crisis was another case where Toyota could have simply written it off as many special interests simultaneously going on the attack over small problems, and creating the myth of a large problem in the electronic systems of vehicles. The NHTSA and NASA reports had absolved the company of any serious safety problems. Yet, when Toyota did its usual deep reflection on the crisis, it was able to uncover some serious problems. We believe that these problems were not in fact the causes of the recalls, but they did lead to failures in responding quickly and appropriately to the growing crisis and especially to customer concerns. It is now clear that none of the recalls had anything to do with what went on in Toyota manufacturing plants or the Toyota Production System. There were some design errors coming out of R&D, but the total number of errors was small, in each case Toyota had determined the cars braked within normal distances, and the design decisions that led to about a dozen different recalls were spread over much of the decade. A couple of errors per year in a product with more than 30,000 parts and hundreds of models globally is far from an epidemic of quality errors. But Toyota still wanted to seize this opportunity to reflect and improve. Various executives we interviewed concluded

1. The time between when a customer called with a concern and when Toyota responded with a design change or a recall decision was too long.
2. The time taken to respond to NHTSA complaints and media attacks was also too long.
3. Most important, Toyota failed to seriously listen to customers' perceptions of features, such as concerns that adaptive cruise control accelerated their cars.

One of the foundations of the Toyota Way, and therefore of lean practice, is *genchi genbutsu*, or "go and see." The principle is that decisions should be made, whenever possible, by those at the work site who have an intimate knowledge of what is happening and what potential solutions to any problem will work. As leaders move up the ladder from the shop floor to executive positions, there is still extreme emphasis on spending time at the *gemba*—the work site, or shop floor—so that the leaders have a grasp of the actual situation.

One of Toyota's clear failures during the crisis was that critical decisions were being made by leaders who were not at the *gemba*. The leaders who were closest to the situation and had the best grasp of the problem of perceived failures of quality and safety were North American executives in Engineering, Sales, Communications, and Government Relations. Yet critical decisions about such things as what information to release about sudden unintended acceleration claims were being made by Japanese executives and Japanese engineers who were very far removed from the problems. The Toyota Way emphasizes that the farther from the *gemba* decisions are made, the poorer the decisions will be—and that proposition was proved in this case.

Another core tenet of the Toyota Way is always driving to the root cause of a problem. In the cases of sticky pedals and all-weather carpets, it can be argued that Toyota did a fine job of finding the root cause of the technical problems, but the bigger problems were in communications and decision making. Following the Toyota Way, it is not enough to say that the wrong people were making critical decisions. We have to ask why the wrong people were making these decisions. This is where the failures of leadership development come in.

While Toyota had long pursued a goal of making its regional operations more self-reliant and less dependent on expertise, personnel, and support from Japan, the company consistently fell short of this goal. Thus, when the crisis struck, the engineering research and decisions were still being handled primarily in Japan. The engineers there were largely isolated from what was happening in the North American news media and public sentiment. As you'll see later in the book, this sort of behavior is not in accord with the principles and practices that Toyota attempts to imbue in its leaders.

What it all adds up to is that Toyota did not develop enough leaders, or did not develop leaders that it trusted sufficiently, in the North American operation to allow decision making and problem solving to be as close to the *gemba* as they should have been. Some have argued that the root of the problem was that Toyota had grown too fast in the 1990s, but in a personal interview with President Akio Toyoda, he refined that diagnosis: "The problem was that the pace of growth was faster than the pace of human resource development. . . . It is not the growth pace itself, but it is the relation between the pace of growth and the pace of [people development]."

Akio Toyoda used all of his powers as president to turn the energy of the recall crisis toward continuous improvement rather than finger-pointing and blame. As he put it in an interview with Liker:

*When I appeared in front of the [U.S.] media in February for the first time because of the recall, I was very harshly attacked, I was almost like a sandbag. . . . I decided* I would never point fingers at somebody else. *And during the congressional hearings, I was not so much worried about explaining to, or convincing, the representatives of Congress. . . . I was thinking about the dealers, and customers, and suppliers, and our U.S. colleagues in Toyota. . . . So rather than trying to be too aggressive, or seeming to be arrogant, I tried to talk to those people.*

Akio Toyoda and those in external affairs sent the message to Toyota team members around the world that the company would accept blame for inconvenience to its customers and focus on what it could do to improve as an enterprise. That continuous improvement had to be more than in product design and key processes: it had to include improved human resource development. It was Toyota's culture of quality and safety that generated the "brand insulation" that kept customers loyal through the recall crisis, and that focus needed to be redoubled. While there were some failures in Toyota's adherence to its own principles that exacerbated the recall crisis, we believe that in the long run the company's response to the crisis illustrated the Toyota Way at its best (see the sidebar, "Toyota's Response to the Recall Crisis").

Certainly Toyota could not find fault with itself over the earthquake. Yet, it once again reflected deeply and learned an important lesson. Back in 1997 there was a huge fire that destroyed the only factory in the world that manufactured p-valves, which are critical to all braking systems. Toyota recovered almost immediately with little loss of production with the help of 36 suppliers aided by 150 other subcontractors. The lesson was to always have at least two suppliers of a critical part in at least two geographic areas. Yet here it was 2011, and the same situation had occurred in a slightly different form. In this

## Toyota's Response to the Recall Crisis

We believe that after failing to recognize and respond to the problems in the early stages of the recall crisis, by February 2010, the company had started down a true Toyota Way path under Akio Toyoda's leadership. Rather than going on the offensive, the company admitted that it had to improve and promised to reform itself. From a public relations perspective, the company adopted the following principles:

- Never blame customers, the government, or partners, such as dealers or suppliers.
- Apologize to customers for any pain or inconvenience that they suffered.
- Do not give responses to the public that appear defensive.
- Work diligently to identify and solve any real problems.
- Admit openly and immediately to whatever problems are uncovered and verified.
- Emphasize positive steps that the company is taking to improve.

While these principles guided Toyota's public communications, there were obviously deeper issues related to how quickly and effectively the company responded to customers who were reporting problems, and even internal issues concerning the way the engineering organization communicated with North American team members and the different regions shared problems.

The steps that Toyota took in response to the recall crisis seem well suited to address these problems. The main focus was on streamlining responsiveness to customer complaints. In organization design terms, Toyota needed linking mechanisms to get information to the right parts of the organization quickly and more local authority so that problems could surface and be resolved within the region where they occurred.

Toyota took steps to make sure that any quality and safety issues could be quickly handled in their respective regions, close to the problem, ensuring that *genchi genbutsu* is possible. The company created the new roles of chief quality officer and regional product safety executive for each region of the world. The chief quality officers are at the managing officer level (one step down from the board of directors), so they have a great deal of power. They also have direct lines of communication to Akio Toyoda and the board of directors, if needed, to ensure that proper attention is being given to emerging issues. Notice that these initiatives are global. Even though the problem was primarily limited to the United States, the root cause of the problem is global, so the response needed to be global.

Since most customer complaints need to be resolved through engineering design, Toyota established a new design quality innovation division reporting to the executive vice president of R&D. This division would focus on streamlining the process of responding to customer complaints with design changes. Many other changes were made in Engineering, such as increasing the number of assistant managers to act as mentors and develop young engineers, adding four weeks to the development process to focus on quality from the customer's viewpoint, increasing engineering trips to dealerships to understand customer problems, and so on.

To help address quick response, Toyota North America created Swift Market Analysis Response Teams (SMART) reporting to the chief quality officer. In the United States, these teams include about 200 highly trained engineers and technicians across the country whose target is to go out within 24 hours to investigate actual customer complaints. Their first task was to focus on SUA complaints, but their mandate grew to any safety-related concerns. During 2010, they investigated more than 6,000 cases in detail, studying the car and interviewing the driver, with no technical problems revealed other than errors that led to the recall repair of carpets or pedals.

They did determine that customers misunderstood some aspects of vehicles that had grown more complex over time. For example, a high-end option on some vehicles is adaptive cruise control, which will automatically slow the car down if the vehicle in front of it slows down. If the vehicle in front then speeds up, the cruise control will accelerate the car back to the speed set by the driver. This appears to some people to be SUA. Simply explaining to customers how the system works resolved the complaints.

In addition, many changes were made to increase regional autonomy, particularly in North America, and to better integrate the different parts of the company. For example, before the recall crisis came to light, Yoshimi Inaba had been brought out of retirement and named chief operating officer of Toyota Motor North America to better integrate Toyota Motor Sales, Engineering, and Manufacturing. This was a longer-term process for getting to the real root cause of the problem.

---

case, the problem was that the suppliers' sources were invisible to Toyota. Some of Toyota's suppliers were relying on a single source or two sources in the same geographic area. Toyota had to dig deeper into the supply chain to ensure that a single natural disaster could not bring global production to a halt.

But a bigger lesson was the benefit of teams working together across divisions and across regions. Throughout the world, each region needed to check in daily on the condition of parts and make decisions about priorities for building vehicles. In Japan, they at first made building hybrids a priority, since they expected these to be big sellers. They had daily meetings to investigate the state of parts, set priorities, allocate parts to regions, and discuss the situation with each region of the world. The daily communication and cooperation needed to deal with this severe challenge both tested the company and strengthened global cooperation.

## So What Can We Learn about Lean Leadership from Toyota's Crises?

We think there are two primary lessons about lean leadership that can be gleaned from Toyota's struggles during the triple crises. The first is a reminder of how crucial leadership actually is in lean. There is no question that Toyota's adherence to the principles of lean manufacturing is as solid as ever. The Toyota Production System still outclasses all of its competitors in terms of efficiency and quality. But being a world-beater in terms of lean process did not prevent these problems from occurring, nor did it help resolve the problems once they had occurred. That's because these problems were in fact leadership problems, not lean process problems. They were a stern reminder that all the investment in lean process in the world will not yield the expected outcomes if it is not accompanied by lean leadership throughout the enterprise, including in corporate support departments.

Second, the crises were a reminder that True North can never be attained—and that no lean leader can ever rest on her laurels, believing that all problems have been solved and all waste has been eliminated. In Taiichi Ohno's inimitable phrase, "There is always waste." Of course, the problems that Toyota encountered weren't ones of waste and inefficiency in the classic sense. But they still involved waste. Overproduction as the recession hit was a fundamental and unforgivable waste. In the recall crisis, Toyota wasted some of its hard-earned reputation for safety, quality, and care for its customers. It was wasteful to have engineers and executives far from the *gemba* making decisions. Despite the lessons of the 1997 fire, Toyota again had this problem deep in the supply chain in 2011 and was not even aware of it. In other words, despite more than 40 years of phenomenal success in building up the global business, there was still waste to be eliminated. One of the key tasks of the lean leader is to help everyone around him recognize that there is a True North—and that True North has not been attained. There will always be problems; there will always be waste; there will always be improvements that can be made. In that sense, every day should feel like an impending crisis.

Part of defining the path to True North is the company's ten-year vision, updated at the beginning of each decade. Global Vision 2020 had mostly been defined prior to the recall crisis, focusing on the integration of cycles of manufacturing and cycles of nature, and emphasizing green manufacturing and green cars. That focus has not been lost, but in the wake of the recall crisis, Akio Toyota realized that there was little involvement from overseas leaders in what was a vision mostly created by Japanese executives. Thus he enlisted the managing officers from all the regions outside Japan and asked them to reconsider the vision. The result was a better response to the issues uncovered in the recall crisis, focusing on customers first, always better cars, a stable base of business, and following Toyota values—all to create sustainable growth. The key tagline is: "Rewarded with a smile by exceeding your expectations."[4] The three main themes of the vision are

- Toyota will lead the way to the future of mobility, enriching lives around the world with the safest and most responsible ways of moving people.
- Through our commitment to quality, constant innovation, and respect for the planet, we aim to exceed expectations and be rewarded with a smile.
- We will meet challenging goals by engaging the talent and passion of people, who believe there is always a better way.

The changes that Toyota embarked on will easily take the rest of the decade. It will take all the company's expertise in lean leadership to make those improvements. And while Toyota was losing its "halo" of clear superiority, its competitors in the United States and overseas continued to get stronger, creating an even greater competitive challenge. We can all learn from watching as the company attempts to regain its competitive advantage by driving true cultural change in a complex global organization.

In the meantime, for companies on their own journey that are struggling to define lean leadership or how to attain it, we have Toyota as a model. Despite the (often misunderstood) issues that led to the problems, especially the recalls and their aftermath, Toyota has been developing lean leaders effectively for more than 60 years—and a lot more if you go back to the automatic loom company. Most of Toyota, including all of Manufacturing, was not implicated in the recall crisis, and just prior to this crisis of reputation, it was operating at a very high level in Toyota history. There is much to learn from this excellent company that has developed exceptional leaders at all levels. There is even more to be learned from the True North principles that Toyota has evolved, whether or not every individual leader in Toyota has lived up to them. For those who are seriously on the lean journey, we believe we have some important insights to offer on what your leadership should look like and what you can do to develop true lean leaders.

# THE
# TOYOTA
# WAY
## *to* LEAN
# LEADERSHIP

# Introduction

# The Roots of Toyota's Global Business Leadership

*Senior management is simply a flag bearer when a business decision is made. It is of no use unless others follow the flag.*

—Eiji Toyoda, former chairman of Toyota

From its humble beginnings in the Japanese rice-growing district of Aichi prefecture almost 80 years ago, Toyota Motor Company developed into the world's leading automobile manufacturer. Toyota's story is remarkable by any measure, but it is particularly remarkable given the volatility that has shaken global manufacturing, and the auto industry in particular, over the last 30 years, plus the daunting challenges of the Great Recession, the recall crisis, and the East Japan earthquake.

Perhaps the most telling statistic is the simplest: Toyota was profitable every year from 1950 until 2008, with the record being broken only when the company was hit by the combination of the global recession and the oil price spike of 2008. Then, after one year, in the wake of the recall crisis, Toyota was again profitable. Such consistent profitability is unheard of at the top ranks of the global automotive industry, where cyclical profits and losses, with major layoffs that are followed later by massive new hiring, are the accepted norm. If you dig a little deeper, the data just get more impressive. For instance, Toyota's per-vehicle profit in 2007 was more than 80 percent higher than that of second-place Honda, and negative per-vehicle earners GM and Ford were not even on the same chart. In 2008, the Camry was the best-selling vehicle in the United States, the eleventh time in 12 years that the car had won the sales crown; Lexus has also been the bestselling luxury brand more years than not since it was first introduced in 1989. And within months of the U.S. recall crisis—the biggest challenge to Toyota's reputation in its history—it was again number one in U.S. retail sales.

Even more important to Toyota is its track record for quality, even at the end of the decade from 2000 to 2010, when critics spoke of Toyota's decline in quality: Toyota (or its Scion or Lexus brands) placed first in six of ten categories on the *Consumer Reports* 2009 quality survey, and J.D. Power has consistently ranked Toyota models among the top five for initial quality (during the first three months of ownership) in nearly every category in which they compete. Other automobile manufacturers have been narrowing the quality gap, to be sure, but after decades of dedicated effort, they still haven't caught up. Again, within months of the recall crisis, Toyota bounced back, and by the fall of 2010, it was leading in 10 of 17 categories in the *Consumer Reports* quality ratings. In early 2011, J.D. Power ranked cars on three-year vehicle dependability (in our view, a far more important measure than initial quality), and Toyota/Lexus brands captured seven first-place awards in vehicle segments, the most of any automaker. We should note that the Lincoln brand was number one overall in three-year dependability. However, by June of 2011, the headlines read: "Ford Scores Tumble, Toyota Rebounds in Initial Quality Survey."[1] Ford's problems per 100 vehicles plunged below the industry average of 107 to an average of 116, and its ranking fell from fifth the year before to twenty-third. At the same time, Lexus topped all brands, and the Toyota brand, which in the wake of the recall crisis of 2010 had fallen below the industry average for the first time in the history of the study, rose to number seven, with 101 problems per 100 vehicles. Despite this, the competition has been getting much better, and Toyota's traditional large advantage in quality has shrunk to precarious levels, so this is no time for Toyota to rest on its laurels. Still, over the long term, Toyota has somehow managed to continuously raise the bar on every conceivable metric: quality, cost per vehicle, profit per vehicle, vehicle sales, residual value of vehicles, innovation, new-model launches—the list goes on.

## The Failure of the Lean Quick Fix

Other companies, in sectors from manufacturing to health care to government, have attempted to learn Toyota's secret. "Lean production," the process management system derived from the Toyota Production System (TPS), is now a global movement in much the same way that the quality movement took hold in the 1980s. Six Sigma, the quality methodology derived from Motorola's Total Quality Management and made famous by GE and AlliedSignal, has become "Lean Six Sigma," inspired by Toyota's success.

A hunger for concepts and "tools" to implement lean has driven the sale of literally millions of Toyota- and lean-focused books (more than one million by Jeff and his coauthors alone). Consulting companies and nonprofit groups run seminars on tools for eliminating waste, one of the key tenets of the TPS/lean philosophy. Companies around the world boast about the results they have achieved from their lean programs. Yet despite all the lean projects that have been implemented over the past two decades, no company in any industry in the world has attained the same level of consistent operational excellence in its field as Toyota has. What are these companies missing?

Every organization has a set of processes that it uses to provide a material product, information, or a service to customers, and if we can make those processes consistent—that is, reduce variability and shrink the lead time—we can get closer to the ideal of giving our customers what they want, in the amount they want, when they want it. So let's train some Lean Six Sigma experts to grab the tools and start hacking away at the variability and waste that stretch out lead time; this will make us more successful, both for our customers and for our business. What could be simpler?

Unfortunately, decades of attempts to do this show that it does not work, at least not in a way that is sustainable for the long term. We measure the process and the results precisely, using Six Sigma, and we develop the optimal solution. We "lean out the process," shifting to smaller batches, moving steps closer together, and eliminating the bad steps, and the key performance indicators go wild, showing improvements that we had never thought possible. Then comes the bad news. As time passes, the processes seem to turn on themselves and degrade, with variability and waste growing back again.[2] As one Toyota master of lean put it: "It is like pulling the weeds, but leaving the roots." So what is the solution? Are there sustainability tools? Do we need more Lean Six Sigma black belts and more green belt training? Do we need tougher senior executives setting aggressive goals and holding managers' feet to the fire to deliver, or else? All of these remedies have been tried, and they have helped for a time, but they still have not produced the sustained excellence that we desire.

The general conclusion that many practitioners of Lean and Six Sigma have arrived at is that sustaining improvements requires a combination of top leadership commitment and a culture of continuous improvement. We have to change the culture from one in which people simply do their own job in their own function to make their own numbers look good (a vertical focus) to one in which people are focused horizontally on the customer and on improving value streams that deliver value across functions. For example, the Shingo Prize, which for more than a decade was awarded to manufacturing plants that followed the principles of the Toyota Production System, was later revamped to add assessment modules for leadership and culture to get at this fuzzy stuff that sustains lean. It was the result of following up on past award winners and discovering that few of them sustained the lean excellence that was evident when the original award committee visited the plant.

Of course, changing a culture is not as easy as instituting a training or communication program. Cultures evolve slowly, and changing them is even slower. Toyota's culture began with its founder, Sakichi Toyoda, known today as the "king of Japanese inventors" and the father of the Japanese industrial revolution. His innovations in developing automatic looms starting in the late 1800s began Toyota's DNA, which has evolved and grown from generation to generation. In Japan, it evolved very naturally through direct transmission in master-apprentice relationships. As Toyota globalized, the company had to adapt to different cultures, hiring leaders with experience in other companies' cultures. There were, of course, ups and downs, but Toyota never gave up on investing heavily to develop the Toyota DNA wherever it set up shop. Its experience in developing Toyota leadership in the United States, Toyota's largest and most profitable market outside Japan, is particularly instructive as a case study of developing lean leadership. In some ways it was Toyota's greatest challenge, as there are such sharp cultural differences between Japan and the United States, in particular strong collectivism in Japan versus strong individualism in the United States and long-term thinking in Japan versus short-term thinking in the United States.[3] Yet Toyota has successfully developed Toyota leaders and culture in America, especially in its manufacturing plants. To better understand the culture and how it evolved, it is instructive to start at the beginning of the company that evolved it.

## A Legacy of Unique Leadership

Despite its global fame today, Toyota's origins are truly humble. The Toyoda Automatic Loom Works began operations in turn-of-the-nineteenth-century Japan as a way for founder Sakichi Toyoda to sell power weaving looms. Toyoda invented his loom in response to frustration over how long it took his mother and grandmother to complete the mundane cloth making that supplemented the family's income from his dad's low-paying carpenter job.

In 1896, Sakichi started with very simple automation of a wood loom by using foot pedals and gravity to move the shuttle of threads back and forth, thus eliminating a large portion of the handwork. Later, he used steam engine technology to automate the wood loom. Eventually the looms evolved to steel construction and, with new automation, ran at startling rates; but quality problems arose when any thread broke. Another major breakthrough came when he developed a device that stopped the loom automatically when a single thread broke, preventing waste from defects. The Type G Automatic Loom of 1924 was a groundbreaking invention that included many new features, such as automatic thread replenishment and automatic shuttle change without stopping operation, and was regarded as the world's best at the time. In fact, the Platt Brothers of England, a world leader in the loom industry, paid 1 million yen for the rights to the Type G loom; this was later used as seed money to found Toyota Motor Company.

Two fundamental principles of the Toyota Production System were created in the process of Sakichi's continual improvement of the loom: stopping when there is a problem, and highlighting out-of-standard conditions so that errors are not carried to the next stage of production. But it wasn't just the Toyota Production System that began in the rural rice fields of Japan. The Toyota approach to leadership was also born there. Toyoda was a big fan of Samuel Smiles's book *Self Help*,[4] which documented how highly successful people, including great inventors, made breakthroughs not simply through a single brilliant inspiration, but through hard work, intensive focus, trial and error, perseverance, and getting their hands dirty. More than anything else, Toyoda valued hands-on knowledge and stepping up to challenges. Though the scale was obviously different, Toyota has never faced challenges more extreme than those that were dealt with during Sakichi's tenure, be it developing the first looms from scratch with no capital or surviving World War II.

More than a hundred loom models and dozens of patents later, Sakichi placed his son Kiichiro in charge of a new division of the company dedicated to developing technologies for the emerging automotive industry. Kiichiro started the automotive company in the 1930s under severe resource constraints. He had to find ways to eliminate all unnecessary inputs and movements just to stay in business. His efforts resulted in the development of the key concept of just-in-time production: "eliminate waste from all work processes." In practice, this meant that parts and materials were to be made available in the exact amounts needed *when* they were needed—the fledgling company simply couldn't afford anything else. Kiichiro's insight allowed Toyota Motor Company to become a major producer of commercial vehicles in Japan and capitalize on the growing demand for trucks and vehicles during the "Pacific War" (World War II).

How Toyota went from being a local player that was unknown outside Japan to being a world leader in just a few decades is rooted in this story. In the textile industry, Sakichi Toyoda was not an outsider; he was an insider who had learned by watching the members of his family weave, weaving himself, and understanding intimately where the opportunities for efficiency could be found. Kiichiro developed Toyota Motor Corporation by traveling to the United States and Europe to research automobile manufacturing and then improve on what he had learned—initially to develop his own gasoline-powered engine.[5]

Toyota's success, in short, is not rooted in its application of a standard "lean" methodology to manufacturing, nor can it be found in any internally implemented equivalent of Six Sigma. Instead, it is rooted in its leaders. More specifically, it can be found in the approach that a Toyota leader takes, seeing self-development and training others as the only possible path, not only for finding the right solution for the problem at hand, but for constantly and consistently improving performance day after day.

## Silos of Lean

Few companies see this connection between Toyota leadership and the company's exceptional results. They see Toyota's methodical approach to everything it does and quickly leap to the conclusion that the technical system is the solution. But replicating Toyota's technical systems without understanding their source—the engine that drives the system, you might say—has largely proved futile. While impressive gains from adopting some version of TPS or lean are common, they are almost never sustained. Why? Because tools and blitz events don't ingrain the leadership needed to coach and sustain a large process change within the existing company culture.

This is not to say that "lean" doesn't work. On the contrary, thousands of companies have derived benefits from lean projects. Those benefits can be significant, as when one of the largest banks in Belgium embarked on a lean program and documented a one-third reduction in labor in one of its largest divisions. Yet these successes can most accurately be described as "point improvements," unconnected to a broader set of business goals. The standard point approach is to implement a process experimentally in a silo of the company. In the case of lean, the silo may see production lead time decrease from five days to three, or production costs be reduced by 20 percent. Everyone cheers these improvements and then turns to the next lean project.

Over time, it becomes evident that these point improvements cannot easily be transferred to other parts of the organization. Worse, they are not even self-sustaining. Without the constant vigilance and dedication of managers and workers alike, without leadership, backsliding is common and rapid, with three days stretching to four and then four and a half. Backsliding is analogous to the months of discipline, dieting, and self-denial required for a person to lose 20 pounds, only to gain it back in piña coladas and desserts during a one-week resort holiday.

Like most people who go on diets, most companies that go lean fool themselves into thinking that the change effort is a time-bounded exercise. The company just needs to eat less and exercise more for *now*. It doesn't understand that if it is to stay lean, a company, like a person, has to *live* lean . . . forever. It is literally about resetting the corporate metabolism, even restructuring its DNA. That cannot be done just by shifting a process, implementing a methodology, or running a change program. Real systemic change has to happen at a company's core, with its people. Most critically, it needs to be embodied in the company's leaders. Adopting Toyota's leadership model and work style is analogous to a committed lifestyle change, not an aggressive diet.

Leaders, and the leadership model that the company cultivates, are the root drivers of Toyota's successful engagement of team members throughout the company. The Toyota Production System is the effect of this engagement, not the cause. Toyota leaders strive for continuous improvement in every aspect of the business, and achieving that improvement requires everyone, from top executives to the heads of small work groups on the shop floor, to work together. That requires consistent leadership over an extended period of time, in every division, and at every managerial position up and down the ladder. In other words, this is the type of leadership that can never be provided by a few stars with extraordinary ability or stunning charisma. It's certainly not the type of leadership that you can hire and just plug in. This type of leadership is what has allowed Toyota to overcome many significant obstacles in a dynamic and competitive industry. It is how the company developed the next generation of leaders to support its global expansion. And it is how it approached the need to survive during the economic crisis that began in 2008.

## More than an ROI Exercise

Perhaps the biggest single barrier to building a viable culture of continuous improvement that we have seen is the ROI mentality. Why am I doing this? Because the costs of doing it will be paid back within two years or one year or even one quarter. Show me examples of organizations like mine that have implemented lean and find out what their ROI was. What was the ROI on that *kaizen* event? How long will it take me to get an ROI from the introduction of a lean training module?

Do not get us wrong. We are not critics of cost reduction; in fact, cost reduction has been a major focus of TPS since its creation by Taiichi Ohno. In the wake of the 2011 East Japan earthquake, when Toyota did not have the parts it needed to make sales, and simultaneously the yen was reaching record highs against the dollar, Toyota undertook yet another major cost-reduction program. This time, the company calculated that if it could reduce Japanese costs by 20 percent in two years, it could be profitable at 80 yen to the dollar.

The problem arises when short-term cost reduction becomes the single focus, trumping any investment in the future that does not have an immediate and calculable ROI—such as training, creating a robust lean system, developing exceptional leaders, and funding long-term R&D based on a deliberate long-term strategy. The concept of a system means that there are interrelated parts; you need all of them to make the system shine. If you expect an ROI from each individual activity, from identifying all potential quality issues, to setting up a cell, to implementing pull, to developing standardized work, to deeply training each and every person involved with the cell, you will focus only on the parts with an ROI, and the process will collapse on itself. Focusing on the ROI for each individual step is like the person who lives for immediate gratification and will not make any investment in his future, such as studying hard and succeeding in school so that later he can go to work and build his way toward a successful career.

We will see in Chapter 6 how Gary and the team he worked with at Dana were able to cut costs dramatically while investing money in developing the future culture that Dana would need if it was to become an excellent company. Cost reduction in the short term is possible, but simply looking at a spreadsheet and picking items that cut costs immediately, as if off a menu, will not lead to building a lean system and a culture of continuous improvement.

## Differing Worldviews

On the surface, it would seem that good leadership is good leadership. Dig deeper, however, and it becomes clear that Toyota's focus on developing people and striving for continuous improvement could not be more different from the traditional principles under which most Western companies operate. The underlying Western management paradigm has its roots in scientific positivism and Frederick Winslow Taylor's scientific management. In Taylor's view, organizations are like machines. If you install the right booster here, tune it up there, and get the right mix of gas and oil, you can go like crazy!

If your worldview involves seeing organizations as machines, then you are likely to view people in terms of the functions that they perform. In practice, this translates into a hierarchical structure, in which educated specialists decide how the company should operate and how each process should be designed; managers make sure that those designs are followed to the letter, guided by targets and metrics; and workers do the work, with no room to make suggestions for improvement. Within such a world, workers are viewed as mindless automatons and managers as bureaucrats who enforce the rules without variation. The specialists, and the specialists only, are encouraged to think.

This worldview is pervasive. It has become so completely the norm within business environments that people don't even see it, just as a fish cannot see water. It is now simply "management," and it is consistently reflected in the five most common questions that conference and workshop participants inevitably ask whenever one of us is invited to speak publicly about Toyota. These questions immediately signal that the inquirer is trying to fit Toyota into a traditional management framework, in which processes are owned and controlled by one person and executed by someone else.

For anyone who wants to learn from Toyota, viewing the company through this traditional lens is a mistake. Simply put, Toyota is not a traditional company. It does not do things the way most other companies (even other Japanese companies) do them. To understand more of what we mean, look at these five most common questions about Toyota, their underlying assumptions, and how Toyota really sees things.

## Question 1: Lean Metrics and Reward Systems

What does Toyota measure to ensure that people follow the right processes and get the right results?

> *Traditional assumption:* The only way for managers to motivate people is to externally control them. Using metrics, along with reward systems based on those metrics, allows you to control workers. Therefore, any company that uses the same metrics and rewards that Toyota does will get the same results.

> *Toyota's view:* Toyota actually avoids tying specific rewards to specific metrics, fearing that people will focus narrowly on what is measured and ignore other parts of the job. The company is as concerned about the thinking behind the group's plans for achieving the objectives as it is about whether the results are achieved. There is also concern that metrics-based incentives drive individualistic behavior rather than a team orientation.

Toyota's philosophy is actually backed up by social science. Psychology experiments show that paying people to do something that they already want to do (either because they enjoy it or because they want to get good at it) can kill the intrinsic motivation.[6] Once that intrinsic motivation is gone, the company will have to continually provide rewards if it wants to continue to see "good behavior."

This is not to say that Toyota never uses metrics and has no reward system. It has both. But the metrics that Toyota uses should be viewed more as tools that help workers measure themselves against a goal than as tools that help managers control the workers. The metrics must be understood and owned by the people who are doing the work, and those people must be supported by a leader who can inspire them not just to "make the numbers," but to take the next step toward perfection (called "True North" by Toyota). Incentives, in turn, are mostly tied to overall plant and company performance, with only a small portion being based on goals set with the individual.

## Question 2: Failure of American Automotive Companies to Copy Toyota

If GM, Ford, and Chrysler were all invited into Toyota's factories and saw for themselves exactly what Toyota does, why couldn't they successfully copy Toyota's approach and get the same results?

> *Traditional assumption:* Toyota's success is based on a set of replicable actions that are transferable one-to-one to other environments.

> *Toyota's view:* The American automotive industry, at least in the past, was characterized by fragmented organizations, with each part working independently to maximize its "silo" goals and preserve past gains. Toyota views a company as a total system, or an organism with two modes: it either grows through daily improvement or it deteriorates; there is no middle ground. For example, Toyota sees a fundamental disconnect between labor and management in the American companies (something that Gary, at least, has firsthand experience with). Implementing some of Toyota's methods in such a fragmented environment would have limited benefit. The proof is in the practice: GM had a 50-50 joint venture with Toyota in California, called NUMMI (New United Motor Manufacturing, Inc.). Toyota ran the plant, so GM had the opportunity to study the Toyota Way up close for years. Visitors from GM even took photographs of every square inch of NUMMI, with the intention of copying everything, but we all know how that story ended.

The root cause of the disconnect between labor and management is, again, management's adherence to Frederick Taylor's philosophy. Management tried to maximize workers' output by using imposed rules and control systems, and the union tried to use rigid rules and policies to limit management's power. Unless labor-management relations are built on trust and cooperation toward common goals, attempts to copy Toyota will be fruitless.

## Question 3: Application of Lean Methodology Anywhere

I make chartreuse, double-bound, gaseous substrates, with inspection done by electron microscopes (for example). Do you have lean benchmarks for a company or process like mine?

*Traditional assumption:* Lean implementation involves finding a best-practice model to copy. If we can find an organization just like ours that has "gone lean" and is getting results, then we too can get those results if we go see it and just copy what we see.

*Toyota's view:* Every organization must identify and solve its own challenges based on the variables of its process, place, people, and any other unique factors. This is as true from one plant to another within Toyota as it is between Toyota and any other company. Not only does Toyota not think that others should copy its processes exactly; it doesn't even think that its own plants should copy processes from each other exactly. Seeing practices that work in other contexts can be useful as a way to stimulate ideas, but it will not produce commensurate results unless a practice solves a real problem and is adapted, or ideally improved on, by the work groups to fit a specific context.

## Question 4: Toyota Human Resource Management Practices

Can you tell us what Toyota's human resource policies (its performance appraisal system, the number of levels in the hierarchy, the size of its meeting rooms, its compensation policies) are so that we can copy them?

*Traditional assumption:* By now, the theme should be clear: traditional companies view HR practices as being context-independent and replicable.

*Toyota's view:* There is no one effective way to align and motivate people within the same company, let alone across completely unlike organizations. Toyota's approach is to create human resource systems and policies that ensure fairness and trust among workers, so as to create an environment in which every team member is willing not only to see and report problems, but to actively engage in solving them.[7]

## Question 5: The Japanese Question

Is the Toyota Way so specifically tied to Japanese culture that its lessons aren't really transferable outside Japan or Toyota?

*Traditional assumption:* Of the five questions, this one at least recognizes the integral role played by a human system like culture. The question is important inasmuch as it recognizes that each context is different. However, it dramatically reduces the nature of Toyota's difference to its *Japanese*-ness. The assumption is that Toyota best practices work in a mechanistic way that is specific to the Japanese environment, as if the company is some kind of exotic plant that can grow only in Japanese soil.

*Toyota's view:* Toyota appreciates the influence of culture on an organization, but it has a much richer and deeper view of what culture means. Toyota assumes that nothing will work in exactly the same way across different factories, even in Japan. Every local social system has its own unique characteristics. It is up to the leaders of that local system, and of subsystems throughout the organization, to encourage team members to adjust and adapt any new procedures to fit the local situation. Toyota refuses to sacrifice certain fundamental principles, such as respect for people, the need for continuous improvement, and the importance of going to see the conditions of work firsthand. But beyond those principles, HR policies must be flexibly adopted, and the leaders who are administering them must always understand their purpose.

These questions, the assumptions behind them, and the real philosophy that is active within Toyota should make it clear that Toyota's founders and current leaders, quite simply, do not view their organization, or anyone else's, as a machine. Recall that the firm came into existence in a poor, agricultural community. Viewing organizations as machines in an environment in which fortunes so clearly rise and fall depending on dynamic variables—workers, weather, inputs, and sociopolitical circumstances—would contradict all known experience. Instead, Toyota's founders viewed organizations as being complex, dynamic, and as unpredictable as the people who operate within them.

The consequences of this view follow a logical pattern. If the world is unpredictable, then the company is going to need to adapt—always. Being adaptable means that all the levels and departments must be adaptable, from Manufacturing to Sales to Engineering, down to the simplest, most basic processes. And who knows how to adapt a process better than the worker who executes that process every day? Certainly it is not some expert who designed it but has never had to use it. Certainly it is not a manager who is only following the expert's script. Adaptability requires that everyone at all levels of the organization and in every department possess deep knowledge about departmental processes and be able to sense change and respond appropriately. To do that, people need to be trained and empowered to think—all of them, all the time.

## The Leader's Role

At this point, many readers may be asking what training and empowering all team members, within their roles and responsibilities, has to do with leadership. The answer at Toyota is *everything*. You see, one of the consequences of the lean approach, with its relentless focus on eliminating waste, is that the company has a very black-and-white perspective on which aspects of the business add direct value to the end customer and which do not. The person who works on the assembly line building vehicles every day adds a huge amount of direct value to the customer; the plant manager does not, except indirectly. Perhaps analogous to a sports coach, the Toyota leader's mission is to put the team in a position to "win," that is, to add customer value. The leader does not "play," but coaches and supports the team members. The leader keeps the team focused on True North—the ultimate goal.

Yet make no mistake; Toyota is not a flat, egalitarian-to-the-extreme organization, nor is it anarchic. The plant manager *is* still the leader. Toyota knows that only exceptional leaders can channel the combined efforts of team members and work groups effectively to achieve larger goals. Indeed, the first three chapters of this book will focus on the active ways in which Toyota develops and cultivates those leaders—primarily by encouraging and enabling self-development and by putting them in a position to develop others. But beyond that, in a system in which the workers provide most of the value, the job of the Toyota leader is to enable that value-added work.

So there it is: if there is a recipe for Toyota's success, it is a deep, time-consuming, and expensive investment in developing everyone in the organization, and truly believing that your employees are your most precious resource. The role of the leader in this context is to be open to the kind of self-development needed to cultivate her own leadership skills, develop subordinates so that they grow and improve, and remove obstacles and set challenges and goals so that teams at all levels of the organization can contribute to Toyota's continuous improvement and attainment of its long-term goals.

## Toyota as a Model

When Toyota launched its first plant in the United States, it went through the difficult process of finding and hiring Americans who had the qualities that would allow them to learn and internalize the company's view of what a Toyota leader was like. In Japan, Toyota developed leaders from within, identifying employees with leadership potential early in their careers and presenting them with challenges that would allow them to grow, develop new skills, and move up in the organization. The company was able to view them up close in many situations in order to understand their strengths and weaknesses, coach them, and select the ones with the most proven potential for higher-level positions. Toyota had never before had to look for and hire employees from the outside who had the skills and mindset that were inherent in those professionals who had already worked for the company for decades.

It was taken as a given that the Americans who were hired for management positions at Toyota in North America would need to have integrity, energy, and enthusiasm. Beyond those fundamentals, the American leaders needed to have open minds: Toyota was expressly looking for people who were willing to question some very basic assumptions about how to manage, how to prioritize problems, and the importance of customers. They needed to be people who truly wanted to learn. When Toyota hired Gary in 1983, it saw these qualities in him. The Toyota "coordinators" who had been sent over from Japan to coach and nurture the Americans believed that they could teach him the Toyota Way.

To understand the core message of this book, readers will likewise need to keep an open mind and question their assumptions. Many of the things that Toyota does simply do not make sense within a traditional Western management paradigm. Jeff was recently giving an intense description of some of Toyota's practices to a colleague and was somewhat taken aback when his associate seemed unimpressed, as if this were common practice in companies. Jeff wondered aloud whether the colleague had ever worked at a large company, thinking that the lack of such experience might explain the lack of reaction. "Actually, I have worked at several large companies," came the response. "It's not that I'm not surprised; it's that I don't believe you. I cannot imagine that any large company really acts this way." The leadership and operations of Toyota often provoke disbelief and to the cynical sound like a fabricated mythology.

Of course, this colleague wasn't the first person to suggest that Toyota's methods and approaches were mere window dressing. Both authors, despite the decades we have spent getting to know Toyota intimately (Gary by working in the company for 20 years; Jeff by studying it as an engineering professor and writing numerous books about it), have had doubts ourselves. But those decades have also given us the chance to see Toyota and its leaders, from the manufacturing line to the board of directors, live up to their values over and over again, not least by admitting that the company never hits the mark and must always strive to improve. This skepticism is one reason why we've approached this book the way we have—primarily through story-telling. The intent is not just to tell you how Toyota shapes leaders and how those leaders, in turn, shape Toyota, constantly pushing it toward perfection, toward True North, but to show you and increase your belief that it is indeed possible. The stories we'll relate in the book are isolated incidents, but they also are not: they really do reflect the way Toyota works on a day-to-day basis.

None of this is to say that companies with more traditional approaches cannot make the same journey toward leadership development that Toyota has made. In Japan, Toyota was allowed to grow up in a greenfield environment where workers could be nurtured and developed, but it did not have that luxury in North America, nor in any other country in which it has established operations. When Toyota launched its joint venture with General Motors in California, it took on an employee base that was steeped in the antagonistic automotive environment of the 1970s and 1980s. It had to work to transform the traditional model of management and labor, leadership from afar, and all the other aspects of traditional leadership thinking, just as most readers of this book who want to emulate Toyota's success will have to. But it managed to prosper nonetheless, and we believe that other companies can do so as well. However, they will have to start, as Toyota did, with a commitment to developing leaders, not just processes, and they must have patience. They will have to take a long-term view. Toyota has achieved the success it has by sticking with a leadership culture for nearly a century. When Toyota decides to start developing a leader, it is making a decades-long commitment, not putting the person through a six-week training course or paying for a two-year, part-time executive MBA. The process of developing American leaders for

Toyota began in 1957 with the founding of Toyota Motor Sales (which imported and sold Toyota vehicles in the United States) and is still not yet complete, in the company's view.

The Toyota story in America can lend inspiration and help provide a road map for the journey to excellence. What exactly the destination might look like, of course, is up to the individual institution. No company should aim to become a clone of Toyota, as each firm has its internal strengths and cultural idiosyncrasies. However, Toyota's path and the development of the people who got it there serve as strong lessons for any company that seeks excellence.

## Toyota's Challenges: There Are Always Weaknesses

At this point, it may sound to you as if we are describing Toyota as the "perfect company." It's critical to understand that, from Toyota's perspective, nothing could be further from the truth. Part of Toyota leadership is the ability to point toward True North (the ideal state of everything, from waste-free manufacturing processes to long-term corporatewide goals) and find the gaps between that and the current situation—which implicitly recognizes that this ideal state can never be achieved. It is never possible to eliminate all waste from a process, perfect quality can never be achieved, and Toyota's corporate performance can always be better. One of Gary's first memories once he joined Toyota was being taken, with other new hires, to one of the production lines at Toyota's flagship plant in Japan. There he and the other trainees were asked to engage in *kaizen* to improve a process at one of the best plants in the company. The most important lesson of this experience was that even a plant that set the standard for the company was not good enough; it could still be improved.

It is common to hear statements from Toyota senior executives that would sound like admissions of complete failure if they came from another company. For instance, in early 2009 (before the recall crisis), Akio Toyoda, soon after being named president of the company, announced a renewed focus on "the basics," noting that rapid growth had caused the company to take its eye off the ball of high-quality production. In isolation, you might think this meant that there had been a surge of quality problems and that Toyota had tumbled down the quality rankings. In fact, a major quality initiative that Gary had started in the United States that reduced warranty claims for defects by more than 60 percent had just been completed.

When we started writing this book in early 2008, Toyota was in the midst of the fastest growth spurt in its history and was forecasting another year of record profits. By the end of the year, Toyota was struggling to get through a global recession and recorded its first operating loss in 50 years. Immediately following this came the recall crisis, which threatened the halo effect of Toyota's reputation for having the best quality in the industry. How would Toyota respond to mounting losses and then a public attack on its core values?

The answer to the question is that it responded in the way it has always responded: it stayed true to the values of the company. That means maintaining respect for people and focusing on improvement in order to get through with as little loss as possible and emerge stronger.

This response was possible only because the company had developed such strong leadership with deep beliefs that change is constant and that only highly developed people can adapt to change. The leaders did not suddenly appear from the outside to navigate through the recession. They had been there all along, developing and growing over decades. Toyota showed its trademark respect for people in the heart of the crisis. There were no involuntary layoffs of team members. Communication was constant and consistent. All the skills of everyone in the company were engaged to cut costs, increase quality, and improve capability. Toyota overall provides a great lesson in how to deal with prosperity and how to deal with crisis.

One casualty of the economic crisis was NUMMI, Toyota's 50-50 joint venture with General Motors and one of the most important learning models for both Toyota and General Motors. In the spring of 2009, General Motors went bankrupt, and in reorganization it decided to drop NUMMI from its portfolio. Toyota tried to convince GM to continue with the venture, offering to build a version of the Tacoma truck as a GM vehicle; when it was turned down, it searched for another partner, even offering to build a version of its popular hybrid vehicle for another company, but the companies that it approached did not agree. Could Toyota afford to buy out GM's 50 percent interest at a time when it had too much capacity in North America even without NUMMI? After agonizing debates within its board of directors, all finally agreed that Toyota had to pull out of the joint venture and let NUMMI close. In one sense, the company was not deciding to close a Toyota plant, but rather pulling out of a joint venture after GM had bailed out. In another sense, Toyota had failed many team members, and all suffered great loss. It was a human tragedy, and it reminds us that Toyota is far from perfect and far from immune to a punishing environment.

## What Follows

Our purpose is to help companies that are serious about operational excellence understand the deep and patient process that is required to develop lean leaders. We will do that largely through telling stories about how Toyota developed American leaders. We will begin in Chapter 1 with an overview of the values that Toyota follows for all its operations and the leadership development model that it has evolved from these values. The chapter will offer an example of how a traditional Japanese Toyota leader experienced that model, and how the model helped Toyota define what it was looking for in its American leaders.

Chapter 2 will follow the parallel development of Gary as a Toyota leader and Toyota in America. In 1984, Toyota launched its first large-scale assembly plant in North America, NUMMI. The venture was established in a former GM plant, which Toyota faced the challenge of transforming from an environment noted for its antagonistic labor-management relations into the best auto plant in North America, with a labor relations climate based on mutual trust. Gary was hired away from Ford into the role of plant manager for NUMMI; this is where Gary was coached by Toyota leaders who helped him get started in "self-development."

In Chapter 3, we move on to Toyota Motor Manufacturing Kentucky (TMMK), where Gary became executive vice president and then the first American president. Many people who toured the plant at the time saw remarkable efficiency and smiling team members, but the plant was not completely healthy. In fact, the level of Toyota Production System skills was at an all-time low for the plant, again illustrating that Toyota is far from perfect. We will describe how Gary's leadership, and that of the other Americans he developed, brought the plant back up to a level that Toyota could be proud of.

Chapter 4 explains how self-development of leaders and their development of others led to continuous improvement in North America, known at Toyota as *kaizen.* Toyota believes that improvement cannot be continuous if it is left to a small number of process improvement experts working for senior management. Continuous improvement is possible only if team members across the organization are continually checking their progress relative to goals and taking corrective actions to address problems. Continuous improvement starts at the work group level, where the value-added work is done. At Toyota, that is at the level of work teams, where group leaders and team leaders facilitate daily *kaizen.*

Daily *kaizen* executed within individual units on individual processes adds up to overall corporate goal achievement through *hoshin kanri,* the subject of Chapter 5. *Hoshin kanri* is the process by which Toyota manages the direction of the company, aligns goals, and controls deviation from those goals. The system of alignment starts with a business vision from the top of the company. That vision is cascaded down through every level of the organization, so that everyone has his personal goals and responsibilities and knows how those actions support the topmost vision.

In Chapter 6, we follow Gary to Dana Corporation, an automotive supplier that hired him as acting CEO after his retirement from Toyota in 2007. Dana offers an object lesson in how the practices outlined in the preceding chapters can work outside the Toyota umbrella. Dana was facing extreme challenges when Gary took the helm. The company had just emerged from Chapter 11 bankruptcy and was just finding its feet when the recession hit. Gary had to draw on everything he had learned at Toyota, as well as help from former Toyota colleagues and hard-driving non-Toyota colleagues, to dramatically restructure Dana so that it could survive the crisis and salvage as much as he could while helping the company grow stronger. It was the challenge of Gary's life, and it illustrates how Toyota-style leadership can benefit a traditional American company in crisis.

The concluding chapter explores the question of how other companies can learn from Toyota's approach and seriously develop lean leaders who can sustain and continuously improve processes to deliver the best value to customers. We will give a few examples of leaders outside Toyota who have had success and raise the question of how realistic it is to do this in a company with a deeply entrenched culture based on assumptions that are directly contrary to the Toyota Way.

We take time at the end of each chapter to offer direct advice to companies that wish to learn from Toyota. Toyota's approach is relevant for any company that is interested in long-term, sustainable competitive advantage. Toyota is unique for its combination of deep investment in people and its focus on long-term continuous improvement. Toyota achieves this focus by developing leaders one by one in a culture that is focused on learning and adapting to change. Through learning, people appreciate in value, and that value makes them long-term partners in a business that consistently makes great products that customers want. If you want to know how Toyota does that, read on.

# Chapter 1

# Leading in the Toyota Way: A Lifelong Journey

*Genchi genbutsu [go and see the actual situation] means imagining what you are observing is your own job, rather than somebody else's problem, and making efforts to improve it. Job titles are unimportant. In the end, the people who know the gemba [where the actual work is done] are the most respected.*

—Akio Toyoda, president, Toyota Motor Corporation, 2009

Perhaps the most difficult task in any book on leadership is defining *leadership*. To use the famous adage, we may not be able to describe leadership, but we know it when we see it. With that in mind, rather than attempting a semantic definition of *leadership* to kick off this book, let us tell you two stories of leadership to demonstrate what it is and what it is not at Toyota.

## What Is Toyota Way Leadership?

In 1970, at the direction of the legendary Toyota research and development executive Masayuki Kato, a young section manager in the overseas sales division named Akira Yokoi was assigned to take over the fledging Toyota operation in Indonesia. The prior manager for Indonesia had become ill, and Yokoi was unexpectedly pushed into action to assume his duties. Indonesia had just emerged from a civil war, and its economy was profoundly damaged. Toyota had made a commitment to the country to help it rebuild and industrialize. Yokoi's orders from Kato did not include specific targets for sales or profitability, but rather were to "always do what is best for Indonesia."

Yokoi began his time in Indonesia with a tour of the country to "grasp the actual situation," as he later wrote in his memoirs.[1] He was deeply discouraged when he saw the barely functional roads and destroyed bridges: ferries were used to cross most of the rivers that he encountered. Yokoi's 150-mile trip took 14 hours. There were no shops open or places to eat; passersby wore rags. In this environment, he was somehow supposed to sell cars.

Yokoi's challenge was all the greater because of Indonesia's industrial policy. The government wanted complete production done in Indonesia, not just final assembly of kits sent from Japan. Yokoi and his team managed to build a plant and introduced four models: large trucks and Land Cruisers for use in construction, the Hi-Ace van for rural areas, and the Corolla for (relatively) wealthy urbanites.

Things seemed to be going well until January 15, 1974, when there was an outbreak of riots in Jakarta, mostly among the poor. The rioters treated Toyota just like every other international company in Indonesia: as an object of wrath. In fact, Toyota's Jakarta headquarters was set on fire. Yokoi thought deeply about this and concluded that the problem didn't lie with the nature of the Indonesian people or the failure of the government to contain the riots; it was that Toyota wasn't connected to the vast majority of the Indonesian population. "Toyota needs to promote understanding about our activities among the poor," he wrote. More than understanding, the poor who were the majority of the country needed to see tangible benefits from Toyota if the perception was going to change. Yokoi became convinced that Toyota needed to build a product for the poor. Of course, there were huge challenges to such a plan, not least of which was how to design a car that Toyota could sell at a profit, but at a price low enough to appeal to, as we would say now, the base of the pyramid.[2]

Selling to the poor meant producing extremely low-cost cars, which was impossible given Indonesia's industrial policy. Indonesia, like most developing countries at the time, charged very high tariffs on imported industrial goods in the mistaken belief that this would help develop local industry. Corolla parts were taxed at 125 percent. Toyota could build the cars internally, but the tariffs made it impossible for Yokoi to get the parts and supplies from Japan that he would need at an affordable price. Yokoi realized he badly needed a lawmaker in Jakarta to act as Toyota's champion. Fortunately, from assignments in Thailand and Malaysia, he had learned the importance of developing direct ties with lawmakers, and early on he had worked hard to develop a relationship with the minister of industry, who was responsible for automobile policy. The minister wanted to help and said he could win approval to waive the import tariffs if Toyota built a car with 70 percent local content that cost one-third the price of the Corolla.

With this daunting vision, Yokoi returned to Japan to sell the idea and encountered great resistance, largely because of the small projected sales volumes. One sympathetic Toyota leader suggested that Yokoi pursue a multiplatform model, so that a car, a van, and a pickup truck could all be built on it, thus increasing the volume at a reasonable cost. This would make it far more likely that production could eventually be profitable. With this starting point, Yokoi looked for other cost-reduction ideas. For example, he studied die making and learned that costs for boxy cars are lower than those for cars with curves. So Yokoi insisted on a boxy design. Even that was not enough, and he finally arrived at the radical idea of removing the glass from the rear doors and substituting clear vinyl covers instead. Based on all this, his final calculations showed that the project could be viable.

He then had to sell his ideas within Toyota in Japan. Many executives objected to making what they perceived as a substandard vehicle. Afraid that it could "damage the brand," Toyota Engineering refused to supply engines or transmissions. Yokoi turned for support to his executive sponsor, Kato, and got it. Kato, who had been closely following everything that Yokoi had been doing in Indonesia through regular calls and meetings in Tokyo, built consensus in Japan to supply the needed components. The Kijang went on the market in 1977. Starting out at low volumes that were not profitable, over the years it became the bestselling vehicle in Indonesia and paved the way for Toyota to become the dominant foreign player in that market. It was dubbed "the people's car," and one million were sold over 25 years.

Around the same time as Yokoi's project in Indonesia, a young manufacturing manager at Ford Motor Company named Gary Convis was confronting the quality problems that were endemic in the U.S. automotive industry in the 1970s. Quickly rising through the ranks of Quality Control, Convis had been assigned to iron out quality problems with a two-door Lincoln that was about to be launched.

As one example, a large interior panel between the trunk and the backseats was connected to the car's steel exterior with a Velcro fastener that was not always in the right spot. The result of the mismatch was that the interior panel often came loose. To repair the problem after the cars had come off the line, the rear seats had to be removed, the panel trim cover removed, and the Velcro reinstalled in the proper location (which was quite difficult to get right after the car was built). In total, fixing the problem with the interior panel took about one half-hour per side. With hundreds of cars rolling off the line each day, many of them with interior panel problems, that wasn't a trivial amount of time or effort.

Today it can be hard to remember what the U.S. automotive industry was like in the 1960s and 1970s. Quality was abysmal. Labor-management relationships were characterized by mutual distrust. Well into the 1980s, the attitude of management toward workers at GM and Ford was that they were lazy and would cut corners every chance they got. Managers watched the line workers like hawks, always assumed the worst, and placed constant pressure on production lines to simply turn out parts. The workers, in turn, had no incentive to do their best for their bosses or their company; the punitive atmosphere killed any desire they might have had to put in a discretionary best effort based on personal motivation and commitment to high-quality work. Even the threat of punishment was baseless, since union rules built out of distrust made disciplining workers a daunting task. In any case, management wouldn't turn off a production line no matter how many mistakes were made or how poor the quality was, because the only metric that mattered was the number of vehicles produced.

Convis traced the source of the problem with the Lincoln's interior panel to the trim shop. He reviewed the details of the Velcro installation and made sure that the workers were properly trained and that the right tools were available. He then announced that any more defects that came out of that area would lead to the line stopping—a threat that few people, if any, took seriously.

About a week later, Convis made good on his threat, stopping the line because of more mistakes with the Velcro fasteners. When the head of production heard about it, he came to Convis's office, yelling, "Why'd you shut the line down?" Convis explained the situation and asserted that the line would stay down until the problem was fixed. The production head responded by kicking Convis's wastebasket through a plate glass window and storming out. It took 45 minutes to get the problem solved and the line running again. Ultimately, Convis won the battle with the production head, and almost all the repair work from this source was eliminated. As a result, the quality control department gained more power in the plant.

Both of these stories would seem to demonstrate leadership. Yokoi stepped up to a daunting challenge; through innovation, building relationships, persuasion, and resolve, he overcame it. In the second example, Convis stood up for what was "right" and faced down tremendous institutional pressure. In fact, in lean terms, he "pulled the *andon* cord" and stopped the line. Many readers who are involved in driving lean and quality concepts at their firms may immediately identify with Convis, recalling very similar situations that they have lived through. So it may come as a surprise that within Toyota, these two stories would be viewed quite differently. While Yokoi's story would be perceived as exemplifying Toyota leadership, Convis's would be seen as a disaster—a failure of leadership, in fact.

## Comparing Traditional to Toyota Leadership

Now, a Toyota leader wouldn't blame Convis for the disaster in this story. In fact, stories like this from Convis's experience at Ford, and earlier at GM, are what got Convis hired at NUMMI (New United Motor Manufacturing Inc., a joint venture of Toyota and General Motors in California). But Convis's "leadership" in this instance illustrates the chasm between what has been traditionally considered leadership in many Western companies and what is considered leadership at Toyota.

We've summarized these differences in Table 1-1, based on the four stages of developing Toyota leaders explained later in this chapter. Leaders at Toyota must develop themselves to a certain level before they can take responsibility for developing others in the Toyota Way and leading the organization to achieve challenging goals. In short, the traditional approach uses the sink-or-swim model to select or hire proven senior leaders who make the right decisions and who either get results through heroic actions or get out. Toyota's approach is to create a challenging, yet nurturing environment that grows leaders from within who follow Toyota values to drive continuous improvement at all levels.

Americans tend to think of leadership as a solo endeavor. We use the word *leader* to refer to people who stand out from the crowd because of their personality, charisma, and sometimes megalomania. The examples of leaders in popular and business literature tend to be of a heroic man or woman who stands against the tide, the solo visionary or the inspirational speechmaker, with thousands of people following him or her.

Reflecting on our years of working at or studying Toyota, we have recognized that this bias toward the individual leader is in no small part responsible for the struggles and even outright failures that most companies encounter when they try to adopt Toyota practices or similar approaches to instituting a lean or high-quality approach to their work. In these companies, a senior executive typically decrees the adoption of a lean system, brings in a consulting team to help the company redesign a few processes and train some internal lean or Six Sigma black belts, and expects this to do the job. Many of the employees are probably left wondering, "Who was that masked Lean Six Sigma man?" as the consultants ride out of town.

At Toyota, the perception of leadership is very different. Leadership is personal, but it also happens within a system. The failure of leadership that a Toyota leader would see in Convis's story at Ford is a failure both below and above Convis in the corporate structure. Toyota would expect leadership in fixing the problem to have come from the local leaders and workers in the trim shop below him. Toyota would assume that leadership from above would not only make quality the priority, but, more important, expect all work groups to find and deal with the root causes of any quality issue without an individual manager needing to be a hero.

**Table 1.1.** Conventional Models of Leadership versus Toyota Way Leadership

| Leadership Element | Leadership Deployment | Conventional Leadership | Toyota Way Leadership |
|---|---|---|---|
| **Stage 1: Self-Development** (Learning True North values through repeated immersion cycles) | | | |
| Capability | Leadership ability and potential | Magnetic quality (charisma) that makes people follow | Natural leaders "see" possibilities for improvement in self and others and instinctively harmonize with Toyota values |
| Process | Learning and growing | Learn from a mentor and/or copy a successful style within the "old boys club" | Go to the *gemba* (where the work is) to deeply understand the actual situation and take on increasingly challenging goals under a mentor's guidance |
| **Stage 2: Coach and Develop Others** (Helping others self-develop) | | | |
| Capability | Develop next-generation leaders | Results-oriented: a laser focus on specific results and driving subordinates with rewards and punishments to help them achieve those results | Process-oriented: learning to see strengths and weaknesses in others, how to create situations for growing, and how to minimally intervene at teaching moments for maximum impact. Develop people in the right way and the results will follow |
| Process | Coach and develop others | Sponsors select similar successors, develop "favorites," or hire proven "heroes" from outside | Take responsibility for helping people advance through the self-development learning cycle |
| **Stage 3: Support Daily Kaizen** (Standards, targets, visual management, daily *kaizen*) | | | |
| Capability | Achievement of goals | Drive to quantify business (unit or process) performance and hold key individuals accountable | Learn how to promote leadership learning several levels down through standards, targets, and visual management |
| Process | Enable process improvements and achieve targets | Hold people accountable for metrics via a system of rewards and punishments | Leader presence in *gemba* to identify gaps with True North and on visual management indicators. Coach others to assume responsibility for closing gaps |

*(continued on next page)*

31

**Table 1.1.** Conventional Models of Leadership versus Toyota Way Leadership *(continued)*

| Leadership Element | Leadership Deployment | Conventional Leadership | Toyota Way Leadership |
|---|---|---|---|
| **Stage 4: Create Vision and Align Goals** (Vertical and horizontal alignment toward True North) | | | |
| Capability | Develop vision and plan | Create and sell a dramatic vision and measurable plan | Participate in a collaborative process to get agreement and align goals and the means to achieve the goals *(hoshin kanri)* |
| Process | Set and align goals and plans for achievement | Drive goals with metrics; aggressive bottom-up accountability to metrics. Identify high and low performers and reward appropriately | Initiate and sustain continuous improvement through visual management of goals; focus on problem solving and developing people |

It took Convis several years at Toyota to begin to move past the Lone Ranger model of leadership. At Toyota, the system requires every manager from the shop floor to the boardroom to take responsibility for driving the company toward perfection. Not only will leaders who thrive on individual action and accomplishment not succeed at Toyota, but they can actually damage the whole system by disrupting the deepening of the leadership bench. This is not to say that individuals must subsume themselves to communal action; remember that the existence of the Kijang car in Indonesia was largely the result of the individual leadership of Yokoi. No one at Toyota would suggest that leaders are interchangeable cogs. Leadership at Toyota is personal, but it is also institutional, and it extends from the group leader on the shop floor all the way to the president of the company: both are expected to develop themselves and improve their personal skills while also leading in a way that builds consensus and develops those around them. Put another way, institutional leadership works only where there is strong individual leadership, with a shared driving philosophy up and down the ranks of the company.

## Toyota Leadership Is Continually Developing

During the process of researching and writing this book, the Great Recession began, and the global automotive industry has been through perhaps the most difficult and harrowing business cycle in its entire history. With the recession still in progress, Toyota faced the greatest challenge to its hard-earned reputation with the North American recall crisis. And as it was becoming clear that the accusations of runaway cars with computer systems taking control were a myth, the greatest earthquake in the country's history hit Japan, causing severe parts shortages. The challenges facing Toyota certainly attracted a great deal of media attention during these turbulent times. On the one hand, you have lots of companies looking for ways to cut costs, improve productivity, and raise quality—all tasks at which Toyota is an acknowledged master. On the other hand, in the worst year of the recession (2008 to 2009), Toyota announced its first yearly loss in more than 50 years, and in the next year it had to apologize profusely for causing its customers concern during the recall crisis. Many people wondered whether the Toyota Way would continue to excel in this new era.

From what we've seen and experienced over the years, as well as what we've seen at Toyota since this series of crises began, we believe that the answer to this question is a resounding yes: Toyota will continue to excel and will outperform its peers in adjusting to the new realities. The reason we are so confident of this is Toyota leadership—not specifically the leadership of President Akio Toyoda (although we both respect him greatly based on our personal experiences with him), but the *system* of leadership that the company has at every level of management. This depth of leadership has been painstakingly built up, at what might seem to others to be exorbitant cost, over many decades in Japan and in the United States. In the difficult economic environment of the present and the foreseeable future, the cost of developing such a deep level of leadership capability has become an indispensable investment that many companies are wishing in retrospect that they had also made.

The point here is twofold. First, Toyota's perspective on leadership and how to develop leaders doesn't offer any quick fixes. Toyota develops leaders slowly and painstakingly over many years because it believes that slow and steady is the only way to win the leadership race (and, of course, it has lots of experience to back up that belief). Second, while there are no quick fixes to be gleaned from Toyota, there are important lessons to be learned that can begin paying off in the short term and that, if followed, will pay off dramatically over the longer term. For example, Toyota's development of leaders enabled it to react to the economic crisis both speedily and with long-term investments in training employees that would be inconceivable for most companies, and then to recover from the recall crisis, and then the earthquake crisis, in an astonishingly short time.[3]

## Toyota Leadership and Leadership Development

So what is the Toyota approach to leadership and leadership development? The first thing to understand about Toyota's approach is that the company is absolutely committed to its core values. Therefore, leadership starts with understanding and living out those core values. It is not a stretch to say that it is impossible for individuals who fail to live up to the core values to advance as Toyota leaders. The promotion process spends as much time looking at *how* results are achieved (that is, in ways that are in compliance with the core values) as at *what* results are achieved.

What may not be clear from the story of Yokoi in Indonesia is that the assignment was as much about his self-development as it was about solving the problem in Indonesia. Yokoi went on to become the top executive in overseas sales and was pivotal in Toyota's global expansion. Each time he met a challenge like the one he faced in Indonesia, he was given more responsibility to take on an even greater challenge. Through this series of planned, yet completely open-ended, leadership challenges, he grew to help transform Toyota into a global company. Unlike Convis, who was struggling against a broken system at Ford, Yokoi was growing within a supportive system, with mentorship that allowed him to achieve seemingly impossible goals. In each step, he not only succeeded in the task at hand but grew to more deeply under-stand the values of the Toyota way that guided his every action.

## Core Values

The five core values were first documented and published internally in 2001 in a document entitled *The Toyota Way 2001*. It may seem strange to claim these values as foundational when they weren't even written down until so recently. The truth is that Toyota in Japan had never needed to write them down. In many ways, these values are derived from Japanese culture and religion. Throughout Toyota's his-tory in Japan, its values were simply understood and inculcated through careful mentoring of each leader as he moved through the company. It wasn't until Toyota expanded around the world and had to operate in other cultures that its management began to consider what made it unique. It was only by working with American leaders to build a modern global enterprise that Toyota was able to identify and codify the defining aspects of Toyota leadership.

It would be inaccurate as well to infer that Toyota has rigidly imposed these Japanese values on its employees in the United States or in any other country. The values are consistent everywhere that Toyota operates, but the way those values are lived out is adapted to the local context. Teamwork, for instance, is consistent, but the way a team operates depends on the local culture and mores. For example, there are more individual incentives in Toyota in America than you would find in Japan, and there is far more emphasis in America on positive recognition for achieving goals for both individuals and groups. Just as important, Toyota learns from and integrates the best lessons from around the world and moves them throughout the company, even back into Japan. One particular example is how Toyota has worked to groom more women for management in Japan based on what it learned about respect for people and gender equality in the American context.

The five values that define the Toyota Way are the spirit of challenge, *kaizen, genchi genbutsu*, teamwork, and respect.[4]

## Spirit of Challenge

Sakichi Toyoda, the founder of Toyota, had the spirit of challenge when he invented his first labor-saving loom to help women in the community who were working their fingers to the bone. His son Kiichiro took a challenge from his father to do something that would benefit society and launched Toyota Motor Corporation. Like the two founding Toyoda family members, every Toyota leader is expected not just to excel in his current role but to take on the challenges to achieve a bold vision with energy and enthusiasm. As *The Toyota Way 2001* puts it, "We accept challenges with a creative spirit and the courage to realize our own dreams without losing drive or energy." One could argue that the spirit of challenge is the core value that energizes leaders and associates in Toyota to strive for perfection. As we will see, it is through taking on successively greater challenges and reflecting at each step that Toyota leaders develop themselves.

## *Kaizen* Mind

Now famous, the concept of *kaizen* is a mandate to constantly improve performance. At the root of *kaizen* is the idea that nothing is perfect and everything can be improved. This is critical to the company, as every leader is taught to remember that the process is never perfect and that the company has never achieved the perfect "lean solution." No matter how many times it has been improved, every step in the production line is full of waste; even if it could be perfect today, conditions will change tomorrow, and more waste will creep in. Similarly, every aspect of the company can be improved, from the way products are designed, to the way they are sold, to the way service parts are stored and shipped, to the performance of every team associate in the company. The recall crisis did not reveal any serious objective quality or safety issues, but upon reflection, it did reveal weaknesses in responding to customer concerns in a timely and effective way.

This value and this way of thinking often lead to a misunderstanding of Toyota in the popular media. You can frequently see statements from Toyota leaders in the press about the need to "get back to basics" or the dire need to improve quality. These statements are usually interpreted, as they would be if they came from a traditional company, as admissions of failure and being on the wrong path. Having a *kaizen* mind, though, means that these statements are as true immediately after a successful quality campaign that reduces errors by 50 percent as they are after a major quality problem is uncovered. In fact, throughout this book, you'll see stories about successful initiatives followed immediately by the launch of a deep reflection to identify weaknesses that lead to a program to further improve.

## *Genchi Genbutsu*, or Go and See to Deeply Understand

It would seem that going to see something firsthand is simply a practical matter—although infrequently practiced in most firms—rather than a value. The value of *genchi genbutsu* is less in the act of going and seeing, and more in the philosophy of how leaders make decisions. Toyota expects all leaders to have a firsthand, personal knowledge of any issue that is in their charge. Otherwise, finding the root cause of the problem and identifying a solution based on facts is impossible. By first gathering facts, decision makers can understand the real situation faster and avoid unproductive debates with peers over proposed solutions that do not target the real problem. As you can see from Akio Toyoda's opening quote, the meaning runs even deeper: *genchi genbutsu* reflects a philosophy of deep respect for the core value-added work of the enterprise. Those who understand the value-added work and contribute to it are the ones who are respected and who advance.

## Teamwork

Most great leaders would say that teamwork is critical to success, but saying this is much easier than living it. Dig a bit below the surface in most areas of human endeavor, whether it's a company or a sports team, and you'll find that people talk a lot about teamwork but are interested first in their individual accomplishments. At Toyota, the view that individual success can happen only within the team and that teams benefit from the personal growth of individuals is constantly reinforced and lived up and down the chain of command. This deep belief is built into the promotion process (which focuses heavily on team behavior) and into incentives for performance (where individual incentives are one small component, while team-based incentives based on the performance of the unit or company predominate).

## Respect

In many ways, this is the most fundamental of the core values and the root purpose of the company. Respect for people starts with a sincere desire to contribute to society through providing the best possible products and services. This extends to respect for the community, customers, employees, and all business partners. Respect for people was perhaps the most fundamental guiding value for Yokoi in Indonesia. His orders from Kato did not include specific targets for sales or profitability, but rather were to do "what is best for Indonesia." Respect is evident in the way team members were treated during the recession. No regular (as opposed to temporary) team members were laid off, and enormous investments were made in their development, and this continued while production was slowed during the recall crisis, then shut down when Toyota could not get key parts as a result of the Japan earthquake. When senior executives from Japan came to factories in the United States that were operating well below capacity, their first question was not about profitability, but rather: "How is the morale of the team members?" It is respect for people that drives Toyota to build vehicles locally in the place where they are sold and to make large commitments to the social and economic well-being of the communities and countries where it does business. And it is that same respect that has led to massive investments in environmentally friendly technology, exemplified in the Prius.

# The Toyota Way Leadership Development Model

These values are the bedrock of Toyota leadership, but adherence to the values, in and of itself, does not a leader make. Toyota does have a systematic way of identifying and developing leaders over their careers, although this process has never been formally codified (unlike the core values). Based on what we've seen and experienced at Toyota, we have created a multistage leadership model that we think accurately captures the Toyota approach to leadership—both what it means to be a leader at Toyota and how to go about developing leaders (see Figure 1-1).

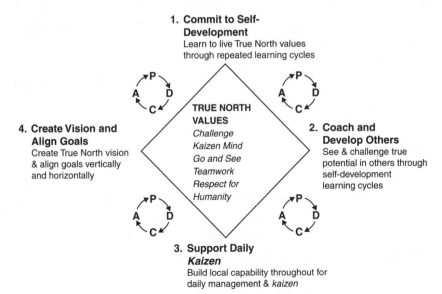

**Figure 1.1.** Diamond Model of Lean Leadership Development

The reality is not as linear as the model suggests and is most definitely cyclical, repeating over and over throughout a person's career, but there does seem to be a logical sequence from developing oneself to ultimately integrating the whole organization to align on goals. It applies to both individual leaders and, by and large, to whole organizations (for example, Toyota North America). So, for instance, the first two stages of the model, self-development and developing others, are focused more at the individual and group levels. Toyota leaders are expected to do both simultaneously (improving their own skills while coaching those whom they manage), although of course a measure of self-development is necessary before one can begin developing others. The cyclical nature of this process means that a leader who led a team toward aligned stretch targets earlier in her career would still be focused on self-development today as she takes on a more senior role in the company. Each leader will go through the stages many times during his career. Only when leaders at every level of the organization have been through the stages several times can we say that the organization has achieved a particular stage. A degree of development of both self and others at the individual level is necessary before one can expect the organization to function as a cohesive whole with a common culture, and there is also a maturation process at the organizational level. For instance, a particular plant may have the leadership in place to be excellent at supporting daily *kaizen* without yet having the leadership in place to fully self-integrate into the alignment of goals and means.

Here we'll briefly describe each stage of the model. The subsequent chapters will fill in the details for each of these stages.

## Self-Development

The first stage of leadership development at Toyota is self-development. Toyota believes that the key trait that distinguishes potential leaders from everyone else is self-development—leaders actively seek to improve themselves and their skills. For a leader or potential leader to self-develop, however, she must be given an opportunity to do so, and she must get support from others. Leaders do not self-develop on their own. This means finding the right challenges for self-development, allowing space for self-development, and coaching at the right times in the process.

## Developing Others

The second stage of leadership development is taking on the task of developing others. It's often been said that the best way to learn something is to teach it. Toyota takes this view to heart and expects that all leaders will be actively engaged in coaching and developing not just star performers or favorites, but everyone on their staff. In fact, it's often said at Toyota that the best measure of a leader's success is what is accomplished by those they trained.

## Supporting Daily *Kaizen*

While the first two stages are primarily about individual leadership, the third stage begins to focus more on institutional leadership—keeping groups of people pointed toward and focused on what Toyota calls *True North*. True North is based on the values of the Toyota Way, which provide a stable vision of where the company should be headed, and it is not negotiable. It does not change with specific goals from year to year. Within this stage, then, leaders are ensuring that their teams are capable of both maintenance *kaizen* (dealing with the daily changes, blips, and bumps of the real world to keep each process performing to its current standard) and improvement *kaizen* (moving each process from its current standard to a higher level of performance).[5] The key at this stage is not that the leader is forcing *kaizen* from the top down, but rather that he is enabling, encouraging, and coaching *kaizen* from the bottom up. To recall Convis's experience with the Lincoln launch, this is the difference between Convis's stopping the line at Ford to force people to do something that they didn't really want to do and Toyota's creating an environment in which each work group takes on the goal of improvement itself.

## Creating Vision and Aligning Goals

The fourth stage involves aligning all the *kaizen* efforts—what you might think of as the small picture—to ensure that the right big-picture goals are accomplished. In other words, the fourth stage is where bottom-up meets top-down. For many who attempt to follow Toyota's lead, it is still difficult to grasp the dynamism of *kaizen* at Toyota. Every hour of every day, processes throughout the company are being tweaked and adjusted to get closer to True North, or perfection. While this is at the heart of Toyota's ability to outclass its competition in quality and productivity, without guidance and channeling of efforts, *kaizen* could lead to chaos: two interlocking processes could be pursuing *kaizen* that takes them in opposite directions. Worse, the resources of the company could be overly focused on the wrong goals. At this stage of development, the leader and the organization are actively involved in what in Japanese is called *hoshin kanri*—the process of setting consensus goals for long-term improvement and deciding on the best allocation of effort and resources to reach those goals.

As we'll see, this is far more than the "cascading goals" process that is common in many companies using "management by objectives." All companies have plans, goals, and targets, but it is rare for leaders to be able to break these down and align their daily efforts in such a way that each work group understands and owns its portion of the big-picture goals and has a clearly defined plan for how it will accomplish them. In fact, in many companies, management does not necessarily know or care how these goals are accomplished as long as it gets the results. For example, simply slashing heads is acceptable, even if in the long term that reduces the capability of the organization. It is the difference between having preset goals and targets that people struggle to achieve and actively participating in translating those goals into concrete targets for improvement and the skills to ensure success. The latter is incredibly difficult and requires leaders and organizations that have mastered the first three stages. As we'll see in Chapter 5, Toyota had had aspects of *hoshin kanri* in place since launching its first plants in North America, but it did not have the maturity to extend this down to every work group on the shop floor throughout North America for 20 years.

## Result: Adapting to Changes in Environment

Only after leaders have developed to a high level are they capable of adapting to the frequent and major changes that the environment will throw at them. In fact, for decades, Toyota's American leaders were buffered from the dramatic changes in the automotive environment in North America by the company's Japanese leaders. They could always fall back on the leadership of executive coordinators from Japan and decisions made at headquarters in Japan. They were even buffered operationally by duplicate capacity in Japan. Up through 2008, most major cars built in the United States were also built in Japan, and dramatic shifts in demand were buffered by the Japanese plants, which could make multiple models (up to six) on the same production line and rapidly shift the mix of car models and the speed of the line. This allowed American plants to operate at a relatively leveled production mix and speed.

The Great Recession was in some ways a blessing in disguise, as it pushed the American Toyota employees into this important stage of being able to flexibly adapt to big changes in the environment and thus to the highest level of self-reliance.[6] Having been through, and matured in, the earlier stages over a 20-year period allowed Toyota in North America to take responsibility for guiding itself through the turmoil of the Great Recession and set itself up for dealing with the rapid ups and downs in the market that will surely characterize the twenty-first century. Individuals and organizations that are capable of leading through major environmental change need less time and attention, thus freeing up the most capable leaders to be more hands-on with the people and groups who need more coaching.

After Convis retired from Toyota, he went on to help lead a traditional American auto supplier, Dana, through a gut-wrenching transformation to help it survive after emerging from bankruptcy. Leaders throughout the company had to lead a radical transformation before they had the depth of training as lean leaders that Toyota provides. Yet even in these circumstances, Convis and the associates whom he brought in from the outside were able to draw on their lean leadership experiences to simultaneously lead the turnaround and begin to lay the foundation for operational excellence at Dana. Chapter 6 tells this story and in many ways reflects a more typical situation faced by Western companies in crisis.

## Can Others Learn from Toyota Leadership?

Compare Toyota's leadership expectations to the leadership models promoted by other companies, and there is a clear pattern. Most companies expect their best leaders to make big changes that show big results quickly, even before they have matured through the four stages of our model (see Figure 1-1). Those who get the results succeed, and those who do not are replaced—often by new blood from outside the company. In fact, there is almost an expectation in American companies that only outsiders can lead turnarounds when the company is struggling through a major crisis. Toyota's success is built on adapting to every major challenge from the business environment—always led by someone with decades of experience at the company. Keep in mind that in its nearly 100-year history, Toyota has never had a president who hasn't spent his whole career at the company.

During most of its history in Japan, Toyota had developed leaders through a process of nurturing employees over the course of their entire career, from novice to leader. Like almost all corporate cultures, Toyota's culture evolved naturally, starting with the influence of its early leaders and their immediate successors. The second generation of Toyota leaders was intimately familiar with the founders' principles, since they learned them directly from the founders. And because all engineering and manufacturing were focused in Japan, the company had not needed to formalize its leadership-development approach or adjust it to account for cultural differences.

Those who are familiar with Asian religions such as Taoism, Buddhism, and Confucianism will recognize close parallels to the Toyota Way. Concepts of a mission of serving society, fostering respect for people, continually striving for perfection, deeply reflecting on where you have just been and what you can improve, always searching for weaknesses leading to problem solving to improve, and taking responsibility for your own development and the development of others are all central to these Asian philosophies. However, Toyota was also heavily influenced by the West. If Japan is a nation of borrowers, Toyota has been borrowing on steroids. Throughout the evolution of the company, the leaders were constantly on the lookout for new ideas, but they would never simply copy general tools or programs. Problems drove solutions, and any new idea was carefully piloted, improved, and fit into the evolving system of TPS and the Toyota Way. The writings of Henry Ford, the teachings of Dr. W. Edwards Deming, and the U.S. military program of Training Within Industry are examples of influences central to Toyota's development. But Toyota selected pieces from each to integrate into its way, such as PDCA from Deming, job instruction training from Training Within Industry, and Henry Ford's concepts of flow and eliminating waste. These were all integrated into a common system and culture, which did not even have to be written down because it was so deeply engrained in the leadership.

That being said, with globalization, Toyota has also had the experience of needing to hire leaders from the outside and develop them quickly, while simultaneously running a highly efficient and successful operation. That is essentially the story of Toyota in North America. The pivotal event that helped launch this globalization took place in 1984, when, in a 50-50 partnership with General Motors, Toyota launched the NUMMI (New United Motors Manufacturing Incorporated) joint venture in California.

The launch of the NUMMI plant was momentous for Toyota. NUMMI was Toyota's first attempt to implement the Toyota Production System (TPS)[7] in America on the scale of a full assembly plant. It was the company's first attempt to transfer its corporate culture, its leadership style and approach, to American managers. Convis was the first general manager of NUMMI, and he had to relearn much that he thought he had learned from GM and Ford about being a leader. The process of learning, adjusting, and developing American Toyota leaders was lived by Convis and studied extensively by Jeff Liker—it's the insights from these efforts by Toyota over the past 25 years that have allowed us to construct a model of Toyota leadership.

The experiences of Toyota in successfully developing leaders in America and in other countries and cultures throughout the world give hope that other companies can also do this. We do not expect every company to teach its leaders to act according to the precepts of Japanese culture. Even Gary Convis admits that the patient process of developing Toyota leaders through questioning and indirect guidance is not his personal style. His style blends a more directive American approach with the Japanese approach. However, Convis has thoroughly internalized the core values of the Toyota Way, especially a deep respect for people and belief in the incredible power of *kaizen*. Investing for the long term in highly capable leaders who grow to live the philosophy is something that any company can do if its senior executives are committed to excellence.

The next four chapters walk through each of the stages of the Toyota leadership model, primarily using stories of how Toyota developed leadership capability in the United States from NUMMI's launch in 1984 through the present. We then step away from Toyota and consider how Convis and others used Toyota-style leadership to set a struggling American company, Dana, on a positive course toward operational excellence. This sets the stage for considering what other companies that have far different histories and cultures can learn from how Toyota develops its leaders.

The most fundamental lessons are not to attempt to copy Toyota's culture or exact approach to leadership development, as that would be contrary to the Toyota Way. Toyota evolved its own culture without copying any other. Nor is it even possible to "implement" a new culture like we might a piece of software. The much broader and more important lessons are to understand the value of a strong and coherent leadership philosophy, investing deeply and deliberately in nurturing a culture and developing leaders, and to have ways in which leaders are intensely focused on self-development and developing others to continuously improve all processes. We see too many organizations with weaknesses in all these areas, so we hope to inspire a new way of thinking about leadership development.

# Chapter 2

# Self-Development: Reliably Identifying and Coaching Developing Leaders at the *Gemba*

*Only that one in the world who is most perfectly sincere is able to give full development to his nature. Being able to give full development to his nature he is able to give full development to the nature of other human beings.*

—from *The Doctrine of the Mean* by Zisi, grandson of Confucius

Are leaders born or made? This nature versus nurture question has been thoroughly debated in leadership literature for at least a century, if not longer. Toyota's answer to this question of whether leadership is innate or learned is a resounding yes. Yes, leaders are born—or, to put it another way, some people simply do not have leadership abilities or aspirations, and no amount of training, in whatever form, will change that. But also, yes, leaders have to learn to be leaders. Taking individuals with leadership potential and telling them, "This is what a leader is like. Please act like this from now on," is useless. The only way to become a Toyota leader is to learn the Toyota style of leadership by doing through a continuous, never-ending process. Mirroring Toyota's dedication to continuous improvement of its products, even the most senior leaders of Toyota are constantly learning and relearning how to be a Toyota leader. When he was president, Katsuaki Watanabe would tell classes of young Toyota executives, "I do not think I have a complete understanding [of the Toyota Way] even today, and I have worked for the company for 43 years."

Confucius saw self-development as a matter of sincere and dedicated practice. In his description on the true quest for morality:[1]

> *One who attains sincerity chooses what is good and holds to it firmly. This involves broad learning, extensive inquiry, careful thought, clear discrimination, and earnest practice. When there is anything one has not studied,…or has studied but been unable to understand, one will not give up.…If there be anything which he has not practiced, or his practice fails in earnestness, he will not give up. If another man succeeds by effort, he will use a hundred efforts. If another man succeeds by ten efforts, he will use a thousand. Let a man proceed in this way, and, though dull, he will surely become intelligent; though weak, he will surely become strong.*

Morality for Confucius begins with "cultivation of the self." This is a "steadfast quest to become fully human."[2] Note that Confucius defined "humanness" as something you have to strive to achieve. We are born animals, and we have to work throughout our lives to become more and more human. There are both vertical and horizontal dimensions to this quest that together form a unified, coherent way. Vertical refers to self-development through intensive self-study and deliberate practice focused on building an ethical and moral base. Horizontal is the need to cultivate harmonious and respectful relations, starting within the family and then broadening to the community, the state, the international community, and ultimately the entire world and cosmos. This happens through education, with support by more senior persons who are further developed and have a moral responsibility to teach junior people who wish to learn. The "teachers" continue to have teachers who are taking responsibility for their learning, as the students must still be responsible for their own learning. We do not claim to be experts on Confucianism or any of the other complex religious and culture influences on Japan. However, we do see striking similarities between the teachings of Confucius and the Toyota Way, such as

- A lifelong pursuit of self-development so that you can serve society
- Striving for perfection, recognizing that humans are never perfect
- Openness to self-development and continuous learning
- Practice rooted in a deep understanding of reality
- A self-critical attitude with reflections every day on your weaknesses and what you can improve
- A deep respect for more senior people who have invested in developing themselves and have something to teach
- The concept of "responsibility," including responsibility for developing others as you develop yourself

Malcolm Gladwell's popular book *Outliers*[2] also seeks to dispel the myth of the individual genius who through sheer natural talent rises to the top of her profession and becomes rich and famous. For example, he quotes a study by Stanford professor Lewis Terman, who asked California schoolteachers to nominate the best and brightest students in their classes; he screened those 250,000 nominees with successive IQ testing and identified 1470 children with IQs ranging from 140 to 200. He expected extraordinary things from this group simply because they had high IQs, and he followed them for many years. Unfortunately, he had to reject his hypothesis when he found that their success was no different from that in a random sample of the population. Gladwell has a different theory: nature is part of the story, but it must be combined with circumstances that allow for deliberate practice (for at least 10,000 hours), hard work, and opportunity. He cites case after case of famous people (e.g., the Beatles, Bill Gates, Steve Jobs) who happened to have extraordinary opportunities to practice their craft for far more hours than their contemporaries and then happened to be at the right place at the right time to exploit those skills. For example, Gates and Jobs happened to be born at a time when their extraordinary computer skills coincided with their becoming of working age at the time of the emergence of the personal computer. He agrees that there is such a thing as native talent and intelligence, but that it must be combined with being in the right environment to motivate hard work with a strong focus and support for learning. He also emphasizes the critical role of culture in shaping the way we approach opportunities for self-development and take the necessary risks to put ourselves in positions to be abnormally successful.

In line with these principles, at Toyota, the first step in leadership development is identifying people who have the potential to become Toyota leaders. A desire, even passion, for self-development is the trait that Toyota uses to identify leadership potential. The focus on self-development as a marker for leadership extends from hourly team members all the way to the highest level of the organization. Only those who show the drive and capacity for self-development get promoted to the next level of leadership. And Toyota provides extraordinary opportunities for developing that talent in the individuals who show the inner drive. But Toyota does not rely on chance, that is, people by happenstance being at the right place at the right time. Toyota deliberately creates situations to challenge people and coach them to routinely produce extraordinary people and leaders.

The extent to which Toyota *allows* self-development can't be emphasized enough, as it is extraordinarily different from the typical American practice, which emphasizes direct and controlled training and development. Nor is self-development at Toyota analogous to the "sink-or-swim" approach, where a company throws those with potential into the deep end of the pool and promotes those who manage to keep their heads above water. From our experience with many companies, the only thing you learn from the sink-or-swim approach is who is most willing to drown his peers and subordinates. While some companies boast about having such a competitive culture, the last two decades have repeatedly shown the dangers of corporate cultures that enable not just the talented, but also sociopaths to ride the fast track to the top of the company.

For the system to work, Toyota has to balance the need to give leaders and prospective leaders the space to self-develop while staying close enough to reliably identify and coach them so that they self-develop in ways that are consistent with the Toyota values.

# Self-Development Begins with Learning

So how does Toyota create the conditions that allow both self-development and close monitoring to identify the self-developers who will live out the Toyota values and become Toyota leaders? Toyota uses aptitude tests for a preliminary screening of new hires,[4] but it does not believe that formal tests are useful for determining who has leadership potential. Coming from a farming culture, Toyota knows that you can tell whether a person is a hard worker only by seeing her work in many challenging conditions. It stands to reason that you can judge leadership only by directly observing how people lead in challenging situations. Of course, people can do only what they have learned to do, so they need teachers to develop them.

## Repeated Learning Cycles

The leadership identification process at Toyota begins with the most junior worker receiving training from a *sensei* (which means both *master* and *teacher*). By American standards, Toyota makes remarkable investments in employee development. All students are given the opportunity to take the initiative under the tutelage of a *sensei*. The role of the *sensei* is to provide challenges, structured opportunities, and coaching, so that the student has an opportunity to learn by doing. It is up to the student to rise to the challenges, however. In many cases, the *sensei* are the student's immediate supervisor and a supervisor two levels up.

To understand the Toyota way of teaching and learning, it is more useful to think about learning a sport or a musical instrument than to think about learning leadership models in a conference room with PowerPoint or in an MBA program. Nobody would expect to become a virtuoso violinist or cellist by watching a video of Itzhak Perlman or Yo-Yo Ma. You must start at the beginning with an instructor who gives you carefully selected drills, and then you must have the initiative to practice and practice until you work your way up to performing entire pieces. The instructor will not follow you around and force you to practice. On the other hand, a master instructor who is trying to develop a protégé feels responsible for the success or failure of his student. Thus, the student isn't left entirely to her own devices.

*Responsibility* is an important word in the Toyota vocabulary, both for the student and for the teacher. The student bears the responsibility for his own desire to succeed. He is responsible for delivering results in the right way, for genuinely reflecting on the feedback from his *sensei*, for taking failure personally, and for striving for self-improvement. The teacher, in turn, is responsible for the student's development, since ultimately, if the student fails, the teacher has failed, and the teacher is responsible for reflecting on the causes of her failure. It is truly collaborative learning between the teacher and the student, and there is joint responsibility.

Too often, companies expect us to learn to be leaders through a short training class. The assumption is that if leaders in training understand the concepts intellectually, their actions will mirror their understanding. Unfortunately, there is often no direct connection between what we conceptualize and what we do. For example, all the intellectual understanding in the world will not automatically make one a great tennis player, a great musician, or a great cook. A set of basic skills has to be learned through repetition and what is now popularly known as "deep practice." The often quoted number of 10,000 hours of practice gets us thinking in the right direction.[5]

One of the clearest instructions on how to practice a musical instrument comes from a summer camp for kids who are budding talents—the Meadowmount school in New York State. They have three simple, logical rules that we believe apply to learning any skill:

- Practice more slowly. Then still more slowly. Then even *more* slowly. The rule of thumb: if a passerby can recognize the song, it's not being practiced properly. Skill circuits don't "care" how fast you go; what matters is firing it correctly—the same rule followed by tennis players at Spartak.
- Break the skill into chunks, and then reconstruct it. Meadowmounters scissor their sheet music into strips, learn each strip, then rebuild the entire piece. This reconstructive act (which, anecdotally, is exactly how the teenage Ben Franklin taught himself to write essays) works because it exactly mirrors and reinforces the desired skill circuits, which are, after all, literal connections in our brains.

- Locate errors. Meadowmounters practice what they call "discernment": finding the mistake and using it to navigate toward the right notes—the basics of deep practice.

Now, of course, to apply advice like this to leadership requires understanding of the fundamental skills required for leadership. Here is a selection of some of the most important skills for Toyota leadership.

- Active and open-minded observing of the work of the organization
- Active listening to hear what people are really saying
- Systems thinking
- Understanding the actual strengths and weaknesses of each person
- Clearly defining problems and identifying the root cause
- Planning
- Creatively identifying countermeasures to the true root causes
- Translating plans into action with clear accountability
- Taking the time and energy for deep reflection to identify further opportunities for improvement
- Motivating and influencing people across the organization (with no direct authority) toward common objectives
- Being able to teach others all of the above

You can take any of these complex skills, break it into pieces, practice it slowly, get feedback on errors, take steps to correct the errors through further practice, and continue until you have reached some level of competency. As with any complex skill, you can continue to refine these skills for decades with a skilled teacher, rather than spending one or two weeks in a leadership seminar. A detailed explanation of how Toyota trains on relatively repetitive manual jobs using the "job instruction training" method can be found in *Toyota Talent*, and the process fits remarkably well with the Meadowmount rules.[6] Of course leadership cannot be broken down into two-second steps, with each step practiced repeatedly. The behaviors are far too complex. But think of the concept of learning over time, practicing, getting feedback, trying again, and repeating the cycle over and over; certainly this can be applied to any of the leadership skills.

## The *Shu Ha Ri* Cycle of Learning

The basic principles of Toyota learning can be traced to the teachings of Zen Buddhism,[7] but they are not unique to Toyota. Researcher and author Mike Rother finds parallels between Toyota's teaching methods and the Japanese concept of *kata*.[8] *Kata*, which literally means "form," is the basis for teaching many Japanese arts like karate, kabuki, or the tea ceremony, and it is the way people learn to perform a highly detailed and scripted task. In the early stages, the student learns the fundamentals through repetition of individual skills that are gradually linked together into the whole. At the beginning, the student must copy the teacher exactly, without questioning or variation. As these routines become second nature, the student can begin to find his own adaptations to improve on what he has been taught— his own interpretations.

The core of *kata* is the layered learning cycle, which is called in Japanese *shu ha ri*. These three terms refer to three stages of learning for the student and three levels of involvement for the teacher: *shu* means "to protect," *ha* means "to break away," and *ri* means "freedom to create."

In the *shu* phase, the student, under the watchful eye of the master, learns the fundamentals by repeatedly performing tasks to precise standards. At this stage, the student is watched carefully by the teacher, who is in a sense protecting him, and the work product, from failure. In the *ha* stage, the student has more freedom to practice unsupervised, although the master checks on her; the student can apply the rules creatively, but still follows the standard form quite rigidly. In the *ri* stage, the rules and behaviors have become so ingrained that the student no longer thinks about them consciously. The actions come naturally, and the student is then in a position to develop her own understanding and to improve on what she has learned. This cycle continues throughout the individual's life. It is a learning cycle because the student is going through *shu ha ri* over and over, more and deeply, periodically returning to the basics.

It's critically important to understand that in the *shu ha ri* cycle, success hasn't been achieved when the student can emulate the master perfectly. That is only the *ha* stage. This is the mistake that many who have superficially studied Japanese culture or Toyota make when they conclude that this approach produces automatons who are incapable of thinking for themselves. The real measure of success in the Toyota learning cycle is reaching the *ri* stage, where the student isn't just mindlessly acting as a clone of the teacher but has mastered the process so thoroughly that he can make changes that improve on what he has learned. To return to our violinist analogy, classical musicians and aficionados know that there is a world of difference between someone who is technically proficient and someone who can interpret a piece with her own unique style. It's the difference between the fourth-chair violinist at the symphony and the acclaimed soloist.

## *Shu Ha Ri* in Practice

*Shu ha ri* is the basis of all learning at Toyota, beginning with the first-day-on-the-job, unskilled line worker. These workers have to learn to assemble parts into a vehicle in a standardized way, the same way every time. A worker on a Toyota assembly line is taught using the job instruction method, which starts with a breakdown of a short-cycle job (one that takes between one and three minutes) into its most basic component parts, with each part lasting only a few seconds.

In the *shu* stage, the worker is taught using a cycle of see, try, say, and practice. The worker sees the teacher do the step and then tries it himself. Next, the teacher repeats the step, this time saying aloud the name of the step and some key points about it, and then asks the student to do the same. The teacher then goes through the step yet again, naming the step and stating the key points, but now adding the reasons why these points are important, and asks the student to repeat all this. Through repetition, the worker learns the step and can move on to the next step.[9]

As the student masters each step, he begins to string the steps together, ultimately learning the whole job. During the *ha* stage, the teacher will still stay around, checking on the student. The teacher continues to bear the primary responsibility for the trainee's performing the job in the specified time with good quality. The trainee is expected to do the job exactly as specified with fine detail until he reaches the point of *ri*, at which he can do the job without thinking.

At this stage, when the actions needed to complete the job are habitual, the worker can focus on observing the overall work procedure and take the responsibility for improving it—and for teaching others. The execution of each assembly-line job with precision, absolute consistency, and accuracy is called *standardized work* in Toyota. Standardized work is a fundamental requirement of the Toyota Production System (TPS) and enables the identification of self-developers. Standardized work is not static, though. As improvements are made to the job by *ri*-stage workers who are doing it, they are incorporated into the standardized work.

Toyota considers every job important enough to teach in this detailed, meticulous way and views it as the job of everyone in the company to become a master of her craft. A one-minute job of installing a seat belt is critical for the safety of the driver, and precision is needed for quality purposes as well as to achieve the highest level of productivity and efficiency. But it's not just assembly-line jobs that follow this pattern.

For example, Kazuhiko Miyadera, former executive vice president for research and development for Europe, told Jeff that his most intense period of learning as a young professional in Japan was when he was assigned to work under a master designer (really drawer) of instrument panels for one year. By the time the design gets to this person, the look of the instrument panel in general has been set, and this person does the full-sized drawing, filling in the details. In many Western companies, people who draw such things as instrument panels (meaning the layout, dimensions, and detailed design of the locations of items on the panel, as opposed to the mechanical or electrical engineering behind the scenes) are hourly employees, and their work is supervised by a degreed engineer. However, even though Miyadera already had an engineering degree and the master designer did not, he was still required to spend one year on what was, from a non-Toyota perspective, a menial task. In the Toyota culture, however, spending a year as the student of one of the company's top designers was a high honor. Miyadera's job during that year was, like an apprentice, to draw a small portion of an instrument panel in excruciating detail under careful scrutiny; the master designer he worked under drew the rest.

Each day Miyadera went to the drawing board, pencil in hand. Occasionally the master would critique something that Miyadera had drawn, but would leave the future VP to consider how to correct the weakness; in other words, the master designer pointed out deficiencies but never told Miyadera how to fix them. Over time, Miyadera gained a master's understanding of the form and function of an instrument panel. He realized that the designer was doing fundamental engineering work. From the perspective of Toyota's learning culture, if Miyadera was going to lead engineers, he needed to master the basic skills of engineering. He was following the *shu ha ri* cycle, starting from the most basic task of an engineer. In fact, Miyadera told Jeff that he learned more about real engineering in that year than in any other year in his life.

## Shu Ha Ri beyond Toyota

Some observers of Toyota question whether these practices, built as they are on Japanese culture, can work at other companies. Certainly Toyota's success in designing and building cars in the United States is a powerful argument for the general applicability of this model. Of course, naysayers argue that although the practices are used in the United States, the overall corporate culture remains Japanese, and this accounts for its success. We certainly agree that Toyota's culture is unique and that it is the basis of the company's success, yet the *shu ha ri* approach is as deeply embedded in Western culture as it is in Japanese culture and was the dominant approach to learning until the early part of the twentieth century. The *shu ha ri* approach has important parallels to the Socratic method and is essentially identical to the apprenticeship model of instruction. Until the Industrial Revolution, when mass production was developed, most skills were taught to apprentices by masters, beginning with the guild system of the Middle Ages; in some trades, like plumbing, this practice continues to the present day. It is certainly highly visible in the sports world. How often do you hear professional coaches or players at the highest level of their sport talk about "getting back to basics" or "focusing on the fundamentals"? Even at the height of his success, Tiger Woods would return to the fundamentals of his swing, reworking it and starting over again to in a sense relearn golf at a deeper level, sometimes going backward in order to move forward. That's the *shu ha ri* cycle, and it never ends.

This approach is also making a comeback, completely independent of Toyota, among those who study educational methods (where it goes by the name of "learning by doing"). Recent scholars have been finding that learning by doing with a coach is a very natural way for adults to learn any new skill. (See sidebar for a summary of the Dreyfus and Dreyfus five-step process, which is very similar to *shu ha ri*.)[10] Unfortunately, Western education has largely abandoned this method in favor of a lecture-oriented model, in which "teaching" is defined as showing or telling the student what to think or do, then providing shortcuts that will speed up the pupil's route to proficiency. This lecture method is now common everywhere in the Western world, from middle schools to universities to corporate off-sites.

Before we move on to discuss how *shu ha ri* sets the stage for self-development and the identification of leaders, we have to emphasize one final aspect of the Toyota cycle of learning. The role of the *sensei* at Toyota is utterly different from that of the modern Western trainer or leadership expert delivering lectures. The lecture-based approach to learning carries the implicit assumption that the lecturer or trainer knows the answers and that her value is in providing shortcuts to the mastery of a skill. Essentially, the message is that if the trainees pay attention to how the master does it, they can bypass the long, arduous process of learning by practice themselves. In contrast, the value of the *sensei* is in making sure that the student doesn't take shortcuts. The implicit assumption here is that shortcuts may produce a short-term gain in efficiency, but they prevent the student from truly understanding and mastering the skill, ultimately resulting in systemic failure. Within the *shu ha ri* cycle, there are no shortcuts; you must demonstrate true mastery of one step before you proceed to the next.

## *Shu Ha Ri* and Leadership

While it's easy to see how *shu ha ri* applies to manual tasks like those on an assembly line, you might question how this approach works

# The Dreyfus Model Compared to *Shu Ha Ri*

Dreyfus and Dreyfus[11] found that in learning skills that require a good deal of judgment, such as playing chess, people advance through five stages: (1) novice, (2) advanced beginner, (3) competent, (4) proficient, and (5) expert. As the learner progresses, she is moving from rigid adherence to a set of rules provided by the teacher to the freedom to use the rules fluidly and innovate:

1. *Novice.* A novice must rigidly adhere to the teacher's rules without deviation. The teacher breaks down the task into individual basic elements that are taught one at a time.
2. *Advanced beginner.* Someone at this level can begin to string together the elements into combinations of steps that make up a routine, but each element is still treated separately. The student cannot adapt the routines to the situation.
3. *Competent.* This person can perform routines comfortably without focusing intensively on them and can begin to see longer-term goals, as well as adapt routines to different situations.
4. *Proficient.* Someone who is proficient has a holistic view of the situation and can apply appropriate routines to solve the problems at hand. She follows basic rules of application as guidelines.
5. *Expert.* The expert no longer needs rules of application to check off and can intuitively adapt routines to each situation. She has a deep understanding of the tools and principles, how they apply, and the reasons for specific courses of action.

The first two Dreyfus stages are similar to the *shu* stage, stage 3 is like the *ha* stage, and stages 4 and 5 seem to correspond to the *ri* stage. One difference is that in the philosophy behind the *shu ha ri* (and the Toyota Way), there are no "experts." No matter how advanced someone is in the skill, there is still much more to learn.

beyond the shop floor. Learning to be a leader is, of course, very different from learning to attach a bumper on a Corolla—leadership can't be broken down into one-minute tasks (no matter how many copies of *The One-Minute Manager* are in circulation). But at Toyota, *shu ha ri* is the basic premise for the training and development of all workers, including leaders. We saw how Miyadera went through this learning cycle in engineering, and it is common for first-year engineers to work in production jobs for months and later to spend up to a year learning the computer-aided design (CAD) system, going through the cycle of *shu ha ri*.

A typical Toyota leader in manufacturing began as a line worker going through *shu ha ri* cycles to perform each job on the team until she reached the point where she could teach those jobs. Once she reached the *ri* stage for every job, she was assigned to perform some of the individual tasks of a team leader, taking on the team leader role while the actual team leader was on vacation. Eventually she earned the right to lead the team full-time under the careful supervision of her supervisor, called the group leader. This cycle is repeated as team leaders become group leaders and group leaders become assistant managers. Even plant managers typically start their careers building automobiles. When a successful leader is promoted into a position of broader responsibility and challenge, she goes back to first principles and starts over through a version of *shu ha ri*: first she learns the individual jobs in the area to standard, then she practices to the point at which leading the area becomes comfortable, and finally she leads a major improvement initiative in the area, all the while developing her subordinates. This model has been followed since the early days of Toyota, when it was laid down by Taiichi Ohno.

Taiichi Ohno is the archetypal Toyota *sensei*. In the 1950s and 1960s, with the executive sponsorship of then-president Eiji Toyoda, Ohno created the Toyota Production System on the shop floor through trial and error. Ohno was also responsible for training the next generation of Toyota senior leaders. He was a harsh but compassionate teacher, and many of his students, like former chairman Fujio Cho, went on to become top leaders in the company. Ohno was not particularly interested in presenting specific terminology and theories to his students. Instead, he aimed to shape the way they thought about problems and how they acted. He did this without doing much "teaching" in a way that Western audiences would recognize. Instead, Ohno believed that the most important development came from daily experiences at the *gemba*—where the work is done.

One of Ohno's most famous teaching techniques involved the use of the "Ohno circle." While working with a particular pupil, Ohno would draw a circle on the shop floor and ask the student to stand in it. Then Ohno would go away, sometimes for hours. Intermittently, Ohno would check in and ask questions: "What did you see? Why did that happen? What have you learned?" Ohno never provided much in the way of feedback to the student's responses. He simply asked challenging questions and grunted disapprovingly when he did not like the answer. There was tremendous pressure, but it came from within the student as he struggled to please the respected teacher. By the end of the day, Ohno usually was satisfied that the student had learned to observe more deeply and simply said, "Please go home." The most unfortunate students had to come back for more the next day. What Ohno was teaching in his unique style was only the first stage of one specific leadership skill—the ability to observe and analyze the actual situation in depth and without preconceived ideas. This is one of Toyota's central values and a critical aspect of Toyota leadership.

## A *Shu Ha Ri* Story of Developing a Young Leader at the *Gemba*

A Toyota leader cannot teach what he cannot do himself, and one of the most basic skills is the problem-solving method that Ohno insisted all of his students master. It may help make this more real to consider an actual example. The *sensei* in this case was a 30-year Toyota veteran and a disciple of Ohno, Rikio Iitaka. The student was Yuri Rodrigues, an employee who had been hired by Gary Convis because of his tremendous leadership potential. At the time Yuri was hired, he had been working for a BMW-Chrysler joint venture that built engines in Brazil and was a fast-track employee. He had an industrial engineering degree from a top university, and he had become a standout in the joint venture, rising to higher and higher levels of responsibility. This plant was viewed by the parent companies as a model of lean manufacturing, and he was viewed as a growing expert in lean methods. In fact, his next opportunity was to come to Chrysler full-time as an assistant plant manager. Gary offered him a job working for Toyota Motor Manufacturing Kentucky (TMMK), but explained that he would have to take a position a few levels below what Chrysler was offering and work his way up the ladder by demonstrating his understanding of TPS. Surprisingly, Yuri had the self-awareness to realize that he was not as much of an expert as Chrysler thought and would develop to a higher level if he worked for Toyota.

Yuri had some visa issues, so Gary arranged for him to work in a Toyota factory in Brazil for the year, with his salary coming out of the Kentucky plant's budget—in essence paying for a year of education. Yuri was made assistant manager in Assembly in the Brazil plant, with responsibility for the trim, chassis, and final lines, despite his having no experience in an assembly plant. In Yuri's first humbling experience with his new mentor, Rikio Iitaka used the famous "Ohno circle," asking Yuri to stand in one place (within the circle on the floor) and come up with *kaizen* ideas for the chassis department of the assembly line. His *sensei* then left. Yuri at first resisted. After all, he was a professional industrial engineer, and he did not need such an elementary assignment. After 20 minutes, when the *sensei* came back, he looked at Yuri's paper and saw five ideas written down. The coordinator looked at Yuri, shook his head back and forth, and said, "Bad, bad, bad! Write 25 ideas in the next 10 minutes." Realizing how hard it was made Yuri reflect on whether he was really the big shot he thought he was.

The next big challenge was solving a real quality problem. About 55 defective cars were sitting outside in the yard waiting for repair. Using his engineering expertise, Yuri figured out that the defects were coming out of the trim department as a result of inconsistent torque in attaching bolts. The team members were using relatively primitive impact wrenches that required judgment in tightening the bolts, something that he had not expected, since in his previous job, the workers had always used more sophisticated torque wrenches that would automatically shut off when the torque reached the precise level required.

Yuri presented to upper management his proposed countermeasure, which was to buy new torque wrenches, expecting that his *sensei* would be proud of his problem-solving prowess. Instead, the *sensei* interrupted Yuri's presentation to say, "Okay, so I see you contained the problem. But do you want me to buy new $400 wrenches for everyone in the whole plant? Because if you are telling me that's your solution for that problem, that's what I'm going to have to do. I suggest you go back and observe the team members to really understand the problem."

This sent Yuri back to the drawing board. The result was a painful odyssey of solutions and negative reactions. For example, Yuri discovered that some of the guns were too old and could not hold the torque and asked if he could replace those. His *sensei*'s response: no, think some more!

Finally Yuri thought back to his early training in problem solving and remembered the Five Whys method: ask why five times to get to the root cause. He came up with two causes. First, the team members were not well trained. When a team member was shooting the bolts using the more primitive impact wrenches, he should be able to hear a different sound when he reached the right level of torque. The team members did not know that. Yuri spot-checked team members throughout the entire line, and about 40 percent did not know how to feel and hear when the correct torque was achieved. The second cause was that the maintenance system for the impact guns was deficient. The guns were getting weak, but no one was maintaining them or changing them out before they got to that stage—there was no preventive maintenance. Yuri also checked the maintenance of other tools, and saw that preventive maintenance was poor throughout the line.

Yuri developed a training program, revised the standardized work to make clear the key point about listening for the sound, and worked with Maintenance to develop a preventive maintenance program. After five months, the faulty cars had disappeared from the yard and the low-torque problems were reduced to almost zero. Quality defects in Trim Assembly were reduced from 0.3 defect per car to 0.1, and the cost of maintenance of the tools was reduced from $9 per unit to $1.50 per unit. Yuri didn't have to buy those expensive torque wrenches after all, and the maintenance program had a broad impact throughout the assembly plant. Yuri had gone through a critical *shu ha ri* learning cycle, and by going through many more, he would become a successful Toyota manager.

# How *Shu Ha Ri* Allows For and Helps Identify Self-Development

We've asserted that the *shu ha ri* cycle of learning is the basis for allowing individuals to have the space to self-develop while also allowing the existing leaders to accurately assess any particular individual's commitment to self-development—and that it therefore helps the leaders to identify the right individuals to move into leadership at Toyota. There are five aspects of *shu ha ri* that deliver these results:

- Standardized work (the form)
- Deep observation by the *sensei* to guide
- No answers to allow the student to learn by struggling
- On-the-job development to get practice and feedback
- Steadily increasing challenges to grow the student's capability

Let's look at each in turn.

## Standardized Work as a Foundation for Learning

Both of us can still clearly remember the first time we visited a Toyota plant operating at the height of efficiency. For Gary, it was just after he'd been hired to become the general manager at NUMMI (New United Motor Manufacturing Inc.), Toyota's joint venture with General Motors), when he went to Japan to visit the Takaoka plant, which would be the training ground for Toyota's new American employees. For Jeff, it was during his first visit to Japan in the early 1980s, when he toured Toyota engine and assembly plants and plants of Toyota suppliers. The impression was shocking compared to what we were both used to in American auto plants. Machines were not stopped, with workers idly standing by waiting for a repair specialist to get the time to look at them. Workers were not walking to and fro in almost random patterns, getting parts and tools. The impression was more like that of an incredibly finely tuned machine—even of a finely trained troupe of dancers.

For Gary particularly, his weeks of training in Japan for NUMMI were nothing short of stunning. After years of working in relatively undisciplined American auto companies, it was shocking to see team members following the standard process exactly every time. For instance, nobody ever lost a *kanban* card (used to track the flow of parts in order to manage just-in-time delivery). Nobody ever forgot to put the card in the chute at the right time. Nobody ever prematurely pulled a *kanban* from containers to advance-order parts. And he could see almost no wasted motions in the workers' carefully choreographed routines. In Japan, allusions are frequently made to the traditional tea ceremony, where the actions of servers are carefully choreographed to create the most aesthetically pleasing experience for the guest. In fact, years later, on a trip to Japan, Akio Toyoda (now the president of Toyota) took Gary to a tea ceremony. He casually asked Gary what he saw. It turns out that it was a favorite way for Akio to teach the power of standardized work.

Yet the system wasn't rigid. On the contrary, as with the tea servers, the precision and exactitude with which team members performed their jobs was a result of a focus on how to get closer and closer to perfection. The standardized approach enhances quality and productivity in manufacturing, and provides the basis for individual team members to improve on the standardized approach.

We've found that for many Americans, the concept of standardized work is somewhat frightening, perhaps bringing to mind either Charlie Chaplin's comic version of depersonalized industrial production (*Modern Times*, 1936) or the more recent *Stepford Wives*. Even those who accept the concept for the assembly line are very resistant to the idea that it applies elsewhere in a company. While these doubts are understandable, they are the result of missing a fundamental part of standardized work: it creates as much freedom as it sacrifices, if not more.

The absolute dedication to standardized work at Toyota grew out of necessity. The company created the just-in-time approach to manufacturing because it could not afford to carry inventory. Just-in-time kept Toyota's limited working capital working rather than sitting in warehouses or in boxes along the assembly line. Of course, there's a huge risk in just-in-time production: if something goes wrong, there is no slack in the system. If you run out of a part, the whole assembly line shuts down. Therefore, it was imperative that Toyota not just reduce mistakes, but eliminate them. Standardized work is first of all a tool for eliminating mistakes.

However, many people misunderstand exactly how it is a tool for eliminating mistakes. If you think of standardized work simply as repetitively following a script, then all it will do is limit mistakes. Human beings are fallible, circumstances are uncontrollable, and therefore no matter how precisely you script the behavior you want, you will still have a large number of mistakes.

To understand how standardized work is really applied at Toyota, first you have to realize that human beings have a limited capacity for paying attention. Without standardized work, all of the worker's attention has to be directed toward the minute details of the job: "Where is the tool? Where is the part? How tight does this fastener need to be?" With standardized work, as the worker moves from *shu* to *ha* and on to *ri*, these minute details can become routine enough that she no longer has to devote attention to them. Those who stop there, thinking that these jobs must be unbearably boring if they are so rote that no thought is required, completely miss the point. At Toyota, the point of taking away the need to pay attention to the details of the job is so that the worker can pay attention to the bigger picture and find ways to improve the process that will not just limit mistakes, but eliminate them. We realize we keep harping on the point that standardized work is not static, but it is critical. At Toyota, in the best plants, every job is constantly under review by the workers performing it and is being improved.

Standardized work also plays an important role in identifying self-developers. It provides a baseline against which to measure improvement in an accurate way. In many companies, processes or goals are fuzzily defined, so that you get a situation in which it is quite difficult to tell whether a proposed change is actually an improvement or just another way to do the job. This is a problem we've frequently seen at companies that are attempting to imitate Toyota, and especially its employee suggestion system, which is in part a tool for improving standardized work. In fact, it's a problem that Gary himself confronted when he first left NUMMI to take a position at Toyota as president of Toyota Motor Manufacturing Kentucky, the first wholly owned Toyota factory in the United States.

Suggestion systems are easy to abuse if you take your eyes off standardized work. Understood properly, the point of a suggestion system is not only to improve a process but also to give employees a self-development opportunity. An individual can take the initiative, identify a problem and its solution, and channel that solution in a way that can actually make a difference. But one of the frequent ways in which suggestion systems break down is that it becomes difficult to tell whether a suggestion is going to produce a measurable and significant improvement.

When Gary first arrived at TMMK, the plant had grown so rapidly for several years that the focus on standardized work and evaluating suggestions against the standardized work baseline had waned. As a result, many relatively trivial suggestions were making it through the system. This quickly eroded the value of the system. It became more difficult for the leaders to distinguish the team members who were taking advantage of the opportunity for self-development from those who were flooding the system with unimportant suggestions in order to reap the small incentive payments that came along with suggestions.[12] Gary's first task at TMMK was to refocus the suggestion system so that it once again became a tool for promoting and identifying self-development. Doing so required adhering rigidly to the policies about how suggestions were to be reviewed and letting only the real contributions pass through, which virtually shut the system down for several months to put it back on the right track.

So, underlying *shu ha ri* is standardized work—the focus of the *shu* stage—which in turn underlies allowing and identifying self-development. Identifying self-development is a key leadership role of the *sensei* in the *shu ha ri* cycle.

## Deep Observation by the *Sensei*

In Chapter 1, we reviewed the values that set the standard for everything that Toyota does. One of these is the principle of *genchi genbutsu*, or "go and see where the work is done." In this context, it is the act of directly observing the actual person in actual situations to understand his strengths and weaknesses for potential promotion opportunities.

In an effort to increase efficiency, a huge number of modern companies have built up departments to handle all aspects of training, from basic job skills to leadership development. The idea is to keep those who are doing the best job doing their jobs; it's perceived as wasteful to have these people train others. Thinking about this construct for a moment reveals that while at first it may seem to be common sense, it's based on highly dubious logic. While trainers often claim to be experts, it's frankly hard to believe that anyone who is not doing a job on a daily basis can be an expert.

Under the *shu ha ri* system, *sensei* are an absolute requirement. The person doing the training and observing the student's progress has to be a master of what she is teaching.

Of course, a huge benefit of this process is that masters are the teachers, and therefore the quality of training immediately goes up. In terms of self-development, though, the benefit is that those who are most able to judge the quality of an employee's attempts at self-development are the ones who are judging them. Who can better see if an employee has come up with a truly meaningful improvement on standardized work than an expert on that standardized work? The chances of a master's recognizing opportunities to meaningfully help the self-development of others is much higher than if the task is left to someone else.

Let's consider an example. For Toyota, the principle of *genchi genbutsu* is a core value, so we would think that any deep involvement of Toyota executives at the *gemba* would be a positive. But in fact there are right and wrong ways to practice this deep value. Executives might feel good about getting out with the people and blending in, but in reality everyone knows who the executives are and the power they have. How they present themselves, what they say, and how they use that power is critical to being effective leaders who add value and are teachers. Without practice, a leader can easily end up solving problems for those that he is trying to develop rather than allowing self-development to proceed. Perhaps the hardest thing for a developing Toyota leader to learn is how to avoid using his skills in a way that provides a short-term benefit but is counterproductive to the longer-term goal of developing others.

A good example of good intentions potentially leading to bad outcomes is one of Gary's missteps during his early years at NUMMI. Just like the body shop, the paint shop at NUMMI had outdated equipment from the GM days. Even with the best paint booth, every car needs some minor repairs of small imperfections or problems with the surface coating. At NUMMI, the inspection and repair of these defects was all done on a moving line; the paint crew had to meet the *takt* time. Because of the equipment, some days there were so many repairs that the regular team couldn't keep up with the *takt*. On one such day, Gary decided to "act like a Toyota leader" and get his hands dirty by personally getting on the line and repairing cars.

The problems with each car were identified by inspectors, who filled out a ticket for the repair personnel to follow. The repair personnel were responsible for either fixing a defect directly or replacing a body panel if the defect couldn't be repaired. Gary leaped right in to make the repairs, helping to carry body panels or buff out paint defects. He was doing well at the repairs, although occasionally he had to call over the inspector to ask him to interpret a particular scribbled note about what needed to be fixed. He was feeling pretty good about himself, thinking he was acting exactly as a Toyota leader should—he was showing his commitment to quality and *genchi genbutsu*, he thought.

After he had been working on the line for more than an hour, the Japanese coordinator for the paint shop (essentially a peer in rank) happened by—and immediately asked Gary to come off the line so that they could have a conversation. The coordinator proceeded to tell Gary a Chinese folktale: A farm manager at a royal orchard was walking through the orchard one day, and it appeared that he was picking some fruit to eat. At the time it was forbidden for anyone to do this because the state owned the fruit, and eating it was stealing from the state. Work came to a halt. It turned out, however, that the manager was not picking the fruit, but was innocently pointing at a rare bird in the tree.

Then the coordinator thanked Gary for his time and walked away. Gary was more than a little confused. Clearly the coordinator was trying to share something important with him—although, in the Toyota

Way, he was not directing but was using a folktale to make Gary think, allowing Gary the opportunity for self-reflection.

Suddenly Gary realized the point: the workers in the apple orchard did not understand what the manager was doing and could easily misinterpret his innocent actions. Worse, the manager drew the attention of all the workers to himself, distracting them from doing their jobs. Gary's participation in making repairs in the paint shop, while motivated by good intentions, was actually disrupting the development of the team members there and distracting them from fixing the problem. Everyone was focused on Gary, not on countermeasures or on finding the root cause of the problem. In addition, when he was asking the inspector to explain the repairs needed, others interpreted that as Gary's questioning the need for these repairs. Gary's responsibility was not repairing cars but developing the team members', group leaders', and managers' ability to solve the real problem. By being too hands-on, he was abdicating responsibility for the development of his staff. The coordinator, conversely, had assumed responsibility for Gary's development by calling him away from what he was doing, but did not interfere with his self-development, since he used a folktale rather than a directive to give Gary the opportunity to reach a conclusion on his own. The more subtle approach created a learning experience that Gary still recalls vividly over 25 years later.

In Chapter 3, we'll continue to explore the role of the *sensei* in developing their pupils and the incredible investment that Toyota makes in ensuring the presence of *sensei*.

## No Answers from *Sensei*; the Student Must Deeply Reflect

The concept of *hansei* (reflection) is key to self-development at Toyota.[13] *Hansei* is the conscious process of looking back at oneself, picking apart what went well and what did not go well, and vowing to be better next time. All Toyota leaders are expected to demonstrate *hansei* in their learning process. We've mentioned before how different the role of a *sensei* is from that of a traditional Western teacher or lecturer. In the Western model of training, each lesson includes a summary of the key points that the student is supposed to learn. The role of the student is simply to memorize these key points. In the *shu ha ri* cycle, there are of course moments when the *sensei* shares "the answers"—this may occur (depending on the style of the *sensei*), but only at the *shu* stage, when the *sensei* is guiding the student in following the standard key points. Once the student is past the *shu* stage, the job of the *sensei* changes from providing answers to asking questions (again, similar to the Socratic method). The student is expected not to memorize key points but to engage in reflection, thinking about the question in terms of the core knowledge that he acquired during the *shu* stage and how it should be applied to future situations.

When Gary's *sensei* stopped his work in the paint inspection process and told him the story of the bird in the tree, he was asking Gary to reflect on what was happening. He could have simply pulled Gary aside and explained to him why it was not a good idea for him to be doing what he was doing. If he had done so, Gary would not have been so confused at first, but he also would not have struggled to figure out what his *sensei* was trying to communicate. It was a key moment of self-discovery for Gary because of his own deep reflection.

*Hansei* pervades operations at Toyota at both the personal and the group level. Many companies put together lessons learned workshops when a project encounters difficulties. At Toyota, *hansei* is expected from every leader on every project. For instance, after each new model is launched, a *hansei* process is kicked off in which the team reflects on how performance can be improved. A program manager for the Toyota Avalon, which launched a new model in 2004 that was widely considered to be a huge success in the market, describes it this way: "We had come in on time and under budget, and the Avalon was selling really well. But right away we had a two-day *hansei* to figure out what we could have done better. It was a bit morbid, like we'd failed instead of succeeded. But as we thought through the process, we found a lot of things we could have done better." The team members then summarized what they'd learned and shared the few most critical learnings with program managers for other vehicles so that they could benefit from the reflection and learning of the Avalon team.

But *hansei* works in terms of self-development only if the prospective leader isn't given answers by the *sensei*. The approach of the *sensei* varies with the situation: feedback can be as direct as asking some pointed questions about how a subordinate arrived at her conclusion and a mandate to look harder for root causes or as indirect as telling a story.

Gary, of course, has many examples of both from his decades of learning TPS. An early example that showed him the power of the approach occurred when he was plant manager during an equipment breakdown in the body shop at NUMMI. When Gary was at Ford, any time a serious breakdown occurred, all the higher-level managers would come to watch the maintenance technician do his job. Newly inducted into the Toyota Way, Gary was impressed by the value of *genchi genbutsu*, or go and see. So when a serious breakdown occurred in the body shop one day, Gary went running from his desk to go and see the problem. On his arrival at the scene, a group of managers was already there, including Seizo Okamoto (who went on to become president of Toyota's plant in Indiana), a Japanese welding expert who had been sent to the United States to be the coordinator for the body shop. Gary, displaying his best problem-solving skills, immediately began asking questions about the situation. Okamoto motioned Gary aside and said, "Gary, I can't fix the machine. You can't fix the machine." Then he pointed to all of the other managers who were standing around trying to use their problem-solving skills. "This is another example of waste. Think about how you avoid waste and how you can add value."

In his role as *sensei* for the body shop, Okamoto belonged there to coach the managers who were most directly responsible. Gary did not. Upon reflection, Gary understood that the body shop manager needed to solve the problem or call for help if he needed it. What the higher-level managers should have been doing while that interruption was happening was looking at the whole plant and asking what could be done to minimize the impact of this problem if it lasted for one hour or two hours or more. Did they need to shut down some of the preceding processes and look for volunteers to go home? Could they make sure they had some training prepared so that they had a productive way to use people's time if the assembly line needed to be shut down?

There's nothing magical about this approach or the insight that it delivered for Gary. But the approach of not providing answers and allowing the learner to engage in *hansei* and come to conclusions for himself is both more effective (that is, the lesson is far more likely to be really learned and become a part of the learner's future "tool kit") and a vital part of enabling and identifying self-development. What Okamoto was hinting at could have been explained to Gary in a lecture about what to do when walking the floor, but he would not really have comprehended what it meant in action. He would not have deeply felt it. Self-development has a huge impact on the learner's actual patterns of thinking and behavior.

## On-the-Job Development

By now, it should be clear from the anecdotes that we've shared that relatively little of the training and development of team members or leaders at Toyota happens in a classroom. There's a certain amount of basic information that has to be imparted at the *shu* stage of learning. Beyond that, the best learning environment, particularly for allowing self-development, is on the job.

On-the-job development also plays an important part in reliably identifying self-developers. Accurately assessing learning and development in a classroom environment is incredibly difficult. Countless education experts spend their entire lives tweaking tests to try to make them valid reflections of student learning; the fact that this tweaking continues unabated decade after decade shows how unsuccessful they have been. On-the-job development is much better for assessing what a student has learned, and whether she can apply her learning, because she is applying the learning. The only assessment of leadership that matters happens in real-world situations. When confronted with a challenge, does the leader step up, behave as expected, and get results in the right way? Once the target is achieved, does the leader take steps to ensure that the problem doesn't occur again and that others learn from the situation? Does the leader engage in *hansei* to reflect on his own performance, and improve that performance when the next challenge arises? None of this can be judged in a classroom environment— nor can it be faked when it happens on the job.

Gary's first experience with training and on-the-job development at Toyota was when he traveled to the Toyota plant at Takaoka after being hired to be general manager of NUMMI. He was in the first wave of what would be several hundred future employees of NUMMI who flew to Japan to be trained. Not surprisingly, the training regimen at Toyota was highly structured: nearly every minute of every day was planned. Most of the "training" wasn't in classrooms, though. It involved spending time performing jobs or participating in *kaizen*. Gary spent time in each of the major shops (for example, stamping, body weld, paint, and assembly), while the department managers spent time in the particular shop they would manage and the team members spent time learning line jobs like those that they would ultimately do. Even as a general manager, Gary was expected to actually perform production jobs to experience the system firsthand.

In addition to performing the jobs, the Americans were asked to study the jobs and find opportunities for *kaizen*—to eliminate waste. They had learned in the classroom about standardized work and other elements of the Toyota Production System.

To their surprise, the Americans were given stopwatches that could measure hundredths of a second (they were used to stopwatches that measured only seconds). The Americans were shown standardized work sheets that listed each work element of a job, with each element broken down into tasks that were considered value-added, or actual tasks that customers paid for, and those that were considered wasteful, such as walking. The Americans were taught how to fill out those sheets, and then they were sent to the floor with stopwatches to observe a process. They were asked to identify all the elements, time each element ten times, and separate the elements into value-added and wasteful activities. As a team, the American managers would then come up with *kaizen* ideas. The act of looking for opportunities for *kaizen* was important training, but everyone was amazed at how many of the ideas were actually implemented on the spot by Japanese team members. The Americans experienced a level of learning by doing that was unlike any training they'd ever had in the United States.

In another training exercise, after a morning spent in the classroom, each American trainee was asked to spend 45 minutes in one place in one section of the shop floor, observing. No one walked around with a piece of white chalk drawing Ohno circles, but the idea was the same: the Americans were expected to observe deeply, after which their *sensei* asked questions about what they had seen. The Americans were asked to go beyond superficial observations and refer specifically to the TPS principles they had talked about earlier in the day during the classroom session, providing examples of where they saw one of the principles in practice and where they were being violated. The Japanese would then ask if the American trainee had any ideas for improvement.

Because this style of learning and leadership development is so different from American norms, it's important to point out some common misconceptions and misunderstandings about on-the-job development. Americans who hear these stories often tend to start thinking of the *sensei* as "all-knowing" and believe that these exercises are set up or simulated. They think the *sensei* already knows how the process can be improved and are testing the trainees to see if they can come up with the "right" answer. In fact, the opposite is true. The trainees were always observing actual production floor processes. The *sensei* didn't have the right answers; they didn't have any answers at all. If they knew of a way in which the process could be improved, it would have been improved already. This is again key to evaluating the skills and self-development of potential leaders.

When the newly hired managers and team members for NUMMI were sent to Japan to be "trained," they learned a good deal through the structured on-the-job development, but they learned even more from the nonstructured daily interactions. In particular, when they were working at General Motors, the former union members had developed very negative ideas of work life in Japan—workers literally working themselves to death in their jobs, completely overloaded with work in each cycle. When they worked in the plant and got to know the people, their attitudes quickly changed and they started to question how American workers who were in constant combat with management could possibly compete with the cooperative relationships they were experiencing between labor and management. One thing that many of the NUMMI "graduates" talked about was the respect showed to them in Japan for their ideas. Joel Smith, the first union president at NUMMI, recalled one such story:

> *One guy's job in the days of old in GM had been putting in the windows, setting the glass in, which was a tricky process, to get the thing in at the right angle and so on. And he had developed a couple of tools of his own that he'd keep in his pocket that he could use. There was a little pry and a little jimmy to get things done. Well, when he went to Japan, he got the job for a day of working with the guys putting in the windows and he pulled out his little tools, and it was amazing: all the Japanese in the area gathered round! Let me see! And before the day was out, which is the Toyota Production System approach, they had made these tools for everybody that had anything to do with that job and [written] it down in the standard work sheets. There were so many stories like that. My members realized the level of appreciation for each other's skills and talents, and the attention they got really puffed them up, and they brought that attitude back to NUMMI.*

## Steadily Increasing Challenges

The final key aspect of the *shu ha ri* cycle in enabling and identifying self-development is that it requires steadily increasing challenges. The challenges increase in intensity within each *shu ha ri* cycle as well as when a leader or potential leader "graduates" to the next cycle. From our experience with Toyota, we have seen that potential can be nurtured by putting students in challenging situations that accelerate and shape growth.

Figure 2.1 summarizes these learning cycles that are embedded within the *shu ha ri* cycle. We characterize these as Plan–Do–Check–Act (PDCA) learning loops. When he is assigned a new task, the leader must first understand the current situation in detail and the gaps between it and the ideal condition. This allows the leader to understand the problems and formulate challenging targets for improvement (Plan). The Do stage involves leading others to work as a team to achieve the challenging objectives. The Check is done with the help and feedback of the *sensei* and is a reflection on the results and, more important, on the process of achieving the results. And finally the student leader is ready for the next challenging assignment, the Act stage.

For a successful Toyota leader, one full cycle (for example, from being promoted to assistant manager to being considered for promotion to manager) would typically take at least three years and probably longer. When the leader has gone through one revolution, she is judged based on the level of her performance and how she achieved her results.

Those who succeed while following Toyota values are then selected to be moved to the next challenging assignment. Success breeds increasingly challenging assignments and eventually moving up the ladder. Those who show greater mastery and demonstrate leadership will progress to a higher level than those who simply do the job as expected. The leader who moves up is taking on a greater scope of responsibility for more people and functions, and also a longer planning horizon.

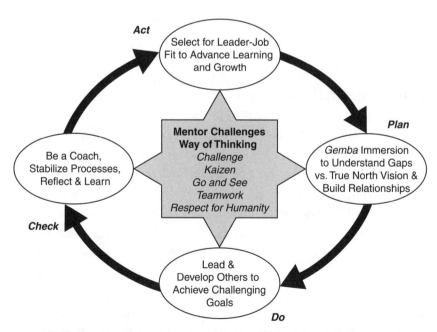

NOTE: Toyota leaders go through repeated cycles of self-development over their careers, taking on increasing challenges under the guidance of a mentor.

**Figure 2.1.** Leadership Self-Development Learning Cycles (PDCA)

In Japan, Toyota has a time-tested method of selecting and developing leaders based on the principle of "grow from within." Up until the 2008–2009 recession, where hiring was frozen for some time, Toyota consistently hired about 1,500 to 2,000 people annually. Those individuals generally stay with the company until retirement at about age 60 (only senior executives stay longer). New hires are carefully observed during the first three years by their immediate supervisors, coworkers, customers, human resource professionals, and managers two levels up in the organization to find those with the most leadership potential. Human resource professionals and direct supervisors spend an enormous amount of time at the *gemba* getting to know potential leaders in action, discussing them, putting them in challenging positions to see how they react, and dissecting their strengths and weaknesses. Sometimes a person is moved laterally to see how he reacts in a new situation where he lacks deep experience and technical expertise. Moving upward means learning to manage a broader span of control across departments than the manager has ever experienced firsthand, as well as managing horizontally by influencing others in a different chain of command. Managers are judged not only by their results but, more important, by their leadership process. As their careers evolve, they settle in at a level that suits their unique strengths and weaknesses.

In Figure 2.2, Leader A has a good deal of work to do on self-development before he can be given significant responsibility for leading and developing others. This person is progressing in pay scales as a result of seniority and is respected for his solid contributions, but through three cycles, he has not established the maturity to develop others. Perhaps this person has superior technical skills, but his social skills are not as strong, so he might have a small group within his technical area assigned to him to mentor, eventually becoming responsible for the group's achieving *hoshin kanri* objectives. By contrast, Leader B is on a faster track, taking on increasing responsibility and more severe challenges. She has been given broader responsibility for leading vertically the people who report up to her, but she also has *hoshin* objectives that involve coordinating with other departments horizontally. Eventually, when there is a need for a major change in the organization, perhaps with a planning horizon of achieving a three- to five-year

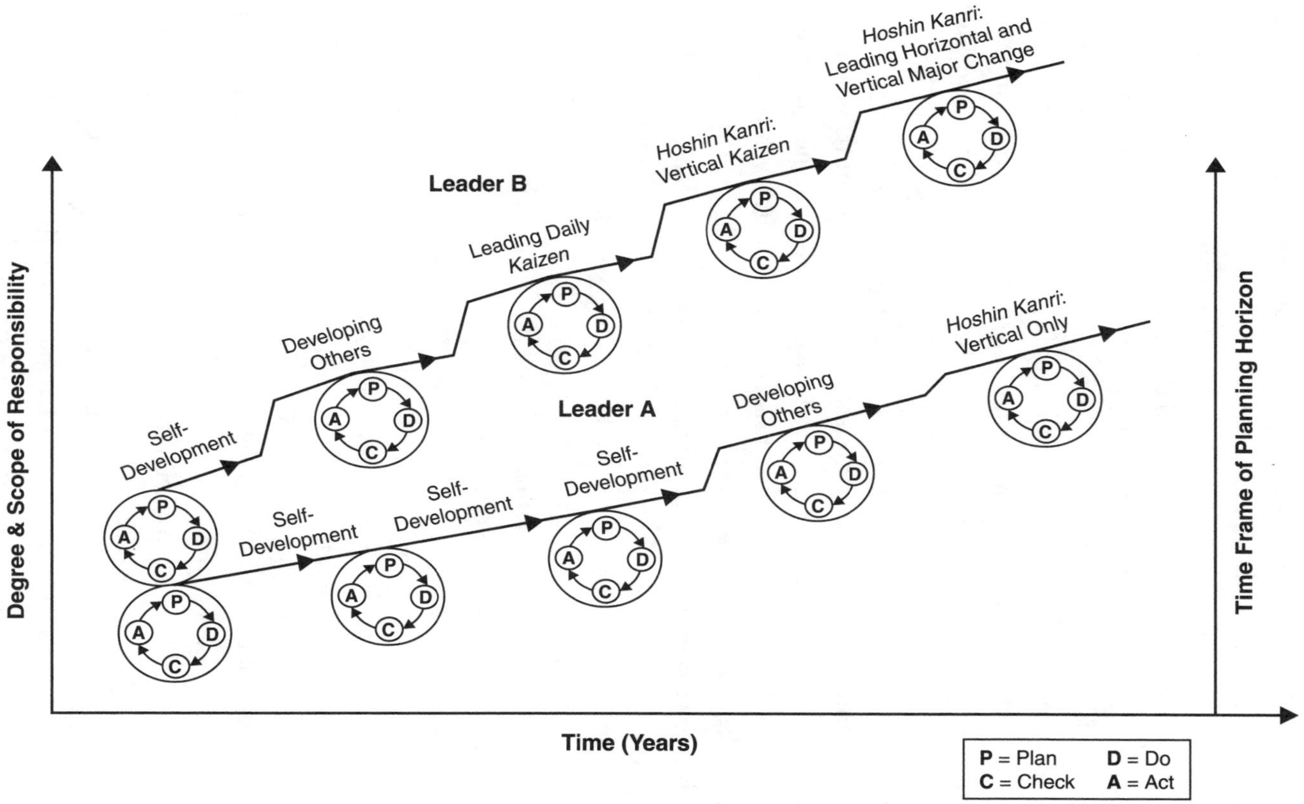

**Figure 2.2.** Comparison of Faster versus Slower Leadership Development Cycles over Careers

**Time Frame of Planning Horizon**

**Degree & Scope of Responsibility**

**Time (Years)**

| P = Plan | D = Do |
| C = Check | A = Act |

**Leader B**

Hoshin Kanri:
Leading Horizontal and
Vertical Major Change

Hoshin Kanri:
Vertical Kaizen

Leading Daily
Kaizen

Developing
Others

Self-
Development

**Leader A**

Hoshin Kanri:
Vertical Only

Developing
Others

Self-
Development

Self-
Development

Self-
Development

Self-
Development

79

vision, she might be promoted to general manager or even vice president to lead a large portion of the organization.

As we already noted, these challenging situations are not scripted. They are based on real circumstances that are taking place in the plant, circumstances for which the teacher himself does not have an immediate answer. It is critical to understand that the student in these instances is being challenged regarding her approach, not her conclusion.

In this sense, there is no "fast track" at Toyota. Existing Toyota leaders take the time to watch candidates in action, because experience has shown that no matter how great one's diligence, no one can judge leadership potential perfectly. Those who are deemed to have high potential may not realize that potential, while others may be late bloomers. As a result, Toyota wants to see people in action over time. Furthermore, the company is interested not just in quantifiable results, but in how those results are achieved—specifically, whether the results are achieved in a way that is consistent with Toyota's values, a topic that we'll return to in the next chapter.

It is always up to the candidate to step up to the challenge. Taiichi Ohno, for instance, would send a student into a parts supplier and give him a severe challenge, such as to eliminate six jobs on a ten-job production line. The student could not leave the supplier until he had achieved the objective, eliminated the six jobs, and trained the remaining four people until they could perform all the required work on time and with perfect quality. Ohno was physically present only for short periods of time, but the student knew he was watching, and Ohno would check in regularly for a progress report. Individuals who failed to meet the challenge did not get fired, but their career progression slowed compared to those who achieved their goals.

The key point here is that self-development is expected throughout the career of a Toyota leader. The challenges steadily increase as a leader takes on more responsibility, and the leader must continually self-develop in order to rise to each challenge and deliver results within the Toyota Way. Promotion to higher levels of leadership is never based simply on time served or on having joined the fast-track leadership ranks. A loyal employee who works hard but lacks leadership capability will eventually get promoted, but he may have few people, if any, reporting to him. Promotion with actual leadership responsibility at every level up and down the corporation is based on demonstrated success and one's self-development efforts on that path.

Virtually every senior leader in Toyota has followed this process, moving up through the company over the course of an entire career. With a handful of exceptions,[14] there are no members of Toyota's board of directors (the highest level of governance in the company) who have served the company for less than 30 years. That's a huge contrast with American companies, which routinely bring in outsiders to become CEO or to fill other C-level positions. Bringing in an outsider for a position of major corporate responsibility at Toyota would have been unthinkable when Toyota was growing as a Japanese company. However, this changed as Toyota grew to be a global company.

## Selecting Outside Leaders for Capability as Toyota Grew in North America

When hiring leaders for NUMMI, the focus was on finding candidates who had demonstrated an inherent capacity for self-development and learning. Unbeknownst to Gary, NUMMI conducted background interviews with colleagues to assess his character and openness to learning.

As we discussed in Chapter 1, Gary's approach to leadership while he was at Ford and GM was admirable, but it was still flawed from a Toyota perspective. You can say that he was getting good results in the wrong way. But, according to people involved in the recruiting process, Toyota was most interested in his excitement for self-development.

At NUMMI, the most important recruit was the first general manager who would run the plant. Toyota intensively interviewed the rather small list of qualified contenders, narrowing its list to six and then four and then two, and finally Gary was selected. Why did Gary squeeze through this ever-tightening filter? Because in many respects, he was already behaving like a Toyota leader during his tenures at GM and Ford.

Conrad Prusac, the executive recruiter hired by Toyota to find its NUMMI general manager, recalled that the Toyota leaders involved in NUMMI at the time emphasized to him that their ideal candidate "is going to have an understanding of the automotive manufacturing process. But they're going to put their biases aside and with an open mind learn about the Toyota Manufacturing method. And then they're going to help us apply this Toyota Manufacturing method to the American worker profile and help us bridge the culture gap."

That lack of bias was Gary's key strength, and it was why the field narrowed to him. "He was obviously a talented guy," said Joel Smith, NUMMI's UAW president, about his impressions of Gary during the recruitment process. "He had the knowledge, the background, and experience. But I think what was more important was his view of where this was going. He wanted to work cooperatively with everybody. He had an openness to learning new stuff and being excited about it."

Joel himself was one of the first people brought into NUMMI— brought back, actually, as he had been the union president at the closed-down GM plant. The fact that a union leader was part of the search process to select the plant general manager was itself a culture shock for Joel. As part of the process of investigating Gary, Joel tapped into his network of union leaders at Ford to find out what kind of leader Gary was. Joel wanted to be sure that he was the kind of leader who would build the culture that they had envisioned in the letter of intent. All the feedback he got supported Gary as the right choice:

> *The letter of intent really spelled out in detail how we'd have to work together, and that really fit him to a T; it's the way he liked to do things. I had talked to some folks at Ford about him and got back positive vibes, very positive.*

Despite all his experience—and his presence on the fast track at Ford—NUMMI didn't just hire Gary and install him as a leader. We've already discussed the extensive training process that Gary and other leaders went through at the Takaoka plant. But Gary was also assigned an "executive coordinator" from Toyota. At Toyota, an executive coordinator is not a personal assistant; it is a *sensei*, a well-regarded and successful leader who can mentor growing leaders. The executive coordinator's job is far from hands-off and far from temporary; the executive coordinator assigned to Gary (and an executive coordinator for every other executive at NUMMI) moved to the United States from Japan (another example of *genchi genbutsu*—an executive coordinator cannot be effective if he is not at the *gemba* with a firsthand view of the performance of the leader he is mentoring). In fact, Gary worked with various executive coordinators for the entire 20 years he served, first at NUMMI and then at Toyota. One can view this as distrustful, but at Toyota, the role is to teach and to communicate with Toyota in Japan.

Sixteen years after being hired as general manager at NUMMI, Gary was asked to join TMMK and soon became president. He quickly confronted a challenge similar to the one that NUMMI had faced when it hired him. The plant had been running very successfully for almost a decade, doubling in capacity since it was opened. However, this rapid growth and Toyota's growing reputation presented a leadership challenge. The combination of very fast growth and a large number of middle managers being hired away by other companies that were eager to learn from Toyota's now famous ability to generate high quality and high efficiency left TMMK with a gaping leadership hole. There were not enough potential leaders internally with enough experience to fill the leadership vacuum. Through an extensive period of *genchi genbutsu*, Gary was appalled to find that a number of key positions were held by internal Toyota managers who had been promoted before they were ready in order to fill an opening. Gary knew that this was damaging to the Toyota system, and he could not perpetuate this any further. Gary and his team at TMMK had to look outside of Toyota to hire leaders who could become Toyota leaders quickly.

Again the search was for potential, but this time Gary had a bit of an inside track. During his time at NUMMI, he had met and worked with a good number of GM managers who had done "rotations" at NUMMI. The idea was that GM managers would spend some time at NUMMI seeing TPS in action firsthand, and then take that learning back to the GM plants. In practice, many of the GM managers did not use NUMMI as an opportunity for major reflection and self-development. In some ways, they can hardly be faulted for this, since the existing structures at GM would have made it difficult for them to apply what they had learned at their own plants even if they had wanted to. However, there were some GM managers who behaved very differently during their rotations at NUMMI, taking self-development seriously. Using this and other channels to find potential leaders at Ford and GM, Gary was able to hire to fill the gaps.

Thus far, the story might not seem to be particularly unique—and up to this point, it isn't. What distinguishes the Toyota approach is that all of these external hires were brought into Toyota several levels below where they had been at their prior companies. In the typical American model, many managers take jobs at other companies in order to get a promotion. Signing on at Toyota, in many ways, meant a demotion. For example, Barry Sharpe was hired from Ford, where he was on the verge of becoming general manager of a plant. His first role at TMMK was as a manager in the paint shop, two to three steps below where he had been within a typical automotive plant hierarchy. In 2005, as Gary was planning for retirement, he actually had to reach outside of Toyota to find the next president of TMMK. He chose Stephen St. Angelo, whom he had worked with at NUMMI. Even Stephen St. Angelo, a high-level GM executive who had spent two years as acting vice president of manufacturing at NUMMI after Gary had moved to TMMK, was asked to spend a year as an executive vice president when he followed in Gary's footsteps. Gary continued in the president's role, freeing Steve to go and see the plant, learn jobs on the floor, and "grasp the situation" in the plant. In all these cases, the new hires were expected to follow the *shu ha ri* process and demonstrate self-development to prove their leadership potential within the Toyota Way.

## Conclusion

The main point of this chapter is that Toyota considers self-development to be the key indispensable trait of leaders. Only those who demonstrate a consistent devotion to self-development will acquire the skills and fill the gaps in their own capabilities to become the effective leaders that Toyota requires to maintain excellence. In this sense, Toyota doesn't believe that leadership can be taught; it can only be learned by those who are willing to self-develop. It is therefore critical to allow self-development and reliably identify it among potential and existing leaders.

Toyota's approach to allowing for and identifying self-development is built into its approach to teaching and learning. The *shu ha ri* learning cycle puts the onus of learning on the student. Only those who have a passion for self-development stand out under this system, but it also requires having masters close at hand to both protect and guide the students and identify the best self-developers among them. There are no shortcuts in this process, and it is a learning system that is virtually impossible to "game" or manipulate.

Too few other companies understand the difference between the "*kaizen* event" as it has become popular in the West and how Toyota uses structured *kaizen* activities. The *kaizen* event as a standard format is five days starting with some instruction, then going to the *gemba* to identify the waste and take quick actions to make changes, then a final presentation on the before and after and results. It has become the main tool for implementing lean in many organizations. There is no question that participants learn a great deal, and it can even be transformative for some. In Toyota there are organized *kaizen* events, but they are called *jishuken*, which translates to "voluntary self-study." There are several-month *jishuken* in Japan, usually led by a Toyota master trainer at a supplier, where the supplier is expected to make a major transformation in an area of the plant to reach targets set by the master. It is intense, and any result short of the target is considered a failure. The goal is to for leaders to step up to the challenge and develop themselves through this intense activity. In Toyota in North America, this got translated into a one-week *jishuken*. While shorter, the emphasis is still on learning and self-development. *Jishuken* is not considered a tool for improvement to get specific results, but achieving the target is essential for learning: one needs to cultivate the drive and passion to reach the target. And the problem-solving process must be followed to the letter—no shortcuts such as skipping problem definition and root-cause analysis by jumping from identified wastes to quick and easy solutions.

One of the key lessons for those who are trying to imitate Toyota is how critical it is to have an approach that allows for self-development rather than having mandated development. Self-development of both thinking and doing is the only thing that ever sticks.

Throughout this chapter, we have emphasized the importance of standardized work, particularly in teaching during the *shu* stage. Standardized work is as much for leaders as it is for those who are doing the work. Standards represent today's best-known way. They provide a teachable methodology and a baseline for improvement. They provide a way to coach leaders on developing others. What should companies do that have not invested in standardized work? The answer is that it needs to be developed. Then you might be thinking that this is nice for a repetitive manual job, but what about knowledge work? In *Toyota Talent*, Liker and Meier[15] provide a method for breaking down any job into the routine and repeating tasks, on the one hand, and other tasks that are purely situational. Even a creative job like the engineering of a new product has some degree of stable knowledge and standard processes. It would not make sense to write out a minute-by-minute script for an engineer, but Toyota does effectively use tools like engineering checklists that specify component-by-component stable knowledge and standard steps that should be part of any good design. There are testing protocols, methods to evaluate a design to meet certain standards, cost tables to estimate the costs of a design, and countless standard tools and processes that are taught to engineers and audited by Toyota leaders.[16]

One of the popular ideas in lean is the notion of "standardized work for leaders." Many consultants sell packages for this, and many companies have been developing their own version. For example, there are standards for the frequency of doing a *gemba* walk and checklists for what to look for while walking through the plant. This would fall into the *shu* stage of *shu ha ri*. It is necessary to start by practicing some basic drills precisely as instructed. Think of this standardized work as one of those basic drills. The problem we have seen is that managers who have had a few successful tours through the plant, all the time pointing out to others the waste that they see and giving orders for fixing these problems, too quickly feel that they are in the *ri* stage and masters of lean leadership. This is a bit like the kid who is first learning to ride a bicycle with training wheels saying, "Look, mom, no hands!" Take off the training wheels and the kid will fall helplessly, possibly doing serious damage to himself and others. It is critical that these early *gemba* walks be supervised by a true *sensei* and that the manager doing the learning is clear that this is just a starting point—and that the idea is to learn to ask questions, not shout out solutions to problems. It will take years of repeated practice with a strong *sensei* for the manager to begin to master even the basic skill of the *gemba* walk.

Few, if any, companies can wait decades to develop a deep bench of leaders who grow up in the operation living something like the Toyota Way. There is a sense of urgency, as we saw there was at NUMMI. What NUMMI did was to carefully select leaders who fit the philosophy, immerse them in understanding the basic principles of TPS and in studying the current situation on the shop floor, give them a stretch challenge with support, and help them reflect on what they had learned. Any company can do this. Few companies will have the resources of skilled and knowledgeable leaders like the Japanese coordinators, but this means that the "expert" lean resources that the company does have are at a premium. In Chapter 6 we will showcase the journey, under Gary's leadership after he retired, of Dana Corporation, an American company that in a crisis had to grow lean leaders fast. It discovered that it actually had some untapped talent inside, and it was able to supplement this with talent brought from outside. In most situations, there are people around who have a deep understanding of the work, and in many cases they have not been challenged to teach and develop others. They can be very valuable if they learn to coach and develop others rather than doing all the thinking for themselves. Toyota's approach to developing others is the topic of the next chapter.

# Chapter 3

## Coach and Develop Others

*I start with the premise that the function of leadership is to produce more leaders, not more followers.*

—Ralph Nader, consumer advocate

When they began launching plants in North America, Toyota executives knew that they must not fail. Their insurance policy was to send over as many Japanese as possible to teach the Americans to lead in the Toyota Way, and if it were necessary, the Japanese could jump in to avoid any major catastrophes. Of course, that was only the first step—seeding the initial group of American leaders. Toyota was growing rapidly globally and could not send armies of Japanese *sensei* to America indefinitely. The long-term vision was self-reliance. To attain this, the top American leaders would have to learn to become *sensei*, and every level of leadership below them would have to achieve a degree of mastery of living the values, leading improvement, and coaching others to improve processes toward clear targets.

As discussed in the previous chapter, self-development as a concept may give the impression of a sink-or-swim mentality: throw out the challenges, and whoever finds a way to succeed gets rewarded and those who do not are let go. The most ruthless American companies use this model explicitly, but this is not the Toyota Way. Toyota strives for the perfect balance between teachers being held accountable for the success of their students and the students taking responsibility for their own development.

In this chapter, we'll look at the flip side of self-development, delving more deeply into how Toyota actively encourages the leadership potential and growth of those who are identified as self-developers. In Toyota, the terms *sensei* (teacher) and *leader* are almost synonymous. Leaders are responsible for creating an environment in which future leaders can blossom. This environment must simultaneously nurture and severely challenge the potential leader, which seems contradictory, but is seen as complementary within Toyota. In manufacturing, a big part of these challenges are naturally generated by the Toyota Production System (TPS).

## TPS Creates Challenges to Force Employees' Development

The Toyota production system itself is largely designed to create continual challenges for leaders and team members. Taiichi Ohno illustrated the fundamental principles of TPS with a picture of a boat traveling on a river that was flowing over rocks. He explained that the water was like inventory. With more water, the rocks are hidden below the surface and become invisible to the boaters. As the water level falls, however, the rocks will break the surface, and the boat must stop until the rocks are eliminated or crash. The rocks signify problems (equipment downtime, quality problems, communication problems, and on and on), and in traditional mass production, they are covered up by inventory: it seems to be smooth sailing despite all the problems. Product is built and inventory is simply pushed to the next process without regard to the actual use of the material.

In a just-in-time system, each process builds at a steady pace to meet the customer demand, called *takt* (see sidebar). The True North vision is to have zero inventory between processes, although there often need to be some strategically placed inventory buffers. With so little inventory, problems are painfully visible, and they must be solved or production stops—if one machine breaks down, the whole production process soon comes to a halt. Jobs downstream can't be performed when

# *Takt* Time

A fundamental concept in just-in-time that we will refer to several times is that of *takt*. *Takt* is a German word (although it has been adopted as a Japanese word as well) that means "rhythm" or "beat" (in music). For instance, a metronome sets the *takt* for a musician. In just-in-time, *takt* is the rate of customer demand. For example, if customers are on average buying a Toyota car every minute, then the *takt* time is one minute. In a just-in-time system, the assembly line would then be set up to finish production of a car every minute (which obviously requires that many cars are being assembled in sequence on the line simultaneously), and ideally all the preceding processes, like stamping and welding, would produce the parts for one car every minute. Using this *takt* time, in the ideal state, every job on the assembly line should be set up so that the team member has one minute's worth of value-added work. Then the car moves down the line to the next one-minute job until the car is completed. Of course, there is always some waste, such as reaching to get a part or a tool, but the goal of TPS is to continue to drive this waste toward zero. Eliminating waste is another form of reducing the water level. With a clear picture of *takt* and no waste, the team members are expected to perform value-added work in perfect synchronization; if they fail to do so, production can stop.

the flow stops; jobs upstream have to stop because there is no place to store what is being produced. As problems are solved (rocks are chipped away at) and flow is restored, the inventory is further reduced (lowering the water level), so more problems surface. This dynamic forces continuous improvement. In a nonmanufacturing process, this would be the equivalent of having frequent tightly timed deadlines for small batches of deliverables (for example, lab test results for one patient at a time), so that each person cannot proceed until she gets what she needs from the upstream process. As we squeeze this linked chain, the problems surface, and we must solve them or stop the project.

This is why so many companies simply cannot bring themselves to fully adopt just-in-time. The safety of having extra inventory is just too hard to give up and adjusting inventory levels takes time and effort. So why does Toyota do it? The difference is between companies that strive to be good at what they do and Toyota's aspiration for perfection. For a company that strives to be "good enough" to succeed, there is every reason to allow a margin of safety in the form of extra inventory. However, for a company that is striving for perfection, there is every reason to make sure that problems become visible as quickly as possible. If a problem remains hidden below the surface long enough, it can stop being perceived as a problem and become part of normal operating procedure. Soon the goal of perfection becomes even more distant and difficult to reach. Without a vision of perfection as the goal, it becomes very easy to let the water level slowly but steadily rise—you might say that it is the path of least resistance. Certainly allowing slack in the system to increase is the easiest solution to most problems that arise.

Ohno used to say that the Toyota Production System is designed to make problems visible to challenge people so that they grow and become better problem solvers and better people. TPS was displayed as a house to illustrate that it is a system and operates fully only if all the elements work together (see Figure 3-1). The two pillars holding up the house are just-in-time, attributed to Kiichiro Toyoda, and *jidoka*, attributed to his father, Sakichi Toyoda. *Jidoka* refers to a machine with the intelligence to stop itself when there is a problem, like Sakichi's famous automatic loom that shut itself down as soon as a thread broke. This evolved into the *andon* system, where equipment or people stop production and signal for help when there is a problem. The combination of JIT and *jidoka* means that problems, when they inevitably occur, can never hide.

This is all well and good, but there are two conditions that turn this fragile system into high performance instead of an exercise in futility. One is a rock-solid foundation of stability in normal conditions, which requires extremely well-trained people who strive to perform their jobs perfectly and extremely well-maintained equipment that rarely breaks down. Without these, the rocks will overwhelm the organization, and production will simply be stopped most

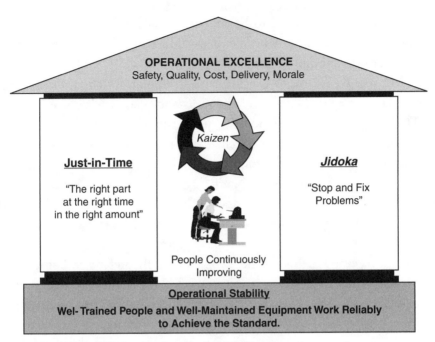

**Figure 3.1.** The Toyota Production System House

of the time. The second is the way people respond when the problems surface. Toyota trains people intensively and repeatedly that in problem solving, they should jump into action, first to contain the problem and restart production, and then to deal with the root cause of the problem so that it will not keep coming back. *Kaizen,* which means "continuous improvement," turns this painful interruption of production into exceptional people and processes for competitive advantage.

One of Gary's early experiences at NUMMI exposed the difference between "good enough," which was the mode that Gary was used to at Ford and GM, and the Toyota pursuit of perfection. During the recruiting process, before he was hired, Gary had spotted that the equipment that NUMMI had in the body shop and the paint shop was old and prone to breakdowns. He also noticed that there was no space to store inventory as buffers. In his first few days as general manager at NUMMI, he tried to demonstrate his commitment to quality and efficiency by suggesting to several Japanese executives that the plan for the body shop needed to be adjusted to allow for more inventory between processes, or any problems would eventually shut down production on the assembly line.

Mr. Kosuke Ikebuchi, executive vice president for engineering and manufacturing at NUMMI, responded to Gary's idea succinctly: "There is no need for extra inventory. Fix the problems!" Ikebuchi-san was expressing one of the core tenets of TPS—if you cover a problem with inventory or a work-around, you take the pressure off of fixing the root cause of the problem. Not fixing the root cause may be acceptable for "good enough," but it doesn't fly in a quest for perfection.

We noted in the introduction that many companies that begin implementing lean concepts see large gains, but all too frequently those gains evaporate over time. People naturally prefer a smooth, easy operation, and it is easy to get accustomed to the status quo. By removing inventory, Toyota makes any status quo other than perfection inherently unstable. An uncompromising commitment to just-in-time pushes everyone to pursue perfection because anything less than perfection becomes obvious very quickly.

What does any of this have to do with developing leaders? In the previous chapter, we discussed the importance of on-the-job development and steadily increasing challenges. TPS, because of its exposure of problems, creates a never-ending stream of opportunities for on-the-job development and increased challenges. Toyota *sensei* do not need to create artificial training situations in which something goes wrong or there is a specific fix that trainees are supposed to find. The daily process of producing cars generates all the development opportunities and challenges that are needed. In a more comfortable environment—one with more water, you might say—*sensei* might need to set a specific target or identify a project to challenge a student's problem-solving skills. There would not be enough opportunities for the *shu ha ri* cycle for students to self-develop, or the development process would take even longer than it does. So TPS not only drives the company toward perfection, but also creates the opportunities for leadership development, both self-development and developing others, that are necessary to fill the leadership pipeline.

# A3 Problem Solving Makes the Thinking Process Visible

In his early days at NUMMI, Gary's worst fears became a daily reality. Since there was no room for inventory in the body shop, getting the people highly trained and the equipment stable was a daily challenge, and TPS provided many, many opportunities for development. With the frequent breakdowns of the machines, fixing the problems at the root cause was essential to maintaining production. In Japan, the vendors who built the equipment regularly came on site to help fix the problems, but NUMMI in California was on its own.

Gary and his team struggled for years to solve one problem after another and did quite a good job of keeping the line running, but there was still a large gap between NUMMI's performance and the level of equipment uptime in Japan. Ironically, the guy who brought the body shop up to a new level was not a manufacturing executive, but someone who came out of finance in Japan. Mr. Fumitaka Ito became president of NUMMI and was not satisfied with the uptime of the body shop. He also noticed the body-shop engineers spending too much time in the office, which of course meant the problems were not going to get solved. In one meeting, he asked Gary to start a new practice. Whenever equipment was shut down for 30 minutes or more, he wanted a personal report from the engineers, with Gary present. The report should be on one side of one piece of paper, the famous Toyota "A3 report" (after the A3 paper size used in the metric system). Ito did not offer a training course on A3, but rather asked for a "breakdown report" for each instance and suggested that the Japanese engineers in the body shop would be able to show the American engineers how to prepare it.

The purpose of the report is to produce, in a single page, a "problem-solving story" that summarizes the problem, its root cause, and the countermeasures taken to solve the problem. Toyota uses a standard approach to problem solving that is now known as Toyota Business Practices (see sidebar). The single-page report details the problem, the gap between the current and ideal states, the root causes of the problem, possible countermeasures, the countermeasures tried, the results, and further actions required. The engineers' job was not only to fix the breakdown but to identify why the breakdown happened (for example, improper maintenance, user error, or defective inputs) and to address the root causes so that the breakdown would not be repeated. The engineers were to present the report personally to Ito and Gary within a week of the breakdown.

By approaching the situation this way, Ito was addressing several needs at once. First, he was addressing the production problems that NUMMI was having in a sustainable way (rather than putting production goals first and just letting the Japanese engineers solve the problems). Second, he was creating a development opportunity for the American engineers to practice their problem-solving skills. By instituting the policy of having the American engineers take the lead and be responsible for the A3 reports, Ito-san was forcing them to learn problem solving and learn the value of *genchi genbutsu*. Third, he was giving Gary an opportunity to be engaged in the problem-solving process and creating an opportunity to coach Gary in his responsibility to develop the engineers.

## Toyota Business Practices

The problem-solving process used at Toyota is currently called Toyota Business Practices (TBP), although it has gone by other names in the course of the company's history (such as Practical Problem Solving). TBP is an eight-step process based on the Plan–Do–Check–Act cycle of quality guru J. Edwards Deming.

In summary, the process begins with a statement of the problem, including the gap between the actual and the ideal condition. This gap is then broken down to determine the most important problems that are actionable. For actionable items, specific targets for improvement are set. These specific subproblems are then analyzed to identify the root cause by asking why until the root cause, and not a surface cause, is found (a rule of thumb suggests asking why five times). Countermeasures are then identified (plan), tried (do), and monitored (check), until, after further adjustments (act), either the problem is solved or new approaches are tried. The problem solver does not leave his role and keeps checking and further adjusting the process until it has been demonstrably stabilized and has run without problems consistently for a period of time, usually months. Then the countermeasures are standardized and may be shared with other plants if they see a need.

The eight steps of TBP are

1. Define the problem relative to the ideal (plan).
2. Break down the problem into manageable pieces (plan).
3. Identify the root cause (plan).
4. Set a target for improvement (plan).
5. Select the appropriate solution among several alternatives (plan).
6. Implement the solution (do).
7. Check impact (check).
8. Adjust, standardize, and spread (act).

Notice that in the Toyota implementation, the first five steps are in the "plan" phase of Deming's process. This reflects the company's focus on ensuring that the right problem is being worked on and thus the problem will be truly solved. It also reflects the emphasis that Toyota puts on gathering information and building consensus for a solution. The target setting is also critical, as it presents the challenge.

Toyota believes that this problem-solving process is essential to leadership—every leader is expected to be a master of TBP, no matter what her role or department. Mastering this process allows a leader with a background in finance or human resources, for instance, to contribute meaningfully on the shop floor, and vice versa. True mastery of TBP means being able to ask the right questions of the domain experts who are doing the hands-on work to ensure that they are truly solving problems and moving the company toward perfection.

During the presentations, Ito would focus on asking questions and critiquing the reports. Was the problem statement clear? Did it lead to the Five Whys? Was the countermeasure clearly connected to the root-cause analysis? Ito had an uncanny ability to pick out key gaps in an engineer's thinking, and to drill down with detailed questions that exposed missing parts of the story, despite the fact that he was not an engineer and did not know the technical details of the problem. Following the standard Toyota practice, he would take a red pen to the report, circling items, putting in question marks, and writing in questions. The goal of filling out the A3 report, of course, is not to fill out the form perfectly, but to serve as an aid to clear thinking and learning in the problem-solving process. By listening to the presentations and reviewing the reports, Ito could assess the capability of the engineers, how they thought, how they reasoned, and how deeply they thought about sustaining improvements. As every developing leader at Toyota learns, the reports are a powerful technique for developing problem-solving ability.[1]

Despite observing Ito-san coaching this process several times, Gary was not picking up on his responsibility in the process. While Ito was critiquing the presentations and reports, Gary simply stood to the side, marveling at Ito's insight and amused at the struggles of the engineers' efforts to learn this way of thinking. After a few sessions, Ito asked Gary how he was coaching the engineers through the process before the presentations. Ito pointed out there was still a lot of red on the reports, and if Gary had been teaching the engineers properly, there would be less red ink. He was pointing out Gary's responsibility for the engineers' development; the problems with the reports were a reflection of Gary's leadership, and he was more responsible for any failures than the engineers were. Quickly, Gary got more directly involved, and soon both Gary and the engineers were sharpening their skills and developing much more rapidly. Eventually Gary became quite skilled at seeing the holes in an engineer's process and thinking and asking questions to expose these holes. He began to understand the reviews as a way to measure both the capability of the worker and his capability as a teacher and coach. Quickly the A3s got much better, and equipment uptime moved steadily up toward the levels in Japan.

Thereafter, when Ito issued compliments on a job well done, they were directed to Gary, but not because he was attributing the success of the problem-solving process to Gary. The real compliment was on the development of the engineers. Any individual report was relatively unimportant in the grand scheme of developing leaders. The steady improvement in the reports showed the more important progress in developing the engineers and in Gary's assuming responsibility for that development: to see how they thought, how they reasoned, how they were going to prevent problems, and how they were going to sustain that prevention.

## Sometimes Leadership Training Must Be Structured

Of course, situations do arise in which additional opportunities and challenges beyond those that daily TPS provides need to be fabricated. Even in these cases, however, leadership "training" should be hands-on, not simply exercises in a classroom. In the previous chapter, we noted that when Gary arrived at TMMK, the leadership bench was underdeveloped because of a combination of growth and the poaching of leaders by other companies. As president, Gary addressed part of this problem by bringing in a few exceptional leaders from outside Toyota, but clearly that wasn't enough. The capabilities of the existing team needed to be developed as well; developing the staff was of course one of Gary's key responsibilities.

Gary felt that there were several impediments to the normal development process that would take place day-to-day on the job. First, development needed to happen even more rapidly than it did normally to rebuild leadership and TPS skills at the rate that TMMK needed. Second, the limited experience of the staff at TMMK meant that even the most senior leaders needed to have their skills refreshed; they weren't in a position to be *sensei* for those they were leading. Gary chose to conduct the training outside of TMMK because leaders might be embarrassed to struggle in front of their staff. Moreover, TMMK was still running full tilt, and Gary was concerned that the leaders who were going through refresher training would be too distracted by the daily demands of their jobs if the exercises were conducted in the plant.

Gary took a page from Taiichi Ohno's book and decided that it would be most effective if the leaders sharpened their skills by working with TMMK's suppliers. This would allow true on-the-job development and also meet a need to improve the capabilities of TMMK's suppliers. He knew he needed help from *sensei*, so he contracted with the Toyota Supplier Support Center (TSSC),[2] a Toyota subsidiary that was training suppliers in TPS, to provide experts to serve as *sensei* for the TMMK leaders during their time at the suppliers. Hajime Ohba, an Ohno disciple, would personally lead the training effort.

The TMMK managers were given a very short refresher course on TPS, standardized work, problem solving, and *kaizen*, and then about three managers a week went to a supplier to practice their skills at identifying waste, solving problems, and improving performance under the guidance of experts from TSSC and a certified trainer from TMMK. There were two stages to the supplier *kaizen* assignment. The first stage focused on "process *kaizen*." One bottleneck process was selected—for example, a machining process. The managers were assigned to work with a team to evaluate the process, identify non-value-added activity, find the root causes, and implement *kaizen* ideas within one week. A few weeks later, they would go back to the plant and lead a one-week "system *kaizen*." System *kaizen* is at a bigger-picture level and employs a tool called the "material and information flow diagram" (more commonly known outside Toyota as value stream mapping) to diagram how material and information flows through the plant. The information indicates what parts to make and move, when, and in what quantities.

Every Friday of every week, Gary went out to the supplier with a department head to see what the managers had learned, what they had done, and what they thought. To encourage the managers to develop the personal hands-on approach, no computer reports were allowed. Gary wanted the managers to explain from handwritten documents the key points of the week: what opportunities they saw, how they thought they could reduce extraneous work, and what they actually did.

When the managers came back to TMMK, Gary sat down with them and communicated his expectation that they would continue to utilize the tools they had refreshed and sharpened at the supplier to lead *kaizen* in their own shop. His minimum expectation was that each department would schedule a review with Gary on the floor four times per year. The managers would be judged on their proactive use of the tools in their own shop to achieve their annual performance improvement goals. All 115 managers and general managers at TMMK went through these opportunities for development over the course of about 18 months.

TPS provides leaders with lots of opportunities to develop the next level of leaders. When needed, a leader can also create opportunities, as Gary did; this is something we'll see more of in Chapter 6. But taking advantage of either the opportunities that arise naturally as a result of TPS or opportunities that have been specifically created to supplement daily experiences also means that you need many *sensei* on the spot to provide either the modeling at the *shu* stage or the coaching and mentoring at the *ha* and *ri* stages of learning.

## Learning to Manage Vertically and Horizontally: T-Type Leaders

The point of *shu ha ri* at Toyota is to develop deep knowledge like that developed by the original apprenticeship system. The "master" is the expert and is teaching the craft to the apprentice. This works very well at managing the daily work of the organization, but at some point in their progression, managers must learn to lead horizontally across the organization to solve larger, cross-functional problems, which means leading people in areas where they are not deep experts and do not have formal authority.

The progression of leaders at Toyota starts very deep within a specialty managing vertically, then those with high potential begin branching out to broaden their responsibility. Top leaders at Toyota must be "T-type leaders," a term used by former President Katsuaki Watanabe to describe the ideal Toyota leader. The concept is simple: a T-type leader gains depth of understanding and experience in a particular technical area (the long stem of the T) and then broadens out to gain exposure across the organization (the top horizontal part of the T). This is sometimes referred to in Toyota as growing deep roots before the tree branches out (see Figure 3-2).

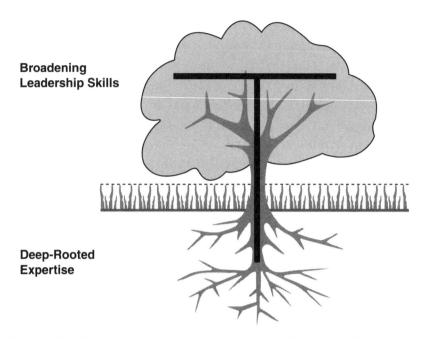

Broadening
Leadership Skills

Deep-Rooted
Expertise

**Figure 3.2.** T-Type Leaders Develop Deep Roots in Their Home Department, Then Branch Out to Lead Other Functions in the Organization

To develop T-type leaders, Toyota emphasizes moving high-potential leaders first up the chain of command in their specialty, then horizontally to often different specialties. The leadership track at Toyota means moving sideways as much as, or more than, moving up. Leaders also get assignments to manage a project that involves a group of peers from other parts of Toyota where they do not have formal authority. In Chapter 5, we will work through a detailed example of how Gary further developed his leadership abilities by working across the entire company to reduce warranty costs. The leaders who advance the furthest in the company have gone beyond their specialty to take on horizontal roles and to manage across departments. Moving horizontally works so well at Toyota because of the emphasis on Toyota Business Practices as the core competency of leaders. As a leader moves up the ladder, the technical details become less important than the approach to identifying waste, improving operations, and solving problems, which is learned in tandem by leaders in all parts of the organization.

In developing others, the role of a leader, especially those at higher levels, is twofold: to coach high-potential leaders as they develop the roots of a technical specialty, and to find the right mix of opportunities that will enable a select group of high-potential leaders to develop into T-type leaders who can make a positive impact anywhere in the company. Of course, some leaders are most effective staying within their home function and continually developing depth, which is highly valuable to the company.

Many companies frequently move high-potential employees from department to department for brief periods to give them breadth of exposure as they rapidly ascend the management ladder. Toyota does move leaders horizontally to areas where they do not have deep expertise, but only after five to ten years, when they have learned a job from the ground up. This early, deep knowledge teaches leaders how important it is that they really understand the processes and become experts on the work. Putting people into situations outside their areas of expertise as they advance forces them to draw on their skills at motivating people and building teams. They have no choice but to lead by listening and coaching, as they are not the experts. Two examples of the T-type leadership development process from TMMK are Cheryl Jones and Don Jackson.

## T-Type Development of Cheryl Jones

Cheryl Jones was one of the first employees at TMMK. She had no technical background prior to coming to Toyota; she'd been a customer service manager at a grocery store. It was, in fact, her people skills that made her stand out during the recruiting process. Cheryl became a group leader in Assembly, managing four team leaders (who, in turn, had a total of about 20 team members). Cheryl went through the usual Toyota training on the shop floor in Japan, and continued with a personal Japanese trainer in Kentucky. She showed particular aptitude for building a high-performing team and was moved to the "pilot team" organization as an assistant manager. The pilot team consists mostly of hourly production team members who are on loan from their work groups for about two years and are responsible for the launch of new models. She then moved laterally as an assistant manager on the team managing the expansion of TMMK to a second assembly line.

By this time, Cheryl had spent nearly 15 years as part of Assembly. She was making a natural progression up the hierarchy toward general manager of Assembly, but she was shocked when then-president Kitano asked her to move over to Paint as an assistant general manager. When she agreed to this move, she had never even been to the paint department before.

Paint had gone through a serious trauma with allegations of sexual harassment, and it needed a supportive, team-oriented leader to help the department move beyond that. There were a good number of experienced engineers and managers who understood the technical side of Paint, so the department didn't necessarily need a technical leader. Cheryl was well equipped to play the team-building role, and if she was to become a T-type leader, she needed to broaden her experience beyond Assembly.

During her first six months in Paint, Cheryl decided that she needed to spend part of her time working on every type of job, on both shifts, to understand the jobs. She struggled, and team members often were concerned about whether she could perform the job, but Cheryl persevered. This experience gave her a way to learn about the paint shop, and at the same time to assess the skill level and capability of the team leaders. One problem she discovered was some weaknesses in how they trained her to do the various jobs. With this knowledge, she began coaching them and putting challenges in place to help them develop further. For example, she was responsible for the paint departments in both of the two plants on site at TMMK, and she realized that the assistant managers were content with leading their own group in their own department. To push them to self-develop, she asked each assistant manager to lead improvement initiatives (such as safety) across the two paint departments so that they would have experience building teams and leading people who didn't report directly to them.

One indicator of Cheryl's success in leading people in the paint department was the proportion of those she led who were promoted. Of the team leaders, senior engineers, group leaders, and assistant managers reporting to Cheryl in the paint department, all but one were promoted. Based on her success in the paint shop, Cheryl was assigned to be a "special advisor" to help lead the launch of a new small-truck facility in Baja, Mexico. When she returned to TMMK, she made yet another move upward to vice president for manufacturing support and power train, which included responsibility for the engine plant, another very different set of technologies. She also was given responsibility for Production Control, Facilities Engineering, and the TPS group. During 15 years in Assembly, Cheryl had developed the trunk of the T; now, with experience in Paint, launching a new plant from scratch, and her new responsibilities, she had made great progress in developing the cross of the T.

## T-Type Development of Don Jackson

Don was hired into TMMK as a quality control engineer responsible for supplier parts. Initially, his Japanese coordinator focused on developing him as an expert within his specialty of quality control, but in a more rigorous way than he had ever experienced. Under the coordinator's guidance, Don had to memorize all the part numbers for the hundreds of parts that he was responsible for, and commit to memory the supplier and the name and the location of the plant that produced each part. He also spent time on the assembly line to gain experience in installing each of the parts, to meet the team members who installed each part, and to become familiar with the standardized work process for each part. The depth of knowledge expected of Don and his accountability for the quality of the part was worlds away from what he had experienced in Quality Control at his former employer, and what we would see in most companies.

When Don moved up the ladder to become general manager of quality, he insisted on following the same approach as he developed another generation of engineering leaders. He was convinced that this in-depth knowledge was one of the real strengths of TMMK because it allowed even the plant managers to identify and implement quick countermeasures to problems, and to avoid most problems in the first place.

After about 10 years in Quality Control, Don was moved horizontally when a role emerged that could take advantage of his skills: the body shop. The major challenge he was expected to take on was managing the transition to an entirely new technology for body welding (the Global Body Line); this transition required that every piece of equipment be changed out while continuing to build on a full schedule and never shutting down production. He divided the body shop into segments and implemented the transition segment by segment. The first area was the most challenging, but since the new body shop took half the floor space of what it replaced, space was quickly freed up, making the task easier. Don had become an exceptional project manager and problem solver during his time in Quality Control—skill sets he would need in the body shop. The move also gave him the challenge of learning a whole new set of skills managing a completely different process.

After succeeding in the body shop, Don eventually went on to become senior vice president of quality planning and production at a new Toyota truck plant in San Antonio, Texas, where under his watch, the plant became the youngest North American facility to win the J.D. Power & Associates Silver Award for production quality. He then left Toyota to become president of a new Volkswagen plant in Tennessee. Was this a big loss for Toyota after all those years of investment? Certainly it was a loss, and more than one Toyota manager has felt despair over the great effort spent on developing leaders to be exceptional so that they can do exceptional things at other companies, even competitors. But senior executives always respond in a similar positive way (a general paraphrase): "We cannot control what people decide to do, but we know we must develop exceptional leaders, and we will continue to live our values and work even harder to retain dedicated and loyal employees. In the meantime, we benefited from years of service and contribution, and we are sending a fine leader to go out into the world and contribute to society. If our competitors get more competitive, it will force us to get even better."

## A Massive Commitment to Developing Leaders

The basic organizational structure at Toyota is consistent around the world, though there may be more or fewer levels in different locations (for example, assistant general manager may exist in an American plant but is more unusual in Japan). A summary of TMMK's structure is shown in Figure 3-3. The first impression of this structure might be that there appears to be a lot of waste. We've frequently encountered executives trying to emulate Toyota who are surprised that a lean organization doesn't have a flat structure, with few managers relative to direct labor. Toyota doesn't believe that flat structures actually save anything; in fact, it believes that they are ultimately more costly than the more hierarchical structure that Toyota uses. In a flat structure, you often see managers who are responsible for 15, 20, even 40 people. Toyota's goal is to have a ratio of about 1 leader for every 5 people, with some variation depending on the level and department. The aim is to provide enough teachers and coaches to support each employee so that actual development of employees and leaders can take place.

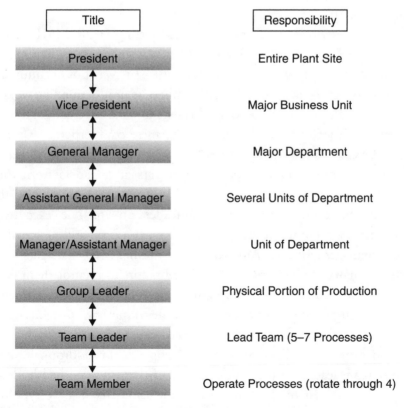

| Title | Responsibility |
| --- | --- |
| President | Entire Plant Site |
| Vice President | Major Business Unit |
| General Manager | Major Department |
| Assistant General Manager | Several Units of Department |
| Manager/Assistant Manager | Unit of Department |
| Group Leader | Physical Portion of Production |
| Team Leader | Lead Team (5–7 Processes) |
| Team Member | Operate Processes (rotate through 4) |

**Figure 3.3.** Hierarchy of Positions at TMMK

The large span of control that is typical of American organizations is in some ways more wasteful than a more hierarchical structure. In such an environment, opportunities to guide people's development and coach potential leaders are inevitably missed. The best performers can leave the company without being noticed, taking valuable skills and knowledge with them. Worst of all, without close attention, relatively untrained employees and managers are likely to find an "easy" or "simple" solution, miss the root causes of problems, and thereby contribute to greater problems in the future.

When NUMMI and TMMK were founded, development wasn't likely to happen very effectively, despite the organizational structure, because too many of the leaders and managers needed to be developed themselves. They were not yet experienced enough to develop others. So Toyota devoted massive amounts of resources to developing the employees of NUMMI and TMMK, just as it does whenever a new plant starts up.

As we described in Chapter 2, when starting at NUMMI, Gary was sent to Japan, along with eight other unit managers. They spent two weeks training on TPS at Toyota City. This was not an unusual step for Toyota. In fact, once NUMMI hired its production line workers, a total of more than 700 were also sent to Japan in smaller groups to learn their jobs firsthand from their Japanese counterparts.

After Gary and his fellow Americans underwent training in Japan, Toyota sent hundreds of Japanese engineers and leaders from the Takaoka plant to get the plant at NUMMI up and running and to continue the training of the American leaders on-site. The "executive coordinators" were sent over for a few years at a time and taught the upper-management-level Americans one on one. Even managers and assistant managers had one-on-one coordinators to mentor them day by day. The trainers rotated through for stays of up to six months to train, through one-on-one on-the-job development, the first-line supervisors (called group leaders) to lead and the hourly team members to build cars. They also taught people in an additional role, hourly team leaders, who built cars part of the time and had leadership roles the rest of the time. Most companies have some type of training program and then send people off to the workplace "trained," but how many would invest in a personal, daily coach for each leader for years?

Similarly, for the first few years of TMMK, hundreds of Japanese swarmed the factory. Every American leader on the shop floor had a personal Japanese trainer, and every executive had a personal Japanese executive coordinator. The sheer number of trainers that Toyota dedicated to the establishment of TMMK is perhaps the best single example of the company's commitment to developing leaders. When most companies talk about training, they mean group sessions that last for a few days. When Toyota talks about it, it means one-on-one attention from a *sensei* for months, or often years. Gary, as we mentioned in the previous chapter, had an executive coordinator working with him continually for the entire 20-plus years he spent at NUMMI and Toyota. The mentor had duties other than just overseeing Gary's training and development, but it was a key part of his assignment. Gary, in turn, had similar responsibilities as a mentor for leaders with less experience and capability than he had. It is literally impossible to move up the ladder at Toyota without being mentored and mentoring others.

The Japanese trainers at TMMK developed the Americans step by step, guiding them through the *shu ha ri* cycle. Reflecting back on this period, most of the American leaders are amazed at how the Japanese coordinators remained calm in a crisis and refused to take over and direct the Americans for fear of short-circuiting their learning. The trainers, working within the Toyota learning system, understood how important it was for the trainees to struggle through issues themselves so that they would truly learn what they needed. The Americans were allowed to face challenges, struggle to meet those challenges, and develop on the job; the role of the trainer wasn't to take over when a problem occurred but rather to ask questions and provide guidance through the process of solving problems (and, of course, to prevent any irrevocable disasters that would hurt either Toyota or the trainee's long-term development). Only when there was a severe problem on the floor would the Japanese engineers take a more active role. The long-term goal was American self-reliance: TMMK needed to be run by Americans who could develop themselves and others, and could improve through *kaizen* without the oversight of their Japanese trainers. But reaching that goal—of essentially turning the Americans into *sensei* for their groups—required years of investment in training and development.[3]

One leader who may have appeared to take a shortcut to a high executive level at Toyota was Steve St. Angelo, who within one year of being hired became president of TMMK. However, a closer look reveals the many years of intensive training that got Steve there. Steve and Gary first met up at NUMMI. Steve was a fast-rising executive at GM and was sent to NUMMI on a two-year stint, from 1995 to 1996, to learn TPS. Steve's title was "senior advisor," and he was eager to jump in and get started. He met with Gary and asked what he could manage. Gary said, "Nothing; you can attend classes and go to meetings, but you cannot manage anything."

Steve was nothing if not determined and explained that he could not learn unless he was actively involved in the plant. After persistent pressure, Gary said that he could get involved, but only if he did it in the Toyota Way like other Toyota leaders. Steve said, "Fine." Gary explained that Steve would have to work on the line. Since Steve had been an hourly production worker on a line at GM for almost three years, he said, "No problem!" Gary clarified that Steve would have to work on the line for eight weeks. Steve said, "Hmm. Okay, I'll do it for eight weeks." Then Gary added that he would have to work both the first shift and the second shift. Steve was willing to do anything to get out of the office and agreed, "Okay, I'll do it." Then Gary brought in the kicker: every day, Steve had to do a different job; he would be rotated throughout the entire plant. By that time, Steve realized that Gary was trying to discourage him. But what Gary did not know was that early in his career at GM, as an hourly person, Steve's job had been as a relief replacement. So he already knew what it was like to do a different job each day and quickly learn to survive.

Steve took Gary's challenge of working a different job every day, both shifts. Though he did it to appease Gary, he found that he was learning more than he had expected. For example, the first time Steve pulled the *andon* cord, he felt, just as Gary had the first time he did it, as if he had done something wrong. But when he saw everyone rushing to help him, he realized the power of a system that gave each worker the right to stop the line if something went wrong. "I realized at that moment that you can read about *andon* and read about the Toyota Production System, but you don't really know lean manufacturing until you actually pull *kanban* cards, stop the line, or participate in a quality circle and then try to get consensus on an idea you think is absolutely the right thing to do. And you know, it's not as easy as people think it is to get total agreement or identify the root cause of the problem."

Steve had great success working all the jobs, to the amazement of Gary and all the team members he worked alongside. He eventually got promoted to group leader and turned one of the worst operations in the plant into one of the best. After working his way up to manager, he returned to GM and applied what he had learned. It was a great surprise, and honor, when NUMMI asked GM to allow him to return to NUMMI as vice president of Manufacturing to run the operation temporarily (from 2001 to 2003), since Gary had accepted the job at TMMK.

Even this was not enough development when he retired from GM and first came to TMMK. Gary made it clear that he would overlap with Steve and continue to run TMMK for one year, and that Steve's primary job was to learn. Steve spent his first year at TMMK essentially in an extended, hands-on training session. This included, for instance, spending 20 days in basic TPS floor training with group leaders and hourly workers. Table 3-1 shows a summary of St. Angelo's training plan.

# Developing Leaders the Toyota Way

When we step back and look at how Toyota develops leaders, there is a common set of expectations for leaders who are developing their staff. The key job of the leader/teacher is to teach the "student" to take responsibility for her self-development, yet remain accountable for the results. The results should be achieved by developing highly capable individuals to work effectively as teams.

## Learning to Take Responsibility for Development

Leadership development at Toyota is a shared responsibility. As we documented in the previous chapter, Toyota puts great emphasis on

**Table 3.1.** Recommended Executive Education, Steve St. Angelo, TMMK
Executive Vice President

| Course/Topic | Next Scheduled Opportunity | Time | Status |
|---|---|---|---|
| Functional Overview at TMMK | April–June 2005 | 3 months | Completed |
| Functional Overview at TMMNA | July 2005 | 2 days | Completed |
| Toyota Quality Way | 5/6/2005 | 1 day | Completed |
| TPS Classroom Training | 8/18/2005 | 1 hour | Completed 8/18 |
| TPS Floor Training | 8/19, 8/22–26, 8/31, 9/7–9/9, 9/26–9/30 | 15 days | Completed 8/19 to 9/30 |
| Supplier Visits | Scheduled individual basis | 1/2 day each | Completed |
| Global Problem Solving | May 2005 | 1 day | Completed 5/5 |
| Executive Development Program | 9/11–9/16 and 10/3–10/7, 2005 | 2 weeks | Completed 9/16 and 10/7 |
| Toyota Way Learning Map | August (approx.) | 2 hours | Completed 8/11 |
| Health Exam | Scheduled individual basis | 1 hour | Completed |
| HR Policies (Systems) | 10/18/2005 | 1 hour | Completed |
| Succession Planning Process | Scheduled individual basis | 1 hour | Completed 8/2 |
| Labor–History/Current Assess. | Scheduled individual basis | 2 hours | Completed |
| Floor Mgmt. Development System | Scheduled individual basis | 1 hour | Completed 6/17 |
| Group Leader 40 Hr. Training | June 2005 (approx.) | 2 hours | Completed 6/8 |
| Work on the Line | Scheduled individual basis | Plastics Body Assembly 1 and 2 Paint 1 and 2 Stamping Power train Quality control Maintenance | Completed most |
| Process Diagnostics | Scheduled individual basis | (2) 4-hour sessions | Completed 9/2 |
| N.A. Toyota Plants Visits | Scheduled individual basis | 10 days | Completed |
| Toyota Sales Customer Sat. Groups | November 2005 | 3 days | Completed 11/11 |
| Toyota Technical Center Review | Scheduled individual basis | 1 day | Completed |
| Cross Dock Visit | Scheduled individual basis | 1/2 day | Completed |
| Go & See: Bolt Counter, Torque Improvement Traceability | August 8–9, 2005 | 1 day | Completed 8/8 to 8/9 |

selecting people who are highly motivated to pursue self-development. However, this does not absolve the teacher of responsibility. If people fail to develop, the blame lies primarily on the teacher or leader for not enabling, encouraging, and inspiring the development of his staff. One reason for this emphasis on holding teachers or leaders accountable for the development of those under their care is related to the point we made at the beginning of the chapter about Toyota's pursuit of perfection. To pursue this goal, Toyota needs capable, highly developed leaders and problem solvers at every level of the company. Therefore, people's development cannot be left to chance or happenstance. And it cannot be the responsibility of anyone other than the leader or manager who is closest to the *gemba* and directly responsible for the people who need developing.

## Leaders Adding Value by "Serving" Team Members

Toyota places so much value on the customers and the value-adding team members who serve the customers that it often seems that the hierarchy is turned upside down: the value-adding team members are at the top and are the most important, and the lowly leaders must prove their worth by demonstrating how they are helping the team members better perform their jobs. This may seem like an alien concept to Westerners, but as we have discussed several times, the Toyota approach is not unique to Japanese culture. The core tenets and approaches are found in almost every culture around the world. One example of that is the concept of servant leadership, a distinctly Judeo-Christian leadership model. Servant leadership emphasizes the leader's responsibility to those who work for her, just as the Toyota Way does. In fact, the concept of servant leadership has been incorporated into leadership development at TMMK in the United States. How that happened is another example of a leader taking responsibility for the development of those he leads.

In Chapter 2, we mentioned Barry Sharpe, who came to TMMK from Ford and, in the Toyota Way, entered the company several levels below where he had been at Ford. One of the challenges facing Barry that quickly became apparent during his adjustment to Toyota was a cultural one. While he hadn't been considered abrasive when he was a manager at Ford, he did bring with him to TMMK a belief that managers direct and staff members obey. In the collaborative and learning culture that Toyota had fostered at TMMK, Barry came off as pushy and disrespectful. Gary was watching Barry very closely, since he personally had brought him in from the outside. He received some negative feedback on Barry's approach and set up a program to help him through this, including a 360-degree feedback process and hiring a professional leadership coach. Meanwhile, an HR executive informally slipped Barry a copy of the book *The Power of Servant Leadership*.[4]

A servant leader supports the people who are doing the work by providing a clear vision of where the company is headed, but focuses primarily on removing obstacles to success and providing each worker with ample opportunities to develop himself. Barry found other books on the topic and began to work on adopting the principles of servant leadership as his guide for self-development. He began to get more positive feedback, but even this did not satisfy him. He saw the power of this approach not just for himself, but for everyone on his staff, many of whom were leading others. First, he created a short training course on servant leadership and taught it himself in shifts to all of the hundreds of people who reported up to him (learning by teaching and further reinforcing his ability to live out the principles). He revised the course based on feedback from each session. He also worked with the people on his staff to practice the principles on the job, mentoring them just as he was being mentored. The insights that Barry developed caught on, and eventually the servant leadership course that he created spread throughout TMMK and became a standard part of the leadership development tool kit.

## Clarifying Expectations and Accountability through Visual Management

Throughout this book, we have emphasized the subtle approach that Toyota takes to supporting self-development by placing leaders in challenging situations and asking questions rather than giving answers and directives. However, this works only in an environment where the trainee has a clear sense of what success looks like. That's the other key foundation for developing others at Toyota: leaders and teachers must set clear expectations for those they lead and be able to clearly judge their progress so that the trainees can measure their progress and be accountable for their self-development.

It's impossible to overstate the importance that Toyota gives to visual management. Every metric that matters throughout the company, especially on the shop floor, is presented visually for everyone who is involved in meeting the goal to see. The A3 reports are often posted on visual display boards; they are standardized and designed to follow a pattern that can be understood and digested at a glance. It is hard to imagine a problem-solving exercise that does not involve creating diagrams and charts of a system or process to help people clarify their thinking and make sure that nothing has been missed.

Many of the tools of the Toyota Production System are mistakenly viewed only as methods for improving the process. In most cases, they are intended to display the standards visually so that any deviations are visible to all. In fact, in Toyota, they say that there are no problems without standards. Problems are the gaps between the standards and the actual. A space marked for one container of parts sets the standard: only one container should be there. A marking on the floor shows where the team member should be when she is halfway through completing the work in one cycle (*takt*). A team member who gets to that spot early or late is out of standard, and that should generate problem solving. And visual displays of data on key metrics always indicate the target and whether the actual condition is within or out of standard.

A key reason for the dedication to visual management at Toyota is that it clarifies expectations, determines accountability for all the parties involved, and gives them the ability to track their progress and measure their self-development. The role of the leader/mentor is to ensure that visual management systems are focused on the right issues (these are usually set during the corporate- and department-level planning process, which we'll look at in Chapter 5) and can be easily understood. In the introduction, we talked about Toyota's use of metrics not to control behavior, as is common in many companies, but primarily to give employees a transparent and understandable way to measure their progress.

One of Toyota's best students at TMMK was Marty Bryant. As we will see in Chapter 6, Marty left TMMK to join a Toyota supplier and eventually was hired by Gary to help lead Dana Corporation to operational excellence. When Marty left Toyota, he experienced culture shock. At Toyota, accountability was simply expected. There were many daily stand-up meetings that usually lasted 30 minutes. Everyone who was invited showed up on time and was responsible for reporting on his progress or problems since the last meeting. The information was displayed on the wall, and it was clear what the status was relative to the target. There was some indicator, a magnet or sticker, showing whether an item was green (on target), yellow (somewhat off target, but a plan was in place), or red (off target, and serious action was needed). For any item that was not green, the person responsible came to the meeting with a prepared set of proposed countermeasures to address the problem. In his new company, it was common for people to come late to sit-down meetings where it was not clear who was accountable for anything.

Marty was also surprised at how little information about the status of operations was visible on walls. The managers at his new company seemed to take pride in having all the data that they could imagine somewhere in the computer system. In fact, the managers reporting to him lobbied strongly to continue to use the computer to display information instead of the "wasteful" practice of hanging charts and graphs on walls. Marty allowed them to go ahead with that and even invested in flat-panel screens to display the data, but he insisted on one thing: for each chart or graph on the computer, they had to identify one key point—the core message that the graph communicated. Then they had to write the key point for each graph on a dry erase board and note whether it was green, yellow, or red. They had to do this every single day, without exception.

Marty would come by and check on this. By asking them to choose what was good or not good and mark it on the board, he was forcing them to pick their target and make whether they were achieving it or not publicly visible. The computer screen is so handy that people stop paying attention to it. By physically writing down the status on each metric, the managers had to take a moment each day to analyze the situation relative to a standard and determine how they were doing. Within one month, there was phenomenal improvement on all the key metrics.

## Conclusion

For many people, the most striking thing about the stories of NUMMI and TMMK is that the plants had so many problems. TMMK holds daily public tram tours, and even in its worst period, people were struck by how neat and orderly everything appeared to be. This was true. By most measures, even on its worst day, it was an exceptional North American manufacturing plant, but that is not enough for Toyota. On any day at a Toyota plant, there is an almost frantic tension below the surface: *andon* cords being pulled, people rushing to fix things, Production Control constantly adjusting the schedule, and people waiting in the afternoon to see how much overtime they will have to work to make up for lost cars. Isn't this the kind of firefighting any company does? Isn't the famous Toyota Production System supposed to eliminate all these problems?

The answer is no. Ohno discovered that one of the strengths of TPS is bringing problems to the surface. Of course, the value of this is lost unless people step up and solve the problems. He put a lot of energy into developing leaders by putting them in challenging situations and then coaching them through the problem-solving process. The leaders who performed the best then moved up and got broader responsibility and more challenges.

We believe the most important lesson from Toyota is the high value it places on developing others. The company is patient and is willing to spend the time and money to do it right. It takes not years but decades to develop senior executives through a process of deep training and broad experience. If things are not going well in the company, the first assumption is not to blame the people who are doing the work, but to hold the leaders accountable.

Most of the examples we have given are of Japanese developing Americans. In the early days of NUMMI, and then TMMK, the Japanese approach of one-on-one coaching was very effective. Fujio

Cho was the first president of TMMK, and as Toyota expanded and there were fewer Japanese trainers and coordinators available for North America, he saw a growing weakness in the 1990s. The intensity of training and development was reduced, and more and more recent hires were lacking the depth of understanding of the Toyota Way.

This led to the start of developing an internal training document, The Toyota Way 2001, introduced when he had gone back to Japan to become president of TMC. Shortly after this general training on the core values of the company, a rapid-fire process of developing formal methods of training and developing people began, including Toyota Business Practices (TBP) for problem solving (discussed earlier in this chapter), the Floor Management Development System (FMDS) to connect problem solving to key performance indicators and targets (discussed in Chapter 5), and On-the-Job Development (OJD) to formally teach how to develop problem-solving capability based on TBP. These programs had a similar format of a small amount of classroom training followed by a great deal of practical application with coaching. They all used cascaded training starting at the senior vice president level and working gradually down through the organization over years, with each level taught becoming teachers and coaches for the next.

## Teaching Development

North America was selected as the global pilot for developing OJD training; it was led by Latondra Newton who was general manager of the Team Member Development Center. The program her team developed in 2007 had as a prerequisite TBP training, including completing a major project using TBP.

The purpose of OJD was to ensure that the skills of TBP were sustained and further developed by leaders. While OJD had been the method of developing people since the founding of the company, this was the first time in Toyota's history that it was in any way formalized and explicitly taught. The steps of OJD were built on the four steps of PDCA. The training included special emphasis on carefully assigning tasks so they are achievable but a stretch and giving the team member enough space to explore and even struggle, so there are coaching opportunities.

The North American organization was selected as the pilot because it was large, had the need, and had the highest concentration of people with the experience and maturity needed to develop OJD. The training itself was based on experiential learning with little classroom lecturing. The first step is a web-based simulation tool that uses scenarios and, based on the choices made, takes you down different paths. The scenarios are video footage from real problems in Toyota organizations acted out by Toyota members.

The second step is classroom training with all students role-playing scenarios and then reflecting and getting feedback. The classroom training includes a module on emotional intelligence and emphasizes understanding the background and perspective of the person coached.

The final assignment for each trainee is picking someone in their group and coaching the person through solving an actual problem. The trainee gets feedback and coaching from their supervisor (who already has completed the training), and from a member of Newton's team assigned to their region rotating among organizations. A final evaluation of whether students have "passed" is based on their reflection, input by the person they coached, and input by their supervisor.

The training started in 2008. Since there were a lot of layers and functions involved, it was a slow process and was not yet complete in 2011.

The formal OJD approach quickly began to spread to other regions, including to Japan, but it was modified by each region. At the point of this writing there was not yet a formal evaluation of the effects of the program, but the training got the highest evaluations of any training program done throughout North America.

Many companies that pursue lean programs experience short-lived success in project areas, but that success often dissipates quickly. After that, the question comes: how can we sustain lean improvements? The only answer is to work harder at developing leaders. The first person who needs development, of course, is you.

Leaders who bring in lean consultants often make the mistake of assuming that they can buy someone to manage the lean effort. They do not see that they must develop themselves if they want to have any hope of succeeding. We have been in companies where it is a big win to get senior leaders to spend most of a week as part of the *kaizen* team. But after the week, the senior leaders go back to their offices, armed with war stories they can tell for years about their experience in TPS. It is hard to imagine many of these executives participating in a 20-day TPS floor training course the way Steve St. Angelo did. It is even harder to imagine them spending weeks personally doing hourly jobs, yet they are expected to lead a lean transformation of something that they do not deeply understand.

There is also far too little time spent on socializing leaders from the outside into the organizational culture. Toyota has shown that this can be done successfully, even though growing from within is closer to the ideal approach. It takes six months to one year and intense attention to the transition to move even exceptional leaders properly into the culture.

The most fundamental lesson from Toyota is to take leadership seriously. It is worth investing in. It is worth having a strong vision of the True North of leadership. What type of leader do you want? What do you need to do to ensure zero defects in leadership capability?

Remember as well that the key point of leadership development at Toyota is to help potential leaders get to the right way of thinking about problems. The teacher must have faith that the student has the potential to think deeply about the problem and come up with creative ideas for improvement. This is the only way in which potential leaders can self-develop and learn to provide the space for others to self-develop, and thereby generate the "raw materials" for never-ending *kaizen* improvements, something we'll look at in practice in the next chapter.

# Chapter 4

# Daily *Kaizen*: Continually Developing Leadership from the Bottom Up

*No institution can possibly survive if it needs geniuses or supermen to manage it. It must be organized in such a way as to be able to get along under a leadership composed of average human beings.*

—Peter Drucker, pioneering management author

In Chapter 1, we made a distinction between Toyota's view of leadership and the standard American view, which focuses on Lone Ranger–type senior executives. What we've discussed thus far of Toyota's model of leadership may not seem that different from the traditional American leadership models, as it has focused on the personal actions of leaders in terms of self-development and developing others. Any successful leader in any company works closely with a tight team that reports to him and to some degree is developing those direct subordinates. At Toyota, however, leaders developing direct subordinates is just a small part of a total system. Toyota also believes that these individually gifted leaders have to be plugged into a larger system of institutional leadership if the firm is to succeed. A quick story to illustrate this point is Gary's "demotion" at NUMMI after several years as vice president of all manufacturing operations.

When Gary first became vice president of NUMMI, every department reported to him, as is typical in manufacturing plants (although

not at Toyota). After racking up what he perceived as numerous successes early in his tenure, Gary had a meeting with his boss, who informed
him that henceforth Quality Control would no longer report to him.
Gary was stunned—not only did this seem an unexpected reprimand,
but it hit him at an even more personal level, since quality control was
the core of his background and was part of what he thought distin-
guished him most as an executive. When he pressed for reasons for the
change, he was told, "You won't always be at NUMMI."

Gary learned that it was not Toyota's practice for Quality Control
to report to the president of a plant because of the inevitable conflict
of interest that arises when a single leader is faced with choosing
between meeting quality goals and meeting production goals. Gary
had been trusted, for a limited time, with managing this conflict of
interest while NUMMI was developing and Quality Control needed a
great deal of attention from someone on-site with Gary's level of experience. But that time had passed. What appeared to be a demotion was
actually a commendation. Through the processes of self-development
and developing others, NUMMI now had the leaders in place to work
the way the rest of Toyota did: the general manager of Quality Control
would henceforth report directly to the president of NUMMI independent of Gary, who was responsible for manufacturing.

This subordination of individual leadership to institutional leadership—via limits on any individual's power and influence—is characteristic of Toyota's different view of leadership. The phrase "roles and
responsibilities" is used often within Toyota. To many people, this may
seem like a call for individuals to assume responsibility and be held
accountable. This is true. At the same time, though, it provides constraints and limits on the power of individual leaders. The leadership
approach, despite its reliance on hierarchy, expects leadership from,
and grants authority to, individuals at much lower levels of the hierarchy than is typical in Western companies.

This approach produces three key outcomes in terms of leadership:
first, the dispersal of power and the expectation that leadership will
come from the base of the hierarchy ensures that there is a constantly
growing roster of potential future senior leaders who are gaining experience on a daily basis; second, it ensures that change is driven by the

people closest to the problem, which results in better problem solving, more sustainable solutions, and the possibility of continuous improvement; third, it ensures that the True North that is being pursued is Toyota's goal, not the goals of an individual leader. We'll look more closely at this third benefit in Chapter 5. In this chapter, we'll look at how Toyota disperses power and authority all the way to the work group level of the company and how that dispersal leads to better, more effective leadership that drives significant change and improvement at Toyota on a daily basis.

# A Better Understanding of *Kaizen*

To those in the manufacturing or engineering world, and to many outside of it, the concept of *kaizen* has become so ubiquitous that it may hardly seem to be a foreign word anymore, much less to require definition. Unfortunately, our experience is that the vast majority of firms and senior executive leaders at those firms misunderstand *kaizen*. Too often it has come to mean assembling a special team for a project using lean or Six Sigma methods, or perhaps organizing a *kaizen* "event" for a week to make a burst of changes. We sometimes hear the phrase "doing a *kaizen*," as if it were a one-off activity. At Toyota, *kaizen* isn't a set of projects or special events; rather, it's an integral part of leadership. It's how the company operates at the most fundamental level. It's what the majority of leaders at Toyota are doing when they are leading: supporting daily *kaizen*.

There are two types of *kaizen* that require daily activity. The first is maintenance *kaizen*: the daily work of reacting to an unpredictable world. No matter what you do, you cannot prevent the unexpected from happening. Maintenance *kaizen* is the process of reacting to the inevitable (some might call it Murphy's Law) mistakes, breakdowns, changes, or variations that occur in everyday life in order to meet the standard (productivity, quality, safety) that is expected. The goal is to bring the system back to the standard, just as a thermostat signals the furnace to bring the temperature back to the standard setting. Visitors to Toyota plants are often surprised by the frenetic level of activity— including *andon* calls—that characterizes a working plant. This frenetic activity is largely maintenance *kaizen*. The system is designed to bring problems to the surface quickly, potentially shutting down the line, so maintenance *kaizen* is urgent and immediate. After the heat of the moment, when the problem has been contained, work groups are expected to select the most frequent or serious problems and through root-cause analysis prevent them from recurring. Those same problems are present in other companies, but they are often allowed to accumulate until a Lean Six Sigma event can be organized.

The second type of *kaizen* is improvement *kaizen* (though this is simply called "*kaizen*" because this is the real goal). This is the work of not just maintaining standards but raising the bar. Again, Toyota inculcates the idea in all employees that the goal is perfection, and therefore that every process can be improved. Put more harshly, no matter how many improvements have been made, every process is still full of waste and ripe with opportunity to improve.

One of the core misunderstandings of *kaizen* is how daily it is. Many people with a superficial understanding of *kaizen* expect Toyota to have perfected most of its processes—after decades of *kaizen*, there can't be much room left for improvement, they reason. It's easy to think this way, and fighting this perception is perhaps one of the reasons that "*kaizen* mind" is a core value of Toyota. You can't even maintain the gains from a lean approach unless you focus relentlessly on continuous maintenance *kaizen*.

We've already made the point that many companies have found that the gains from lean projects are hard to maintain—but they fail to connect their struggles to maintain their gains with what would happen at Toyota if it did not practice daily *kaizen* so rigorously. Human activity seems to be just as subject to the law of entropy as chemical reactions are: unless you add new energy to the system, it slows down and halts. Daily *kaizen* can't happen without adding new energy to the system. This is the role of the leader in supporting daily *kaizen*: making sure that the new energy is added, not doing the work directly.

This last point is critical. Contrary to popular belief in management circles, when a senior executive is the "change agent," often jumping in to direct and "supervise," her actions tend to steal energy from the system rather than add to it. The people closest to the process lose ownership and incentives. They aren't revitalized by a leader who tells them what to do and how to do it; they are paralyzed. This is the scenario we see play out over and over again in companies that hire lean consultants and train a few lean "black belts," then set those people loose to redesign processes. Their presence brings energy only so long as they remain in the room. When they leave, all the energy is sucked out of the room, and the improvements, following the law of entropy, quickly decay back to the original steady state.

This definitely goes against the grain of the dominant models for driving change in American companies. Some people simply don't believe that the excellence Toyota has achieved in so many processes can possibly be the result of small, incremental changes led by the lowest level of management at the firm and driven by the people doing the value-added work. But in fact, this is the only way that sustained excellence can ever be achieved. A famous quotation of anthropologist Margaret Mead captures this perfectly: "Never doubt that a small group of thoughtful, committed citizens can change the world. Indeed it is the only thing that ever has." Top-down-driven initiatives can create a "big bang" in the short run, but they cannot deliver the long-term sustained excellence that characterizes Toyota.

Now this does not mean that Toyota engages only in small changes that lead to a lot of small, incremental improvements. Daily *kaizen* is carried out at different levels by different functions. *Kaizen* in a small work group running a part of the assembly line is likely to be localized to processes on the assembly line. But senior managers are also expected to lead *kaizen* activities that have a broad impact across many functions, leading to major systems change. Functional groups also lead major changes within their function, such as production control transforming the logistics and delivery system to a new level of performance. But even these major transformations, as we will see in the case on *minomi* in the next section, are broken down into many small steps, and the next steps are "discovered" because there is learning (PDCA) from the earlier steps.

To illustrate the power of truly engaging the people who do the work in continuous improvement, it's helpful to look in detail at exactly how a series of small innovations (improvement *kaizen*), guided by a broader vision, led to major gains in productivity and quality at TMMK and ultimately spread throughout Toyota.

## Minomi—A Material Flow Revolution in Small Steps

The most complex activity in an automobile assembly plant is not making the cars—it's getting all the parts and components into the right place as the production lines move inexorably on. When a car body is made, the parts are first stamped from rolls of steel, the overall body is welded together to create a shell, and then the individual parts are welded together into the body on a moving assembly line. Many of the parts of the steel body are large enough that moving them to the assembly line has been a problem since Henry Ford. Getting the logistics of parts management and delivery right is even more difficult in the Toyota Production System (TPS) because of the downsizing or removal of inventory buffers that cover up any problems in handling parts and delivering them to each station on the assembly line. This process, understandably, has been a focus of *kaizen* for many years.

Traditionally, small and medium-sized body pieces are placed in four-foot-square baskets, and large parts are moved in huge containers with custom-made "dunnage"—packing and packaging to protect the parts. These baskets and containers are moved via forklift to the appropriate place on the assembly line. Having forklifts moving four-foot-square baskets loaded with expensive and heavy parts around a moving assembly line adds a lot of complexity and cost. Additionally, forklift accidents occasionally happen, hurting people or damaging the forklifts or other expensive equipment. Because of the expense of operating and maintaining forklifts, and the many safety risks, Toyota has worked for many years to reduce their use.

Toyota first piloted *minomi*, a word that implies conveying parts without a container, in a major way as a solution to this waste at a subsidiary named Central Motors, based in Japan, in the late 1990s. Central Motors gained a lot of notoriety for its success in building five different steel bodies on the same line in a very small plant. The plant had evolved the *minomi* system out of necessity so that it could move the many different parts from one point to another in a confined space, which required eliminating large containers and forklifts. The *minomi* system at Central Motors employed racks on wheels and an overhead track with "meat hooks" to hang car body parts that delivered the parts to the assembly line.

On one of his visits to Japan in 2000, Gary visited the Central Motors plant and was understandably impressed by the gains in productivity and the cost reduction that Central Motors had achieved using *minomi*. The next step he took illustrates one of the key differences between Toyota's approach and that used by so many other companies that we've seen attempt to implement lean. While Gary thought *minomi* held great promise for TMMK, what he had learned at NUMMI had taught him that since he was not the leader at the *gemba*, he was not the right person to decide whether *minomi* was right for TMMK or whether Central Motors' approach was the right way to implement it. Mindless copying is always strongly discouraged at Toyota. Instead, Gary put together a team to examine *minomi* more closely and engage in *kaizen* of the parts-handling process at TMMK to determine whether and how TMMK's process could be improved. The team was made up of people already in the body shop who would feel ownership of what happened there: four hourly team members, one hourly maintenance team member, and the group's leader, Vahid Javid, an engineering specialist commonly called V.J. The team visited Central Motors in Japan for two weeks to study the *minomi* system in person. We haven't come across many companies that would even consider sending hourly employees on a business trip across the country, much less on a two-week learning trip to Japan. It's just another example of the commitment Toyota has to bottom-up leadership.

V.J. and his team spent the full two weeks at Central Motors studying every aspect of *minomi*, learning about the choices the Central Motors team had made, the problems the team members had encountered, and the hiccups they were still having. They returned home excited to begin a pilot project at TMMK. Gary provided space in the plant for the team, a budget for the cutting and welding tools that they would need to build prototypes, and the time and manpower to get to work right away.

## Phase 1: Copying on a Pilot Basis

V.J. and his team first tried using the same "meat hook" system they had seen at Central Motors, but it didn't work very well for them. The center of gravity of the different parts varied, so at times they would swing and hit one another, and some corners would bend. This created welding problems, since the bent corners could not mate properly. This happened at times at Central Motors, but it had a different welding system that pinched the body parts together during welding, and this compensated for some of the bends; TMMK's system did not do this. In addition, workers had to walk among the parts to take them off the hooks, causing safety risk and wasted motion—certainly not ideal. Given these problems, the benefits of replicating the *minomi* system as it was employed at Central Motors weren't enough to justify overhauling the parts-handling process. V.J. and his team realized that they couldn't just copy what they had seen; they would need to innovate on the basic approach.

## Phase 2: Innovating to Fit TMMK

V.J. and his team then began trying different methods. A breakthrough came when they thought about the root cause of the problem (the expense of moving large parts in baskets with forklifts) rather than copying the Central Motors approach. Instead of hanging the parts, they came up with the idea of placing them on something that held them from the bottom. They developed the idea of a cartridge system that held the parts tightly from below using metal "fingers," the way you might hold CDs or DVDs in slots on a tray. The parts on the cartridges could then be fed by gravity down a roller-type conveyor to deliver a part right to the team member, reducing the amount of walking, lifting, and maneuvering that the team member would have to do.

At this point, the team showed its prototype to Gary, and he gave it the go-ahead to move forward with a more significant test. Within a month, the team had fabricated the first cartridge system to hold the parts and slide them down to the operator. Because almost all of V.J.'s team members had personal experience on the production line, the system anticipated one of the most important factors in reducing waste and increasing safety: it delivered parts at the best height and orientation for the team member on the line to pick them up or simply begin working with them. The operator at Toyota is viewed like a surgeon in an operating room. He needs to have his tools and materials handed to him in exactly the right orientation. The result was that a great deal of wasted walking and handling was eliminated, without any damage to the parts.

In the new process, parts from the stamping press were hand-loaded onto the cartridges. The cartridges were placed on a rolling cart by a material handler and placed in a storage buffer—a supermarket, in Toyota terminology. When a welder needed a part, the appropriate cartridge was pulled from the supermarket and delivered in the orientation that allowed him to put the part in place with little extraneous motion and effort. The time needed for a welder to unload a basket had been measured in minutes; the time needed to unload a cartridge was measured in seconds. In addition to the benefit to the team members, the cartridges reduced the required space for parts in the welding area by half. In the old system, there were always two baskets side by side, one to work out of, and one waiting when the first ran out. This required walking to one or the other basket to get parts. In the new system, a team member had each cartridge of parts fed to her in one location, reducing walking and creating a more standardized rhythm for the work.

Once the team members had proved the concept on the working line, *minomi* implementation proceeded on a part-by-part basis based on an analysis of cost-reduction opportunities. Common sense at first suggested that this system would work only for small and medium-size parts, not very big parts like major body panels. But V.J.'s team members now had the bit in their teeth. They had figured out how to make Central Motors' concept work at TMMK, and they weren't going to let a simple detail like the size of the part stop them. Each month, through continued experimentation and innovation, they figured out how to handle taller and wider parts.

## Phase 3: Automating the Loading and Unloading

Soon the team from Central Motors that had originally invented *minomi* was paying a visit to TMMK to see what V.J. and his team had done.

Central Motors quickly adopted the cartridge system, seeing that it was superior to the overhead system that they had developed. But they also took the process another step further, working out how to automate (using robots) the process of loading parts into the cartridges.

V.J.'s team soon copied Central Motors' automation and added some automation of its own. The team members built new carts for the cartridges that could be pulled by an automated guided vehicle (AGV) that could follow magnetic tape on the floor of the assembly line. In essence, they automated the cartridge delivery process.

## Phase 4: Extending Automation to the Stamping Department

V.J.'s team members had all come from the body shop, since the original focus had been on the process of moving body parts from the stamping process to the welding area in the body shop. Gary created a new *minomi* team from stamping team members and put them under the leadership of a group leader from Stamping. The stamping *minomi* team was very impressed with the automation that V.J.'s team had achieved and wanted to automate the process of moving parts from the stamping presses directly into the *minomi* cartridges (prior to this, the body parts had been manually moved from the stamping press to a rack where a robot could load the cartridges). In their early experiments, the stamping *kaizen* team found a problem: unless the parts were perfectly spaced side by side on the *minomi* cartridges, they could be damaged. The main innovation the team members developed to solve this problem was the use of a machine vision system (based on a camera) to judge whether the parts were lined up correctly, with proper spacing between parts; if they were not, the robot could adjust for the part location and pick it up properly.

The new automation system allowed one person running a sequence of stamping machines to do what before had taken three people. Rather than being a burden on the one person, it actually increased job satisfaction because the team member now could see the process from start to finish and got a much greater sense of accomplishment from single-handedly turning raw materials into ready-to-use parts.

Additionally, the time savings allowed the stamping teams to devote more time to preventive maintenance, which allowed them to increase the productivity of the stamping machines by almost 50 percent.

It's worth pausing here to contemplate the huge difference between manually loading four-foot-square baskets of parts, driving them via forklift, and manually unloading them and an automated system that loads parts onto cartridges, moves the cartridges onto carts, and then delivers the parts to the right location on the body welding line. And all of this change was driven by two small groups of hourly team members led by engineering specialists through a series of many small discoveries and occasional breakthroughs.

## Phase 5: Delivering Parts in Sequence Just-in-Time

V.J. and his team, meanwhile, had turned to another challenge: delivering more than one type of part on each cartridge. Each team on the welding line typically was installing more than one part. Under the first iteration of the *minomi* system, the welding team was moving among the cartridges to select the right part to put on next. The next generation of cartridges allowed the delivery of, for example, the hood, luggage rack, and fender together on one cartridge so that the operator could get all the needed parts from one place. Once they were able to deliver multiple parts on the same cartridge, V.J. and his team evolved the system even further to a form of kitting that had a full set of parts needed for one car body. They figured out how to put together full kits of parts for one car and deliver them on a single AGV in the same sequence as the car bodies coming down the line, then traveling alongside the car body, further reducing wasted effort and mistakes.

## Phase 6: Connect to Supplier, Then Sequence

Even after all of these evolutionary steps, there were some parts that hadn't benefited from the *minomi* approach. Some steel parts were being manufactured by outside suppliers, and these suppliers were still delivering parts to TMMK in the large four-foot-square baskets. So the team members designed special pallets for selected suppliers to use (where cost-justified) that would make it easy to move the parts to a cell, where a person loaded them onto the *minomi* cartridge. The suppliers shipped the parts on these specially designed pallets, which were removed from the truck by forklift and placed onto flow racks in a sequencing cell. A TMMK team member could then pick parts from these flow racks and load them onto *minomi* cartridges in the sequence of the car bodies going down the welding line.

By December 2008, the progressive *kaizen* to implement and expand *minomi* in the body shop had eliminated about 40 forklifts and freed up about 100 line jobs. And these savings were based on the implementation of *minomi* on just 154 of the 326 stamped parts used in the production of a vehicle. As the *kaizen* teams continued to innovate, these gains would more than double.

*Minomi* spawned other opportunities for *kaizen* as well. Toyota had been buying the carts and AGVs, but at some point an hourly team member asked why the company was spending so much money to buy AGVs from external suppliers—Toyota manufactures vehicles, after all. Team members found that they could buy the little robotic device that pulls the carts and custom-make the carts themselves. Later they discovered that they could buy inexpensive, generic circuit boards of the type used in the AGV and program the boards themselves so that the AGVs would stop and wait at certain points along the line. Programming the AGVs themselves was a breakthrough, since it cut out licensing fees and added the flexibility to reprogram them. The original AGVs cost about $25,000 each; the ones built in-house cost under $4,000. With more than 100 AGVs in use, the team members' *kaizen* initiative saved TMMK more than $2 million.

## *Kaizen* and Leadership

Traditional American leadership models focus on an executive as a visionary, or "change agent," who then drives change through an organization by force of will. Even "enlightened" leadership theory focuses on how to convince employees to sign on to the leader's vision. What happens in Toyota leadership is radically different and is the only way to generate the kind of continuous improvement that is necessary for lean. Gary didn't have a complete vision for *minomi* at TMMK that he wanted to convince V.J. and his team to get excited about. He saw possibilities, but from there, he turned over leadership to the group—those at the *gemba*—and asked them to figure out the vision that was right for TMMK and evolve it through planning, doing, checking, and acting—PDCA. As a result, V.J. and his team didn't slavishly follow Central Motors. Because of Gary's trust and his willingness to allow V.J. and other group leaders to really lead, they had the passion and the drive to continually improve, innovate, and solve problems. The end result far exceeded Gary's initial expectations of what *minomi* could do for TMMK; in fact, there is no way that Gary, or anyone else who was that far removed from the *gemba*, could have anticipated all the different little innovations that would be needed along the way if *minomi* was to amount to anything other than a small experiment.

None of these innovations and improvements could have been driven from the top. But that doesn't mean that senior leadership doesn't have any role to play. Gary played a key role in supporting the daily *kaizen* activity needed to implement *minomi*. He was not involved on a day-to-day basis, and he certainly was not telling the team members and group leaders what to do. But he was coaching them and encouraging them, spending a great deal of time reviewing their work and asking questions, reinforcing how valuable their accomplishments were, and pushing them to even more improvement—adding energy to the system. As V.J. explained: "It is not every company that would have the president come down to the floor every month and review our work, ask questions, and support our imagination. The meetings with Gary always inspired us to do more."

## Organizational Structure Based on Work Groups

We opened this chapter with a quotation from Peter Drucker about the inevitable failure of any management system that depends on superhuman leaders. Part of the intent in telling the *minomi* story is to illustrate that large-scale change and dramatic improvement can happen from the bottom up without requiring such superheroes. V.J. and his team accomplished extraordinary things, but they were not extraordinary in and of themselves. Perhaps what is most extraordinary is

Toyota's investment in and trust of group leaders and team leaders. This investment is most clearly seen in the work group structure, without which daily *kaizen* would be impossible.

The fundamental organizational unit in Toyota is the work group. There are work groups in Engineering, Sales, Finance, Service Parts, Logistics, and Marketing. In Manufacturing, there is an ideal standard work group structure that consists of about 20 hourly production workers, known as *team members*; an additional 4 hourly production workers known as *team leaders*; and 1 salaried *group leader* (GL). In reality there is variation in these numbers. Team leaders begin as team members and rise by performing all the production jobs in the team at a high level, working on *kaizen* projects, and going through voluntary team leader skills training. They split their time between full-time production work some days and full-time team leader functions other days: responding to *andon* calls, for example, or doing quality checks, solving production problems that come up through the day, or working on *kaizen* projects to improve the group's processes (see Figure 4-1). At any time, two team leaders might be working a line job and two might be fulfilling team leader functions off-line.

The group leader, in relation to the team leaders, is the first level of management—the point at which Toyota begins to think of its employees as having the formal authority to manage a major process. In many ways, Toyota views its group leaders as its most important leaders: they are members of the work group, and thus have the greatest amount of direct influence over team members, and they are the part of the management team that is most responsible for delivering business results to the company. In the Toyota mindset, team members, by building the cars, deliver the greatest direct value to customers. Therefore, it is hugely important to cultivate strong group leaders and allow them, and their teams, to have ownership of their area and its strengths and problems.

Many who have taken an organizational behavior course will recognize the model in Figure 4-1 as Rensis Likert's "linking pin" model of management.[1] The manager in Likert's model is more than a daily controller of disturbances to the system. She is a linking pin that connects the team she leads to the leadership team that she is part of.

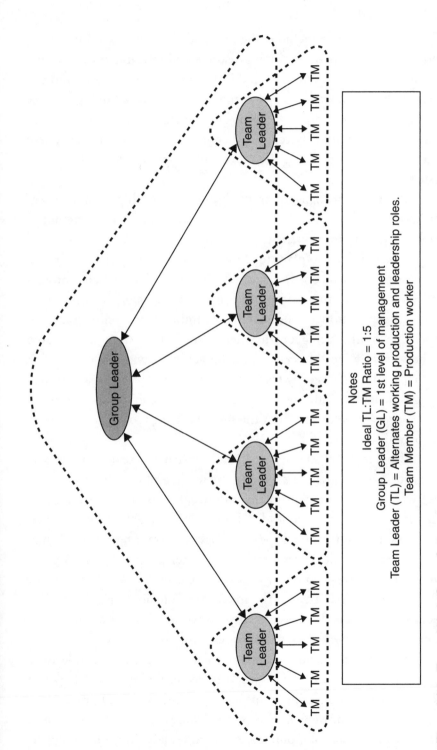

**Figure 4.1.** Toyota Work Group Structure

Notes
Ideal TL:TM Ratio = 1:5
Group Leader (GL) = 1st level of management
Team Leader (TL) = Alternates working production and leadership roles.
Team Member (TM) = Production worker

The linking pin role includes aligning goals, communicating policies and operating status, developing team members, and providing the resources that team members need if they are to perform and improve their work. When leaders develop the ability to play a linking pin role effectively, then the organization is positioned to mature from a controlling, authoritative system to a consultative management system and ultimately to the highest levels of a true participative management system.

The reason for focusing on work group leadership is simple: senior leaders do not build cars. More explicitly, senior leaders are not in the best position to properly identify problems and sources of waste at the *gemba* and develop plans to eliminate them. The group leader is in the best position to do that. Indeed, the group leader leads through daily *kaizen*. Continuous improvements made through *kaizen* are critical to the evolutionary and sustainable implementation of lean concepts in manufacturing or anywhere else. Lean cannot be achieved without *kaizen*, and *kaizen* cannot be achieved without the explicit participation of the hourly team members; therefore, real leadership at the group level is absolutely critical. If the capability at the group leader level is weak, than even the most brilliant idea from the top of the organization will fail.

At Toyota, group leaders teach and coach the team leaders who support the team members who do the work, and together those people own, operate, and continually improve their processes. Real *kaizen* happens only when group leaders lead and their teams truly own their processes. No motivational speaker, classroom training, quality initiative, or lean consultant can replace fundamental investment in training the people who do the work to lead *kaizen*. As we've seen in the last few chapters, at Toyota, the role of the "outside expert" from the staff or from outside the company—anyone who is not the leader closest to the *gemba*—is to ask questions, to coach without commanding, and to encourage, not to take over. There is a role for a technical specialist who has a deep understanding of technology (for example, V.J.'s engineering of material handling systems) or technical approaches to improvement (for example, Six Sigma), but that role is to pull together a team of group leaders, team leaders, and team members and, by coaching them through transformative *kaizen* projects, further develop their capabilities for leadership and *kaizen*.

These skills of leading *kaizen* and coaching *kaizen* can never be taught in a certification class. Classes teach the tools at a superficial level, but not real *kaizen*. Toyota leaders grow their understanding of daily *kaizen* first by developing themselves, and then by coaching and developing others. It's what makes *kaizen* a leadership development process. The act of deeply thinking through problems, energizing people, and aligning them toward a common goal is the only way to practice and develop real leadership ability.

At the end of a *kaizen* project, there is a report with the results of the process improvement, but a Toyota leader is also looking at how the people involved were transformed. If the business results were achieved, but the people involved have not developed, the *kaizen* is considered a failure.

If we return to the case of V.J. and *minomi*, there is a story behind the story. When Gary first selected V.J. to lead the team, others had some concern about how he would lead the team. V.J. was known as an exceptional engineer technically, but some people felt that he had not self-developed sufficient people skills to lead such a high-profile team. However, V.J. turned out to be a dynamo, not only in getting the job done, but in developing team members and their *kaizen* capability. In fact, V.J.'s team became a sort of training ground for those hourly employees who wanted to deeply learn *kaizen*. His success at developing others earned him the right to select the people who would join his team: applicants had to prove that they were serious about learning. V.J. grew tremendously over this period and earned a promotion, and those who learned from him went on to become recognized *kaizen* experts throughout TMMK.

## B-Labor and Kaizen

When hourly team members are doing their production jobs as part of a work group, they are known as A-labor. But at any given time, Toyota has a percentage of team members who have been pulled out of their work groups to participate full-time on *kaizen* teams as "B-labor." The hourly team members who worked with V.J. were B-labor. Many companies would call the B-labor indirect labor, or overhead.

Barry Sharpe recalls that at Ford, getting Maintenance to make improvements to equipment or build something required a bureaucratic request to Maintenance or Engineering, followed by a long wait. Once someone arrived, the problem was almost never handled on the spot. The maintenance worker or engineer would spend time diagnosing the problem, then leave to file another request for the labor and parts necessary to actually perform the fix.

At Toyota, because of the B-labor system, there is always a ready pool of knowledgeable team members and team leaders ready to take on any project immediately. Daily *kaizen* at Toyota doesn't just mean a daily process of identifying problems and opportunities for improvement. It means daily action to implement changes and improvements immediately; if the change requires effort beyond what the A-labor team members can take on, the B-labor team can be scheduled to handle it. When a new product is launched and production must be prepared job by job to build the new product, it is B-labor in a "pilot team" that does the detailed preparation work of setting up the jobs and training team members. The pilot team becomes a full-time job, usually for two to three years, for these hourly employees. The team has representatives from all relevant areas of the plant. *Kaizen* is part of the way the company is run, and Toyota makes it easy by having B-labor teams available all the time. Keep in mind that the B-labor teams are not *kaizen* specialists or lean black belts in the way that most companies conceive of them. A B-labor team is generally led by a manager or engineer, but the members of the team are hourly employees. The B-labor teams come from the same people who are working on the line day in and day out; the whole system would break down otherwise.

## Supporting *Kaizen*: Adding Energy and Developing Leaders

So how do you add energy without taking over *kaizen* and develop others' ability to engage in *kaizen* when they don't have the requisite experience? That's the challenge that Wil James, a general manager at

TMMK who preceded Gary's arrival in Kentucky, faced during the "renewal" of Toyota leadership and TPS at TMMK.

Wil was in charge of Assembly, the part of the line that takes a chassis and installs all of its inner workings, from the radiator to the carpeting. When Wil took over, it might be described as a classic example of a group where entropy had pulled performance down. Turnover and fatigue from running flat out for years had brought *kaizen* to a halt. Wil and his executive coordinator knew that they needed to inject energy, retrain team members and group leaders in TPS and *kaizen* thinking, and get daily *kaizen* rebooted. The approach they adopted was implementing a tool known as process diagnostics.

Gary had seen process diagnostics used at several Toyota plants in Japan, mainly as a tool for engineering specialists developing work processes when launchng a new vehicle. They used it like a pilot's pre-flight checklist—"Did we forget anything?"—when setting up a new process. The checklist included items like the range of cycle times for different car models or different options, orientation of parts and tools to limit walking, ergonomic considerations, and so on. Gary was amazed by how the tool focused attention on all aspects of the work process as a system. Wil and Gary saw in process diagnostics a tool that could provide training, guidance, and energy for *kaizen* in the assembly shop.

Wil and his team, supported by TBS master trainer Hideshi Yokoi, simplified the checklist and added a few items. Most important, to aid in the training process and to add energy to the effort, they converted it into a score sheet. Each item (such as distance walked by the team member) had a score range, with the total score from 0 to 100 percent (where 100 percent meant that there was nothing to improve). The score sheet provided a defined process for evaluating each job on the assembly line, which would help identify *kaizen* opportunities.

An example of several of the factors in an actual process diagnostics case (installing a radiator) is presented in Table 4-1. It shows the scores before and after some focused *kaizen* activities along with a description of the changes. (Note that this is not an actual process diagnostics form, just excerpts from one.)

With the draft of the process diagnostics score sheet in hand, Wil selected a group leader and 24 team leaders from Assembly to be the

**Table 4.1.** Example of Some Process Diagnostics Factors for the TMMK Radiator Install Job (Biggest Before and After Improvements)

| Metric | Description | Before Change | After Change | Describe Change |
|---|---|---|---|---|
| **Process WACT**<br>O = WACT ≤ takt (4 max)<br>X = WACT > takt (0) | Weighted average cycle time (if it is higher than takt, operator is overburdened) | 2 | 4 | There was a difference in the cycle time between the two models, with one being under takt and one over takt. Improved the process so that both cycle times were below takt. |
| **Start/Finish Marking**<br>O = 2 (marks correct and used)<br>X = 0 (marks out of date or not used) | Marks on floor show operator start of job and where he should be when finished | 0 | 2 | There were different start and stop lines for two different vehicles, so not used by team member. With changes in process for WACT, were able to use one start and one finish. |
| **Dolly/Table Parts Quantity**<br>O = 2 hours or less of parts and only major parts needed within cycle (2)<br>X = > 2 hours of parts or more parts than can handle in a cycle (0) | Too many parts to handle (overburden) or more than 2 hours' worth of parts (excess inventory) | 0 | 2 | Too many tasks in the job required too many different parts for a dolly, so delivered extra numbers of some parts on one round and extra of the others on a different round. By reducing excess motion in other processes, could rebalance work and move some parts to another process. |
| **Value-Added Work Ratio**<br>O ≥ 60% value-added (2)<br>● = 40–59% value-added (1)<br>X = < 40% value-added (0) | Higher ratio of value-added work to the total cycle time is desirable. | 1 | 2 | Had excess walk time to pick up and handle radiator. Tray to present radiator better was built to reduce handling by 50%. |
| **Self Quality Confirmation**<br>O = can self-check (1)<br>X = cannot self-check (0) | If root causes of potential defects not fixed, operator must self-check quality | 0 | 1 | Because process was over cycle, could not self-check quality. With extra time freed, added quality check to standard work. |

Note: Overall improvement in process diagnostics score went from 51.5 to 60.5.

first trainees in the scoring system—they became known as the "smooth motion team." The training, including a TPS refresher, was conducted in the standard *shu ha ri* fashion we discussed in Chapter 2. Each classroom session was paired with opportunities to practice the skills on the shop floor.

The team's first chance to put process diagnostics to work was evaluating carpet install. Carpet install was a manually challenging process involving several team members; managers in Assembly nearly unanimously agreed that it was the job that needed the most improvement. Using process diagnostics, the team in training spent a week evaluating the process and brainstorming and testing improvements. The initial score for the process was 19 out of 100. The smooth motion team used the process diagnostics approach to eliminate five miles of walk distance on an eight-hour shift, fix numerous ergonomic concerns, and cut the people required per shift from five to four. Within a week, the process diagnostics score went from 19 to 89. Through trial and improvement (which, of course, the score sheet was subject to as well), process diagnostics evolved into a system of 30 or more checkpoints summarized on one side of one sheet of paper (11- × 17-inch or A3-size paper). The back side of the sheet describes how to score each metric and the ideal state of the item.

Now the challenge was training everyone in Assembly on the tool so that the whole team could be involved in daily *kaizen*. Wil split the 24 team leaders on the smooth motion team into two groups of 12, one for each assembly line. These 12 trainees turned trainers were responsible for teaching the tool to all the group leaders (even though the leaders were at a higher rank). Wil and the smooth motion team prioritized the jobs and processes (there are more than 1,000 in Assembly) based on those with the greatest opportunities for improvement.

To address a problem process, the smooth motion team would work with the group leader and one of the team leaders to train them on using process diagnostics to evaluate the job. Once the group leaders had finished training in their own group by working on a problem process with the smooth motion team, they were then assigned to a different group, where they had to use the tool for a problem process in an area that was not so familiar to them. Finally, they had to pass a test to be certified on process diagnostics. Following this process, eventually every manager, assistant manager, group leader, and team leader in Assembly was trained in process diagnostics.

To continue adding energy to the system, Wil would add more items to the score sheet as soon as every process had achieved high scores on all of the existing items. But it wasn't just Wil who was improving the tool. One of the things that surprised the team members was the way in which process diagnostics could be applied to reduce not only physical waste in the process but mental waste as well. The initial tool focused on physical waste, such as unnecessary walking and difficult-to-reach parts. But it didn't take into account another source of problems—mental errors. While performing process diagnostics on all the jobs in the assembly shop, the smooth motion team found a key pattern in the data: the more decisions team members had to make (for example, between two different models of the same part or among several colors of seat belt), the more mistakes were made, which led in turn to time spent correcting mistakes, falling behind on the *takt* time, and eventually an *andon* call. They concluded that it was just as important to make the job cognitively simple as it was to make it physically efficient.

Based on this breakthrough by the team members, the smooth motion team ran some experiments. In one, they put colored Ping-Pong balls into a box and asked a team member to pick up balls according to colors that were called out—for example, pink, then green, then yellow—within a time limit. The experiment showed that when there were six colors, an average team member would make a mistake on the fifth cycle. With five colors, the team members on average made a mistake on the tenth cycle. Ultimately, they concluded that only when they got down to two colors were mistakes all but eliminated.

This experiment led the assembly team to establish as a standard that the number of decisions had to be two or less for a job to qualify as "simple." So, for example, if a team member had to select the two right color seat belts for the front seat and then the two right color seat belts for the rear seat and then the right color cup holder, that was five decisions—three decisions too many, and out of standard. The item was added to the process diagnostics sheet as "simple job," requiring two or fewer decisions.

The use of process diagnostics led to many small improvements that added up to major gains. But entropy always remains a danger. With a scoring system like process diagnostics, the way entropy enters the system is typically via "grade inflation." Team members can easily slip into a process of raising scores for relatively insignificant improvements. The role of the group leaders is to ensure that energy doesn't slip out of the system via such processes. In terms of process diagnostics, the smooth motion team decided that it was important to take two steps to keep the energy going.

First, the team members created a certification for process diagnostics. To become certified, a team member had to be able to apply process diagnostics to a series of processes and score the processes correctly within 90 percent accuracy, based on the scoring of a process diagnostics expert. The requirement is at 90 percent because process diagnostics is not entirely objective. There is some judgment involved, and there will not be perfect agreement between people, so 90 percent accuracy seemed a realistic expectation. Second, they set up an audit process so that every job was regularly audited by a team member who was certified in the use of the tool. These two initiatives kept the tool useful for continuous improvement. A process diagnostic audit can still add energy to the daily *kaizen* process.

## Conclusion

In conclusion, we have to make one point absolutely clear: it's not about the tools. Toyota's success is not the result of TPS, Toyota Business Practices, process diagnostics, or any other tool. For example, process diagnostics evolved as a method for supporting daily *kaizen*. In fact, when the San Antonio plant was initially set up, the leaders there considered and rejected process diagnostics as a tool, deciding that it was too complex for the typical team member. They chose a simpler tool that also allowed them to analyze waste and opportunities for *kaizen* of the work process. Gary was the head of North American operations and past president of TMMK, but he still allowed San Antonio to go in its own direction. As long as the people there had a reason and an alternative tool that they were seriously using, he was content to let them learn in their own way. Interestingly, several years after Wil left TMMK, in the midst of the recall crisis, when there was an intensified focus on quality, Yuri Rodrigues became quality manager and with a pilot work group developed an alternative to process diagnostics. The plant had also concluded that process diagnostics was more of an engineering tool and was too complex for the typical team member. So it developed a simpler version.

No matter what tool is used, the determining factor for success is leadership at every level, but particularly in the groups that do the value-added work. Does the organization have group leaders who are committed to self-development and who invest in developing team members? Does the organization have senior leaders who are willing to let group leaders lead and are committed to doing what it takes to inject energy into daily *kaizen*? If not, no tool in the world can create sustainable gains from lean approaches. If so, there's no shortage of useful tools and approaches.

Companies throughout the world are "implementing lean." They hire a few consultants, "train up" some internal lean experts, and "deploy the methodology." This is the common language of such initiatives. Many companies invest in "lean certification" programs to create black belts. The internal experts like the certification credential because it gives them something to put on their résumés when they seek out another job in another company. But these actions cannot replace fundamental investment in training the people who do the work to lead lean through *kaizen*. Unfortunately, that investment all too often is not happening. Professionals outside of Toyota are constantly struggling—and failing—to sustain the changes from lean, and no amount of certified black belts can help them.

Toyota takes a different approach. The people who manage the work day by day, the group leaders, teach and coach the team members who do the work, and together those people own, operate, and continually improve their processes. The role of the outside expert is to ask questions, to shake his head when things are not being done right, and to smile a little and say, "Please continue," when the student is learning. The outside expert needs to understand *kaizen* deeply enough so that he knows when to nod, when to disapprove, and when to jump in with a suggestion. This skill can never be taught in a certification class. Classes teach the tools at a superficial level, but not real *kaizen*. And for *kaizen*, that cannot be handled by the work groups: a manager or engineer and "B-labor" works across groups.

The idea that a group of engineers from Corporate would arrive at the plant to make a bunch of improvements, without direct involvement and ownership of work groups, and then leave is hard to imagine at Toyota. Toyota wants the ownership and understanding of processes and improvements to reside in *gemba*, in the work group.

In *The Toyota Way*, Jeff told the story of all the material logistics changes that V.J.'s team developed over a five-year period could perhaps have been implemented in one year by a team of engineers from Corporate led by a black belt, and perhaps construction of the devices could have been contracted out. Speed of implementation is fine, but not at the cost of sacrificing the learning, development, and commitment of the team members who need to maintain and continue to improve the system. If *minomi* had simply been implemented without the work having been done to adapt it so that it became the right solution for TMMK's needs, TMMK would not have improved the system that Gary saw at Central Motors. It would have copied that system at every welding process in the body shop. It would never have advanced to the point where Central Motors could learn from TMMK and then learn to automate the process. TMMK would not have gone from Phase 1 to Phase 2, and eventually up to 6, and then kept on going. It would have stopped in the early stages, declared that it had *minomi*, and then wondered why the process was not being sustained. When Toyota makes a process improvement, it has two goals: to improve the process to get better results and to develop the people.

We expect that by now, readers are convinced of the power of delegating responsibility for *kaizen* to the work group, with strong coaching support. In a traditional company, there are "supervisors," and most large companies have at some point tried to "empower" teams by giving them targets and "getting out of the way." Often autonomy is granted by flattening the organizational structure, eliminating layers of management and increasing the supervisor's span of control from, say, 20 people to 50 team members per supervisor. A different trend creeping into lean practice is companies attempting to "deploy work groups wall to wall in a year." They set up the HR definition of the team leader role and put group leaders through a short classroom training course.

Unfortunately, both options are doomed to failure. Reducing management does grant autonomy, but it is undirected autonomy without leadership. Where are the teachers? Where are the people with the natural ability to inspire others? "Deploying teams wall to wall" is no more effective than deploying a tool like *kanban* end to end. You can have the formal structure, and it can look good on paper, but in reality you do not have the capability. *Kanban* requires a very disciplined, stable set of work processes to function properly, and work groups require highly developed and skilled leaders at all levels. A work group is only as strong as the self-development of the leaders above it, and group leaders and team leaders must go through *shu ha ri* to develop themselves.

This is recognized inside Toyota. In *The Toyota Way*, a story was told of a Toyota service parts operation.[2] The executives of Toyota Motor Sales and the warehouse manager agreed to phase in work groups with team leaders over a three- to five-year period. At first the group leaders were supervisors who were deeply trained in TPS methods, and they had to self-develop as leaders before they were allowed to appoint team leaders. In this early stage of self-development, they were told that they needed to be directive until their teams experienced TPS and matured to a given point. A report card for judging the performance of the work groups was put together, and the score needed to be achieved before group leaders could designate individuals as team leaders was determined. It took three years for the first work groups to achieve the maturity needed to appoint team leaders and make the transition to a more bottom-up style of management.[3]

Can other companies meet the long-term challenge of developing true *kaizen* capability in their people year after year? It requires a level of patience and a level of financial investment, for example in B-labor, that is not characteristic of many companies, whose cowboy-style leaders have a short period of time to get results or move out of the way. The alternative is to give up on developing daily *kaizen*, give up on sustaining improvement, and give up on establishing a true lean enterprise.

# Chapter 5

# *Hoshin Kanri:* Align Vision, Goals, and Plans for Continuous Improvement

*Vision without action is merely a dream. Action without vision just passes the time. Vision with action can change the world.*

—Joel A. Barker, futurist

In Chapter 4, we looked at the "grassroots" nature of Toyota leadership. Leadership of daily *kaizen* by group leaders, and the support of leadership coming from the base of the organizational pyramid, is responsible for much of Toyota's success. The development of continuous improvement isn't restricted to technological visionaries and executive-level "change agents." While there certainly are breakthrough innovations coming out of Engineering, most day-to-day improvements in processes are driven from below by committed group leaders and team members, who are given both the latitude to constantly improve their domain and the responsibility for doing so.

It doesn't take a leadership expert, though, to point out the limitations of a solely bottom-up approach for a global company. For one thing, in a system in which each work group operates semiautonomously, owning its own process, *kaizen* projects do not necessarily complement one another. Every organization, Toyota included, needs to prioritize its initiatives and to adjudicate and resolve the differences between competing or conflicting efforts. In the *minomi* example that we looked at in Chapter 4, for instance, there were times where increasing productivity in one area required adding personnel in another. At first, both Stamping

147

and the materials handling department had to add people so that the body shop could use *minomi* to save resources. Not until the stamping department joined in to automate the loading of the *minomi* cartridges and suppliers moved to send parts in on *minomi* cartridges was overall waste reduced. While several of the steps seemed to add as much waste as was being eliminated, when all the pieces were in place the system was far more productive.

If different departments are working on disconnected projects, one reducing costs, another on safety, another reducing inventory, it is likely that no overall large benefits will accrue to the company. But having high-level business targets that get broken down to more specific targets for each department, with well-developed plans of action, and then rapid-fire *kaizen*, will allow the separate efforts to add up to meaningful results for the business.

Every organization needs a vision and a set of goals. At Toyota, where the entire leadership process is centered around the pursuit of "True North," this is more critical than it is at most companies. Setting True North at Toyota is the role of the board of directors; it is a top-down leadership process. Where does top-down leadership meet bottom-up leadership? How does Toyota pursue the holy grail of leadership: coordinated action across the entire global company?

Toyota's approach to the universal challenge of coordinated, directed action across the corporation is *hoshin kanri*. Literally translated, *hoshin* means "compass," or "pointing the direction," while *kanri* means "management" or "control." *Hoshin* is the term used for the annual plans and goals up and down the company. *Hoshin kanri* is the process of setting goals and targets and, most important, the concrete plans for reaching those targets. It's another example of personal leadership being guided by institutional leadership. But, as we'll see, it also works only because of the high level of personal leadership that Toyota develops.

In a formal sense *hoshin kanri* only refers to the alignment of breakthrough goals and objectives that take the company to a new level (sometimes called *kaikaku*), while stretch objectives on KPIs aligned with these goals are part of daily management of *kaizen*. There is not much concern, in practice, with distinguishing *hoshin kanri* from daily management and *kaizen*: they are both part of the company's commitment to continuous improvement. When individual leaders in Toyota write out their objectives for the year, they do not distinguish the breakthrough *hoshin kanri* initiatives from the daily *kaizen* targets. We've used this pragmatic approach, referring to both breakthrough initiatives led at Gary's level and the breakdown of objectives from the President to the work group, as *hoshin kanri*. The blending of *hoshin kanri* and daily management to drive *kaizen* illustrates once again that it is not the particular tools in use but the leadership approach that all initiatives are grounded in that makes the difference in sustaining continuous improvement.

As goals move down through the company, they become more specific. "Become best in class in quality" at the top level can work its way down to very specific targets on very specific measures, such as, "a 5 percent improvement per year over three years in first-time, defect-free welding." Improvements in quality in welding can be translated into even more specific actions. For example, it may be determined in the first year that many defects occur in welding when tools are worn and should have been changed out. Thus, the more specific target for that year might be: "implement a predictive tool change system to change 100 percent of tools on a planned schedule." This is something that can be easily measured day by day, work group by work group.

The movement down the organization can be thought of as a big triangle that relates broad goals at the top leadership level to concrete actions taken and measured by the working teams (see Figure 5-1). In this way, *hoshin kanri* links the leadership together in a tight chain of goal setting and goal achievement. Vertically, goals cascade down the organization and are turned into innovative thinking about how to achieve the goals. Horizontally, different functions coordinate their plans to achieve the broader goals. Vertically and horizontally, however, this chain is only as strong as the weakest link in the leadership chain, which is why Toyota works so hard at leadership development. Unfortunately, too many companies adopt something that they think of as *hoshin kanri*, but they lack the leadership and the engaged work groups to work effectively to translate the high-level goals into concrete changes. Or worse, middle management cuts corners to meet metrics endangering the future of the company.

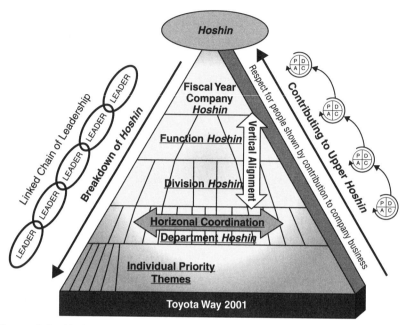

**Figure 5.1.** *Hoshin Kanri*: Direction Management Vertically and Horizontally

# *Hoshin Kanri*: Management by Objectives by Another Name?

Those who are familiar with approaches such as "Management by Objectives" (MBO) or other methods that use a cascading goals process to communicate corporate objectives and develop business unit–level means of achieving them will recognize the process of *hoshin kanri*. In some ways, *hoshin kanri* is not particularly different from many tools used by other companies in their attempts to align corporate, business unit, and individual goals. Familiarity with those tools may lead many people to be somewhat skeptical about *hoshin kanri*; while compelling at the theoretical level, such tools have a decidedly mixed record in practice. However, there are some subtle but absolutely critical differences that distinguish between checking off on achieving metrics (MBO) and thinking deeply about innovative ways to achieve results (*hoshin kanri*).

Aligning efforts across an organization is the dream of every executive; that's what makes Management by Objectives and *hoshin kanri* so appealing in theory. We've worked with many companies that have seen such tools and adopted them immediately, mistakenly believing that it is the tools, rather than the people using them, that are responsible for the outcome. There are nice forms and charts showing how the objectives at one level are connected, or not connected, to the objectives of the next level up.[1] However, adopting *hoshin kanri* after visiting Toyota, or expecting that simply using these forms will lead to aligned goals and high performance, is the equivalent of Alexander Graham Bell seeing a modern phone and deciding to implement a touch-tone keypad on his first prototype. It might look nice, but the buttons won't work.

For example, Jeff's consulting firm recently worked with a company to help teach basic lean tools at its work sites globally. Each site received a four-week course that included hands-on *kaizen* to improve operations. Encouraged by the results of some initial efforts, in the second year the CEO got enthusiastic about using *hoshin kanri* to drive more aggressive goals. At a corporate off-site, he worked with the vice presidents of business units to set aggressive targets for quality and cost reduction; the vice presidents were then held accountable for achieving those objectives—at all costs. Since the vice presidents lacked mature skills in process improvement, however, this aggressive goal setting mostly meant head-count reduction and hammering on supervisors to improve customer evaluations of quality. Ironically, many of the lean coaches who had been trained in *kaizen* in the initial phase of the project were among the casualties of the head-count reduction. Most of the disciplined lean processes that had been developed during the training period disintegrated into daily firefighting during peak periods of demand.

In another case, Jeff received a confidential letter from an executive at a hospital that had received quite a bit of praise in the press for its seemingly successful implementation of lean concepts and *hoshin kanri*-type processes. This executive told Jeff that he believed the company was on the verge of collapse. The lean objectives had been mandated by the CEO with minimal input from business unit leaders, let alone from the leaders and managers who were closest to the work. The objectives had been met, but only through unsustainable cuts and nonrepeatable projects. The big "lean" gains came from a huge capital expense to renovate the entire hospital complex to improve flow; in the recession, the debt incurred to finance the renovations was weighing the company down to near bankruptcy.

There are three main differences in the way Toyota executes *hoshin kanri* that account for its success as compared to the Management by Objectives/cascading goals that are too frequently practiced at many companies. The first difference is the way in which the *hoshin* goals are identified and vetted. Specifically, the corporate *hoshin* is developed through an intensive process of data gathering and consensus building engaged in by the 20 to 30 top leaders within Toyota, people who have intimate knowledge of the present state of the company at all levels— knowledge built by spending time at the *gemba*. This is a substantive difference from the five- or eight-member executive teams that so often set goals in large companies without having much insight into how work actually gets done and what opportunities for improvement there may be.

The second difference is the level of collaboration and give-and-take that occurs as the goals are cascaded down through the organization and get turned into innovative approaches to process improvement. *Hoshin kanri* uses the term "catch-ball" to describe this process. In essence, the process of setting goals and targets in support of the corporate *hoshin* is a two-way conversation, not a one-way mandate. Senior leaders (at whatever level of the company) engage the next level of leaders in considering what goals are achievable and what would be the best options for approaches to achieving them. Of course, senior leaders are not held hostage to the willingness of more junior leaders to sign on to the targets. At the same time, the catch-ball process, which we'll look at in more detail later in the chapter, is a real conversation based on facts, not just lip service. Executives at the top of the company know what the business needs if it is to be successful, but the people in the trenches know what they can do to improve their processes. In the right environment, the creativity of the working levels is unleashed to create true innovation and sustainable process improvement to achieve goals.

The third difference in Toyota's approach is the point at which the company engages all levels of the organization in *hoshin kanri*. At

Toyota, the company invests in developing leadership first; leaders then develop more junior people, so that everyone, from team members up to senior leaders, has the requisite skills needed to engage in the process of cascading *hoshin* goals and identifying the means that will be used to achieve them. This is why Toyota can use the catch-ball process and engage more junior leaders in real discussion and innovation: it trusts the leadership skills of these junior leaders. The requisite skills for self-development and *kaizen* include standardized work and problem solving done in the right way so that it engages and develops others; and it takes years to bring a company to the point where these skills are strongly enough in place that engaging all levels of the organization, especially the team members doing the value-added work, in *hoshin kanri* can be done. If the leadership of a particular group, plant, or even country is not yet sufficiently developed, Toyota doesn't use the *hoshin kanri* process in its complete form of top-to-bottom participation. It uses a top-down structure that is more similar to Management by Objectives. For instance, during the early development of leadership capability in North America, Toyota corporate in Japan identified the *hoshin* and then communicated what the Americans needed to do, while the Americans, with strong coaching, worked out the details of implementation; there wasn't a great deal of catch-ball down through the American organization. Similarly, we will see in the next chapter that when Gary ran Dana, he was using a modified version of *hoshin kanri* that included top-down objectives and plant managers developing the plans for attainment.

Most firms that try to transform to lean have the process backward. They set the goals and push targets down through the organization *before* they cultivate the skills that lower-level leaders need if they are to identify the best means for achieving those goals. It is somewhat like requiring a pianist to perform Chopin before she knows her scales; it sets the bar too high, sets the leader up for disappointment when he fails to meet his objectives, and creates a dynamic of distrust that is hard to undo. More important, it frequently leads to disaster for the company, as short-term decisions trump long-term considerations. It's striking that so many companies trust managers to, for instance, cut costs by 10 percent year over year, but do not value them enough to invest in their leadership ability or to solicit input from them on the consequences of such cuts. Thus you get situations like the one noted earlier, where a "lean" initiative leads to laying off the people who have been trained in "lean" methods.

# The *Hoshin Kanri* Process

Just like the cyclical leadership development model, *hoshin kanri* operates at many levels and in many cycles. It starts with a long-term corporate vision, typically with a ten-year time horizon, and an intermediate five-year business plan. The five-year plan is then broken down into annual *hoshin kanri* plans that ultimately support the ten-year vision. The president makes a state of the company speech each January, laying out his vision for the company, and a high-level business plan, which leads to a process of developing specific *hoshin kanri* by different parts of the company. Then these annual plans are cascaded down through the various levels of the organization. Again we must emphasize that "cascading down" is not a passive process. At every level, work groups are constantly thinking about what can be improved in their processes and are getting hints throughout the year as to where the company is headed. Often their ideas for improvement for the next year are well developed before the formal *hoshin* are announced from the top.

Throughout the year, progress is reviewed against the targets, and adjustments are made through many reflection events. At the end of each year, progress toward the ten-year vision is reviewed, and new annual plans are set based on the achievements and learning from the prior year and a forward look at the environment. Thus, as with so much else at Toyota, the *hoshin kanri* process can be thought of in terms of W. Edwards Deming's Plan–Do–Check–Act (PDCA) problem-solving process (see Figure 5-2). A plan is developed at a high level and broken down into finer and finer levels of detail, the doers execute the plan, progress is checked at each level and the results are rolled up to higher levels, and further action is taken based on the continuing gap between the targets and actual conditions. Part of the Check stage halfway through the year is setting the foundation for the next year's *hoshin kanri* planning. Throughout the company, there are many smaller PDCA

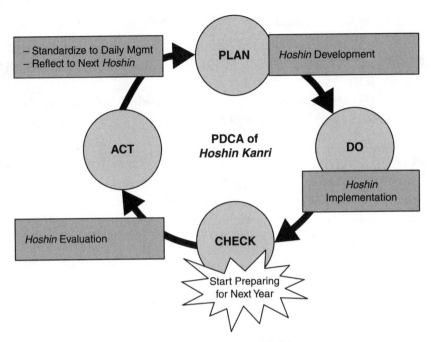

**Figure 5.2.** The *Hoshin Kanri* Process Follows PDCA

cycles throughout the year. Every attempt to improve a process, guided by the *hoshin* goals, is a PDCA process.

## Long-Term Vision Set by Internal Board of Directors

The Plan stage begins with the ten-year vision and goals for the company. The current vision guiding Toyota is Global Vision 2020, as we discussed briefly in the prologue. It replaces Global Vision 2010, which was announced in 2002. We'll use Global Vision 2010 as an example of the *hoshin kanri* process, since implementation of Global Vision 2020 is still in its early stages.

The way Toyota builds the ten-year vision is unique among companies that we have studied. The board of directors sets the ten-year vision, which in itself doesn't sound particularly unique. It is the makeup of the board (which violates the commonly accepted "best practices" for corporate governance) and its decision-making process that stand out.

Toyota is one of the holdout companies in Japan that still relies on an internal board of directors made up of the company's senior executives, with no external board. Having only an internal board used to be common in Japan, but during the 1980s and 1990s, many Japanese companies switched to the Western practice of having an external board of directors.

The theoretical benefit of the external board is that it creates a system of checks and balances to offset the internal executives' potentially self-reinforcing methods and blind spots. The last decade has yielded plenty of examples of this theory not working particularly well in practice, as outsiders with a very superficial understanding of the business can drive it in ways that destroy its internal competencies. Yet Toyota's rejection of an external board has little to do with the failures of American-style boards. Its stance is based on a set of risks that are less recognized, particularly for a company like Toyota that is built around a strong culture. External board members, while bringing an outside perspective, are only part-time decision makers and, as such, are less able to communicate with a company's leaders beyond the executive team in order to deeply understand the current state of the firm. Outsiders are also less likely to be committed to the company as an institution with a distinctive culture. At Toyota, having an external board would mean that key decisions were being made by people who are not governed by the Toyota Way or deeply trained in the rigorous, highly disciplined Toyota Business Practices process.

Toyota is risk-averse enough that it would hate to leave so much to chance when making key strategic decisions for the company. However, Toyota understands the dangers of blind spots, particularly since the board of directors is almost exclusively made up of long-term Toyota executives.[2] To counteract this, Toyota has put countermeasures in place that bring data and divergent viewpoints to the board. In fact, Toyota leaders go out of their way to get dissonant data, usually through first-hand visits to Toyota sites around the world, including Manufacturing, Engineering, Sales, and dealerships. Toyota board members travel around the world and spend time at actual work sites to an extent that would be inconceivable even in many "international" firms.

To supplement these direct observations and the data presented to them in meetings, Toyota board members rely on the opinions of "experts." The first expert opinions come from leaders within the company. In preparing for his presidency in 2009, Akio Toyoda developed a hotline network of leaders at all levels, from executive vice presidents to managers on the shop floor. He gave these people a special cell phone number and instructed them to call him regularly with any observations or thoughts. He cannot be in touch with hundreds of thousands of people all the time, but he does not want to be insulated from the reality of daily life on the shop floor. And, of course, internal experts from functional areas (Quality, Finance, Human Resources, Purchasing, Business Planning) put together detailed reports based on data in their areas.

Outside experts also have a role to play. At many board meetings, Toyota invites a world expert to report on some topic. Topics are selected based on trends that Toyota believes are important to its future, such as world fossil fuel supplies or global demographic trends. With their finely honed skills in listening, sorting through information to identify key points, and openness to good and bad news, Toyota leaders are able to put together a comprehensive, yet focused picture of an issue.

In the past, Toyota board meetings were led by the current president of the company, and the board included the former president, vice chairman, and chairman. Other former executives were often on the board as senior advisors. For example, Hiroshi Okuda, who was chairman between 1995 and 1999, was still on the board as a senior advisor in 2009, as was Dr. Shoichiro Toyoda, who ended his term as chairman in 1999 and became honorary chairman. All of the executive vice presidents who run global operations (for example, Global Manufacturing, R&D, Sales, and Human Resources) were also on the board. This group had already been shrunk over time from a peak of 60 members, which was unwieldy to manage. By 2009, there were 25 members of the board of directors, and 13 managing officers from the local regions.

The managing officers obviously have a detailed understanding of their respective domains and report in at each board meeting; they also take the high-level *hoshin* goals to their area of responsibility and begin to cascade them to more specific plans. Gary recalls that soon after he was made a managing officer, when he participated in his first board videoconference, he was amazed at the intensity of interest in everything he had to say when he was asked for input based on manufacturing conditions in North America.[3]

In 2011, Akio Toyoda and the executive team made the radical move, by Toyota standards, of reducing the board from 27 to 11 members. This was part of the planning (actually replanning) for Global Vision 2020 in the aftermath of the recall crisis (discussed in the prologue to this book). In the deep reflection on the recall crisis, one issue that emerged was the slow speed of decision making in response to the crisis. Faster decision making and giving more power to those for whom the problem was local might have at least dampened the crisis. The 11 members consist of a chairman, president, five executive vice presidents, and four officers who are responsible for business development, accounting, finance, and external affairs. While shrinking the board of directors, Toyota increased the regional managing officers group from 13 to 15 as part of a process of "regional autonomy," giving more power to the regions to make local decisions—decision making closer to the source of a problem.

In the old and the new systems, all of the board members have been through the leadership learning cycle many times, and have achieved success at every level of the company. For example, board member Takeshi Uchiyamada led a major reorganization of global R&D into vehicle centers, was the father of the first Prius hybrid vehicle, led Production Engineering and then Production Control and Logistics, and then became chief officer of global vehicle engineering. It would be very unusual in any other company for a senior executive to have such a wide range of experience, but the Toyota board members are examples of T-type leaders who can quickly understand a function, build winning teams, prioritize activities, and lead in very different environments and specialties. In fact, at Toyota the only way to become a member of the board is to be a phenomenally successful T-type leader.

It is the board of directors and the managing officers who establish Toyota's top-level *hoshin*, not just the CEO and a handful of his closest associates. The deep involvement of the board in personally investigating the state of the company and its various operations is another reason why Toyota's process is unique. In keeping with the value of *genchi genbutsu,* each member of the board spends time at the *gemba* regularly. The actual planning for next year's *hoshin* starts in the Check process for this year's *hoshin.* When Americans in plants, engineering offices, and dealers see Japanese executives coming to visit, they know that a key reason that the Japanese are coming is to see things firsthand to confirm actual progress and prepare for the next *hoshin.* In the months leading up to Akio Toyoda's appointment as president in June 2009, Americans were often surprised to see him popping up in unexpected places. He would show up in Toyota sales offices, at plants, and at individual dealerships. These were not ceremonial visits. He was asking detailed questions and checking processes. He was doing the same thing in Europe, China, and other parts of the globe.

The meetings, formal and informal, between members of the board of directors are important, but what goes on outside the boardroom is far more important. Because all the board members are deeply steeped in the Toyota Way, the board operates quite differently outside the boardroom from the way most American managers would expect. At Toyota, individual board members or managing officers take responsibility for a particular issue, work on it outside the meeting, gather many opinions and work to build consensus, and then report back at the next meeting.

This is all part of the process of testing and evolving ideas through *nemawashi.* Translated literally as "digging around the roots of the tree to prepare for transplant," in Japanese culture, *nemawashi* is an informal process that goes on in the background to lay the foundation for some proposed change or project. Meetings in Japan are very formal and public, and it would be embarrassing for a well-vetted proposal to be rejected in this setting. Thus, before any formal proposal is made in a meeting, a leader practices *genchi genbutsu,* gathering the necessary information and then discussing his analysis and proposed solution one-on-one with various people in the company. Through a series of these discussions, the proposal is modified and consensus is built.

It is worth expanding on what consensus is and is not in the Toyota context. Consensus does not mean that everyone agrees—that would be impossible. Consensus at Toyota means that each person feels that she has been respectfully heard, and that her ideas have been seriously considered. Through *nemawashi*, a leader tests, modifies, and improves a board proposal at all levels of the organization *before* it gets to the board. This helps the idea get board approval, and it helps prevent any unpleasant surprises at different levels of the company; leaders have had their chance to share their thoughts, and so any proposal adopted by the board will be familiar to those who are given the task of implementing it.

The corporate *hoshin* is therefore created not by a small group of insiders or by a group of knowledgeable but distant external board members, but by a collection of the most knowledgeable and experienced people in the company. This process of developing the plan and gaining agreement is critical to the success of *hoshin kanri*. It is often said in Toyota that when there is a good plan, at least 60 percent of the work has been done. The developmental process of getting agreement and getting people to think deeply about what is possible and challenge themselves is as important as the specific goals that are set. As a result, the phrase "cascading of goals" is something of a misnomer: through *nemawashi*, ideas are tested down within the organization before they are sent back up for final approval. While the ten-year vision (and five-year goals) is definitely set at the top, it is so thoroughly based on input and information from throughout the company that it can be said to be bottom-up as well. This is another example where top-down meets bottom-up at Toyota. Then the annual detailed plans are like stepping-stones to ensure that methods are implemented and actions executed to achieve the overall targets.

This process at the turn of the millennium is what created Global Vision 2010. In the media, the announcement of Global Vision 2010 was grossly oversimplified, focusing almost exclusively on President Fujio Cho's statement that Toyota would seek to achieve a 15 percent global market share. The real vision was much broader: to become the most respected and admired firm in the automotive business while following the guiding principles of the company.

The guiding principles, adopted formally in 1992 and modified in 1997, were based on the five main principles first set out by founder Sakichi Toyoda. They spoke of being honorable, contributing to society, pursuing growth through innovative management, creating a corporate culture that enhanced individual creativity and teamwork, and working with all partners for mutual growth and benefits. Global Vision 2010 reflected these principles with a focus on three main elements:

1. Demonstrate responsibility as a world leader.
2. Benefit society through *monozukuri* (or "the art of making value-added products") and technological innovation.
3. Share prosperity with employees.

## From Long-Term Vision to Intermediate Plans

The core of Global Vision 2010—becoming the most respected and admired company in the automobile industry—is a fairly vague goal. The next phase of *hoshin kanri* is turning that vague goal into more concrete terms and from there creating a midrange plan covering four to five years that is clearly actionable. The 15 percent market share target announced by Fujio Cho was a way of making the goal of being the most respected and admired company into something tangible that everyone in the company could grasp. It was also a forecast, since demand for Toyota products was already growing at a sufficient rate to justify doubling the size of the company by the end of the decade. The goal wasn't truly a 15 percent market share (that's not the metric that the board was focused on); achieving a 15 percent market share would be an indicator that Toyota was succeeding at the important tasks necessary to become the most respected and admired automotive company. However, when you put a numerical target out there, it does become a focus, so you have to be prepared to coach leaders to do it in the right way.

This is another example of why the success of the *hoshin kanri* process depends on having developed leaders throughout the company. There are plenty of examples of companies that have been thoroughly derailed by the pursuit of market share at all costs (one need look no further than GM for an example). Pursuing market share could have led Toyota to cut costs by sacrificing quality, cutting back its investment in people, or pricing cars below the cost of manufacturing them. For example, American auto companies typically sell at cost to rental car companies (called "fleet sales") to boost volume, a practice that is not profitable and can tarnish their reputation. Of course, such actions would have been counterproductive in achieving the real goal of Global Vision 2010, but, more important, they would have violated the principles of the Toyota Way. The board could set a goal of 15 percent market share because it was confident that throughout the company, the goal would be pursued in the right way.

Outsiders have frequently misinterpreted this goal and Toyota's actions since it was announced. When it leaked out early in 2009 that Akio Toyoda would replace Katsuaki Watanabe as president of Toyota, the immediate reaction from the newspapers was that Watanabe was being replaced as a consequence of the fact that his pursuit of this goal had left Toyota overextended when the global recession hit (in fiscal 2009, the company posted its first annual loss in 50 years).

Inside of Toyota, the board of directors recognized that under Watanabe's leadership, the company had achieved its growth targets and had the four most profitable years in its history. As the earlier explanation of how goals are set in the company should make clear, no one person at Toyota makes major decisions. Watanabe, as president at the time, would certainly assume responsibility for the major financial loss in the recession, but the reality was that in many ways he was no more or less culpable than the rest of the board for any mistakes that were made. For example, when Fujio Cho announced the 15 percent goal (actually carrying on the push for growth under his predecessor, Hiroshi Okuda), Watanabe was a member of the board that built consensus on that goal; while Watanabe was president, Akio Toyoda was a member of the board. However, in an interview with Liker in November 2010, on the recall crisis, Akio Toyoda did reflect that his agenda was to reemphasize the true purpose of the company.

*I realize that sometimes our people were mixing the goals and the means. For Toyota, the goal is to contribute to society through the automotive business. As a means to get to that goal, we need to sell more so that we have resources to reinvest. But if you put more sales and profit in front of the goal, we are going to make a big mistake.*

The 15 percent market share goal was one of many goals and metrics created in the process of turning Global Vision 2010 into actionable plans. One consequence of crystallizing this vision of a larger global company was to communicate the urgency for each regional operation to become self-reliant. Essentially, the board concluded that the continued commitment of resources from Japan to support, for instance, the North American operation by providing trainers, technology, engineering, and manufacturing capacity put a limit on the company's ability to grow elsewhere. North America, Europe, and other regions would have to take major steps toward self-reliance so that resources at global headquarters could be deployed to support growth in other, less mature markets. Figure 5-3 shows the overall cascading from the broad vision based on the guiding principles to a five-year medium-term plan to the annual *hoshin kanri* for all team members.

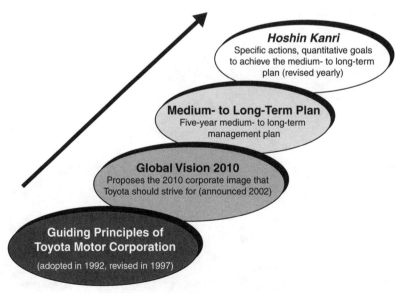

**Figure 5.3.** Cascading from Global Vision to *Hoshin Kanri*

## Translating Global Vision 2010 for North America

A specific example of this process is how the North American organization took Global Vision 2010 and converted it to an actionable plan for the decade; this plan would then be broken down into annual plans based on the annual corporate *hoshin*. In North America, the president of the North American organization, Atsushi Niimi, took the entire North American leadership group off-site to discuss what North America would do to achieve Global Vision 2010, including, but not limited to, achieving its part of the goal of a 15 percent market share. The group developed its own visual image to reflect what the 2010 vision should look like in North America, as shown in Figure 5-4. It was designed to look like a bird's-eye view of a car. At the center was the vision of "one Toyota," with each regional operation of Toyota being capable of self-reliance. The difference between the current and ideal states in that respect was large: at the time, Toyota's North American operations were fragmented into many different parts, many of which were highly dependent on technology and leadership from Japan. Engineering, each manufacturing plant, and the sales organization were set up and run as separate companies. As one of the most mature

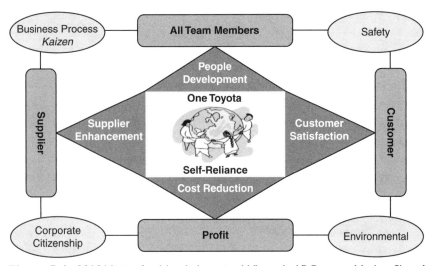

**Figure 5.4.** 2010 Vision for North America: Where Is 15 Percent Market Share?

overseas branches of Toyota, the Americans were going to have to take the lead and become self-reliant, and to do this, they needed one integrated Toyota for North America.

The North American leadership team examined Global Vision 2010 and identified the four areas it would need to focus on if it was to achieve its part of the corporate vision: customer satisfaction, supplier enhancement, cost reduction, and further development of team members. For Toyota in North America to grow, it had to make even higher-quality and more cost-effective products and develop the current leaders so that they could develop new members as the company grew. For Toyota to grow globally, the North American organization had to mature to self-reliance so that the headquarters in Japan could focus on developing Toyota leadership in other regions of the world. The most striking thing about how Global Vision 2010 was translated is that nothing in the North American vision specifically mentioned a 15 percent market share. In fact, as time went on, it was rare for the leaders in North America to even talk about a 15 percent market share. If they did all the right things for the customer, developed team members, made a profit to fund growth, and developed the supply base, the result would be increased demand for products and the capability to support that demand with high-quality products.

## Toyota's *Hoshin Kanri* Calendar

Each January, the president of Toyota Motor Corporation (TMC) makes a speech in which he reviews the prior year, summarizes the business environment and trends, and paints a picture of the future and what the challenges facing the company are for the year to come. This is an integral part of *hoshin kanri* target setting. January through the end of March is the window for detailed *hoshin* planning, starting with global headquarters in Japan and cascading to the countries and divisions, and down through the plants to the work group level. By the beginning of

April (the start of Toyota's fiscal year), the *hoshin kanri* plans are in place around the world.

From the point of view of North America, by mid-February, the targets for Manufacturing, Sales, and Engineering have been set. By the end of February, the North American targets for Manufacturing have been broken down by plant. The plants then start an internal process to allocate the targets across departments. Agreements are reached at each level, both on what the department targets are *and* on the methods to achieve those targets; it is critical to agree on both target and method, or there is no real plan, just a wish. Managers and executives at all levels take on initiatives they are responsible for—the higher the level, the broader the initiative.

There is a great deal of catch-ball at the level of breaking down the North American targets across the various plants, as well as when deciding how the targets will be allocated across departments. By the time a target comes to a work group, the main issue is the methods by which that work group will achieve the targets and how the targets are broken down to specific key performance indicators at the process level. In many ways, this is the most creative part of the process: understanding the current problems deeply and the methods by which processes can be improved to achieve the breakthrough targets.

By the end of March, in time for the new fiscal year starting April 1, the *hoshin kanri* at all levels globally has been set. So it is about a three-month process, although in reality much of it started in the preceding fall. We have seen companies try to do the whole thing in a single off-site. Obviously, there is no catch-ball, and in fact they are missing the most important part: the creative thinking involved in breaking down the broad targets to specific metrics and detailed plans for action that apply to each specific work group. True *hoshin kanri* is a process of innovation and of developing people at all levels, and it takes time and commitment.

# Catch-Ball to Agree on Actual Targets at Every Level

The catch-ball process that we discussed earlier has an important role not only in refining the corporate and regional *hoshin*, but also as a check on the whole *hoshin kanri* process. While the spirit of challenge is one of Toyota's core values and Toyota expects each team member and leader to push himself, it also recognizes the futility of "stretch" goals that are impossible to achieve. Thus, the catch-ball process provides feedback through the ranks about whether annual and medium-term goals are achievable and whether priorities need to be reshuffled or resources reallocated to meet the specified goals.

In general, the catch-ball process is a lot of discussion and planning as the high-level goals are cascaded down through the organization and turned into more specific, actionable plans. At each level where the *hoshin kanri* process is active (and, as we've noted, it cascades only down to levels where Toyota is confident that the leaders have sufficient skill and experience to manage it properly), a senior leader works with the leaders beneath her to create a plan for achieving a specified goal. For example, a plant may have a goal of reducing injuries by 15 percent. That does not necessarily mean that every part of the plant has to reduce injuries by the same amount. Some areas of the plant may already have made major gains, so that a further 15 percent reduction is unrealistic, while others may be behind and have the opportunity to reduce injuries by much more than 15 percent. During catch-ball, the senior leader negotiates this allocation of responsibility for achieving the plant's target. Again, the success of the process depends equally on the senior leader's having deep knowledge of her domain so that the goal for the plant is actually achievable and on the junior leaders' willingness to take on a challenge and pursue improvement in the right way. In an organization with a zero-sum culture, where each junior leader was simply trying to set his target as low as possible, catch-ball would never work.

To clarify how it does work, consider an example of catch-ball in action: negotiations over productivity goals at TMMI (the Toyota plant in Indiana) in 2005. The productivity targets for the North American region (set during a catch-ball process between the North American leadership and headquarters) were initially divided up among the different manufacturing sites by the functional group responsible for productivity at North American headquarters. The North American functional group had developed the targets for each plant based on what its members knew about each plant's condition. That information had led them to assign TMMI a higher-than-average goal for 2005. TMMI had launched a new model of the Sienna minivan the previous year. When a new model is launched, there is understandably a lot of waste—the new jobs have yet to go through much *kaizen*. In the second year after a new model launch, there are usually major productivity gains to be had, and the functional group expected TMMI to make such gains. The leaders at TMMI, however, had set a relatively low 2005 productivity improvement target. They felt that because of the popularity of the vehicles being manufactured at TMMI, the team members were working overtime each day, and were simply too busy to deliver the kind of *kaizen* that would be necessary for a major leap in productivity. As the executive vice president for manufacturing, Gary's role was to engage in catch-ball to reach an acceptable target—one that was achievable by TMMI and that contributed sufficiently for him to achieve his North American goals.

On the surface, this sounds very traditional: corporate demands extreme improvement and the plants hold back, so the executive charges in to negotiate a compromise or simply make the decision. But the situation in fact was not traditional. To understand what actually happened, we need to go back to a moment in 2004 when Gary was touring TMMI with the executive team. During the tour, he stopped to watch team members assembling the Sienna. He knew that the plant was struggling to meet its *hoshin* productivity target for that year, and he saw many opportunities for waste reduction. He pointed out some of what he saw to Norm Bafunno, the senior vice president of TMMI, and estimated that they could easily take 50 or more positions off the line.

Gary proposed that TMMI use a *yamazumi* chart to find opportunities to take processes off the line. The *yamazumi* chart is a visual method of showing the amount of work involved in each job compared to the line speed, or *takt*. Basically, it is a bar chart, with each bar representing all of the work elements that are either value-added or extraneous for a given process (for example, the work of one assembly-line job). Value-added work has a direct positive impact on the customer; extraneous work includes elements that are wasteful, such as reaching and walking. The height of any given bar is determined by the number of seconds it takes to perform all of the work elements for that process. Toyota uses a magnetic strip for each work element that is proportional in height to the number of seconds, so that workers can physically put the work elements on a whiteboard and see which bars are over (too much work) or under (too little work) the line speed. They can then move the work elements from job to job to see how to balance the work so that all jobs are at or near *takt*. Green magnets are value-added steps and red ones are waste, so at the same time the team works to eliminate waste and thereby often eliminates a process.

This is a great tool for getting a group of people (team members, team leaders, and the group leader) to look at how the individual work elements are allocated to jobs, and to figure out how to eliminate waste. Gary was still president of TMMK at that time, and he offered to send several of his people from TMMK's smooth motion team (see Chapter 4) to TMMI for a few weeks to help in a pilot area and teach the team members how to take out waste and rebalance the line. As expected, they were able to remove an entire process from a small pilot area.

Thus, when it came time to set the *hoshin* for 2005, Gary knew that TMMI had plenty of opportunity and that the team members there had seen the smooth motion method in action and were capable of applying it themselves. But he also knew that they had a lot on their plate. TMMI ran a complex product mix, making Tundra trucks and Sequoia SUVs on one line and Sienna minivans on the other. There were a lot of variants of all these vehicles, so there was tremendous parts complexity. There was no warehouse attached to the plant, so the thousands of parts needed for the line were stashed in various places. Parts shortages were all too common, and the plant was spending a lot of time fixing this problem (which meant less B-labor and leadership bandwidth to focus on productivity). In addition, production volumes were high, since all three vehicles were selling well, and the plant team members were working a great deal of overtime to keep up. These factors, coupled with the fact that the workforce was relatively young, led Gary to conclude that the productivity target set by the corporate group at Toyota Engineering and Manufacturing of the Americas (TEMA) was indeed unrealistic, but that TMMI could do better than the original estimates coming out of the plant. The catch-ball process thus ended up with a new target that was still a stretch for TMMI, but that the plant leadership was comfortable signing up to meet (and that the plant ultimately succeeded in meeting). The factors that made this situation different from the average executive negotiation were

1. Gary had an unusually deep knowledge of the plant because of his visits to the *gemba*.
2. He had walked in their shoes, as he was going through the same process of target setting and achievement as a leader of TMMK.
3. He was able to offer concrete support to teach the team members skills that would help them reach their targets.
4. The tools, in this case *yamazumi* charts, were designed to allow team members to see and agree on the waste and focus their creative energies as teams on coming up with process innovations to achieve the targets.

# Doing and Checking through Visual Tracking

*Hoshin kanri* continues on down to every value-added worker in the company. Finally the work groups are involved in setting specific targets for the year and detailed action plans for achieving the targets. *Target* is an important word. Ultimately, each team member in each work group must be able to understand in concrete terms what the target is and how she is doing relative to the target. Think about any sport: if the targets were not clear, we would be without focus. In some cases, the gap between the target and the actual can be clear as the work is being performed—for example, through a simple counter that shows the number of units produced compared to the target based on the *takt*. In other cases, the target must be represented on a chart or graph. It is for these reasons that Toyota puts a great deal of emphasis on daily management based on visual tools (see Chapter 3). Daily management focuses the team on the *hoshin* goals through the review of the prior day's performance and meetings to discuss the goals versus the target as the day goes on.

One tool that TMMK uses to facilitate the daily management process is the "floor management development system" (FMDS).[4] The centerpiece of FMDS is the visual management system that links daily performance in every work group to plant-level metrics. Space near the work areas is set aside for daily meetings, and in those spaces, leaders post charts and graphs and color-coded information. At the work group level, the metrics are organized by the major headings of safety, quality, productivity, cost, and human resources. As you move up the hierarchy, the data are rolled up first to the department level and then to the plant level (see Figure 5-5). The charts and graphs all show status relative to a target—the standard to be achieved. Magnets are used to highlight which processes are performing up to standard (green), which are out of standard, but on track for improvement (yellow), and which are out of standard and in need of immediate action (red).

As we've mentioned, Toyota deploys *hoshin kanri* only at a level that matches the maturity of the leaders, so that they are able to contribute to and appropriately manage the process. A specific example of this is TMMI. While the senior leadership of the plant participated in the *hoshin kanri* process, the goals were not cascaded down to the work group level for many years after the launching of the plant. The lack of a fully developed daily management system was the primary reason for this: the capability of visual management was weak, and those at the group and team leader levels had not been taught Toyota Business Practices. There were boards with measures, but they were different in each department, and they did not show a clear connection to the *hoshin* of senior management.

TMMI took the economic downturn as an opportunity to introduce FMDS and improve its daily management capabilities. Toyota Business Practices were, for the first time, taught all the way to the team leader and team member levels, and each work group did multiple projects using Toyota Business Practices. With this capability now in place,

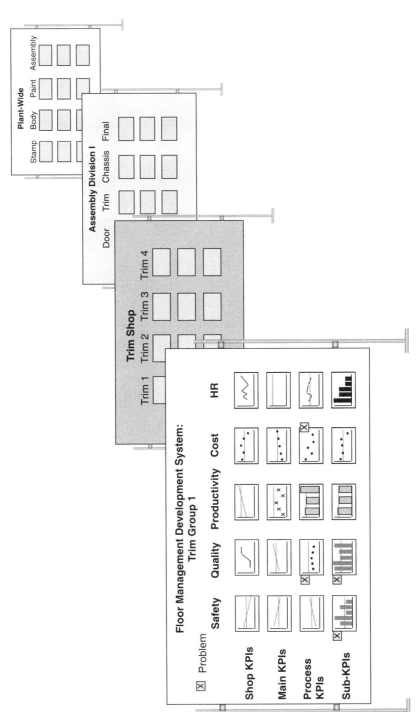

**Figure 5.5.** Visual Metrics Aligned from Top to Bottom

TMMI is fully participating in *hoshin kanri* down to the work group level for the first time—ten years after the plant's launch. It is not that TMMI was backward, although its great success in winning quality awards almost every year and its off-the-chart sales, which drove constant overtime, did delay the investments needed to drive *hoshin kanri* to

---

## *Hoshin Kanri* and Incentives

It is clear that *hoshin kanri* requires motivation at all levels. Indeed, many companies ask how they can get people to have the daily discipline to maintain all of these detailed metrics, carefully work through a very structured problem-solving process, and make improvements while still focusing on daily production. This brings us to one of the most intriguing topics for many companies: recognition and rewards.

Toyota tries to avoid the practice of giving out a doggy biscuit every time someone behaves in the right way. There is a great deal of satisfaction that comes from contributing to the team and seeing the needle move on the trend charts. Leading a quality circle is often the most rewarding experience of a team member's career. This is not to say, of course, that people don't want to be recognized and rewarded for accomplishing goals. However, since Toyota wants commitment to the team and the company, not simply individual goal accomplishment, the measures focus on larger units than the individual. There are usually substantial bonus pools assigned to plants based on company performance and plant performance. Management bonuses are proportional to salary and are based on company performance, plant performance, and individual achievement of *hoshin* objectives. Even the individual *hoshin* objectives cannot be accomplished by a person working alone, so the raises, bonuses, and promotions always reflect team accomplishments. In fact, how a person works toward the goals (the process) is as important in performance evaluation as achieving the goals (results).

the work-group level. The larger point is that it takes relentless development of people to make *hoshin kanri* a real, living system—development that many companies never even attempt. And those companies that simply laid off workers during the recession missed a golden opportunity.

Unfortunately, too many companies adopt *hoshin kanri* as a quick fix to get easy bottom-line results. We have heard many executives say: "That is what we need, *hoshin kanri*, to finally get this lean program to deliver real business results." They see it as an extrinsic motivation tool to get the troops focused on the business results. They are quick to find a consultant and get started on this "*hoshin kanri* thing." Fortunately for them, or maybe unfortunately, there are many consultants who will be glad to facilitate *hoshin kanri* for a tidy fee. They will promise executives quick results, perhaps through a series of two or three off-sites. The main focus is on filling out the right kinds of forms—matrices linking goals at each level that are sometimes called "X-charts."[5]

We would love to say that *hoshin kanri* is a silver bullet and that setting the right goals, objectives, and metrics guarantees long-term competitiveness. But fancy charts linking objectives at one level to those at another does not produce a disciplined and creative focus on improvement. Even neat-looking visual metric boards will not deliver without group and team leaders who are highly developed in problem solving and can actively lead the team to make improvements. Standardized work is also critical, as without a standard it is impossible to judge progress.

We have never seen X-charts used at Toyota, and Gary never filled one out. To check to see if this has changed we spoke to Mark Reich, who had managed the *hoshin kanri* process while he was in the planning department at TEMA. His answer was predictable:

*This is not used at Toyota. This sounds like another "consultant" generated method that maybe looks good, but isn't necessary. In Toyota, first and foremost,* hoshin *is a tool of [vertical and horizontal] collaboration and people development through problem solving, so linkage is not achieved through a matrix, but through face-to-face discussions (vertically manager to team member) and horizontally (across functions) in order to break down and achieve corporate goals. The X matrix could become a "check a box" type approach.* Hoshin kanri *is not about the format of the paper, but the management structure and culture. Without that, X's or any type of matrix is a waste of time.*

What it boils down to is that without an effective system of daily management and *kaizen*, any *hoshin* improvements will be short-lived and unsustainable. Daily management is the process of checking actual versus target results and engaging the team in creative problem solving. The goal is as much to develop people as to get the results. We illustrate this in the hypothetical graph in Figure 5-6. From our experience, *hoshin kanri* plus daily management with *kaizen* can lead an organization toward continuous improvement and competitive advantage. Even without *hoshin kanri*, a company that has taught *kaizen* and established a good daily management system will make continuing progress, but at a lower level. The worst case is a company that introduces *hoshin kanri* with no daily management system and weak leadership of *kaizen* at the work group level. Such a company may, through sheer force of will, achieve big *hoshin* objectives, but as soon as senior management and the process improvement specialists look the other way, the systems will collapse and performance will move backward.

We commonly see that there is a weak link in the leadership chain at the middle management and first-line supervisor level. Often companies have "leaned out" these layers to an anemic level, and those who are left can barely keep up with the daily firefighting needed to keep production running. These companies' experience starts and stops in lean deployment that matches the ups and downs of the business cycle. During the down times, they lay off people, and, in the up times, they bring in raw talent, so that development has to start from zero. Unfortunately, they want the quick results, and they lack the patience to invest in people who are capable of delivering the results. If it took TMMI a decade to get this degree of alignment, even with its highly consistent and skilled leadership aligned under a common philosophy, then other companies should not expect to "implement *hoshin kanri*" in a few well-facilitated off-sites.

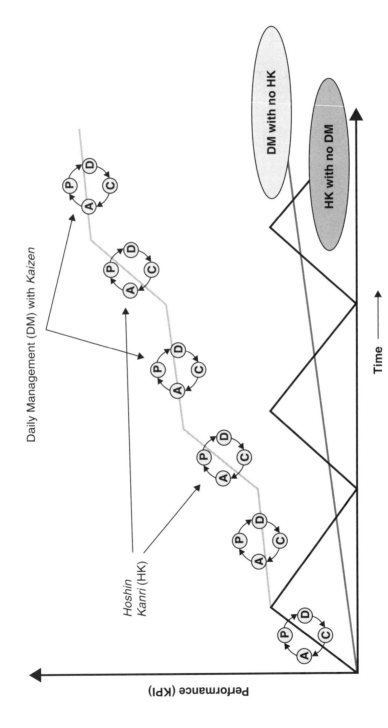

**Figure 5.6.** Relationship between *Hoshin Kanri* and Daily Management

# Hoshin Kanri in Action

To understand the *hoshin kanri* process at Toyota more clearly, it may be helpful to follow one example from beginning to end. In this case, we'll look at how Global Vision 2010 was cascaded down to shop-to-shop benchmarking among North American plants. As we noted earlier, one of the outgrowths of Global Vision 2010 was an emphasis on self-reliance. Expectations were highest for North America, which was the most mature of Toyota's overseas operations.

## Achieving Self-Reliance via Internal Benchmarking to Develop Leaders

Why would Toyota think of internally sharing best practices as a solution to the problem of self-reliance? The goal was to increase the learning that North American plants were getting from one another. As you can imagine, the "go and see" approach leads to lots of plant-to-plant visits as team members, group leaders, and executives learn from more seasoned Toyota plants. Yet, when these activities were examined through the lens of self-reliance, it became clear that the transfer of knowledge was essentially happening in only one direction: from Japanese plants to individual American plants. Even the American plants were not adequately sharing with one another what they had learned from Japanese plants.

Senior leaders believed that if specialists and managers across North America were having deep discussions about best practices, this should increase the rate of innovation and reduce the reliance on Japan for new ideas. Thus, a *hoshin* was set for intensive study and transfer of best practices across shops at different plants with similar technology, such as paint to paint, stamping to stamping, or plastics to plastics.

Gary and Ray Tanguay, who was president of Canadian operations, were asked to be champions for self-reliance in North America in 2005. Gary took four divisions—Quality, Plastics, Power Train (all of the engine lines and transmissions), and Stamping—and Ray took the remaining four divisions, including Production Control. They chose an appropriate vice president from each plant to be responsible for each of these divisions. This also would become a stretch assignment for those vice presidents, as they would have to lead their peers across North

America horizontally. Gary and Ray realized that encouraging learning from plant to plant wasn't sufficient; it could easily lead to conversation for conversation's sake rather than generating improved performance. It was also unclear who should be learning from whom.

So Gary and Ray gave the lead vice presidents a very fundamental first task: to standardize the key performance indicators (KPIs) for their function. This would include both core KPIs, like cost, quality, and productivity, and process KPIs, which defined how well a specific process was operating. Once the KPIs were determined, they could be used to assess the performance of each shop and could help identify for each shop what practices it wanted to learn from others. If a best practice was learned from one shop and brought to another, this should lead to a measurable improvement in the KPIs.

The processes were broken down into two categories: daily management and new model preparation and launch. For new model launches, whoever was launching a product would include new model representatives as part of the team; those people could focus on the tools, the methods, and the visual management approach for the launch.

In Toyota, the name given to spreading best practices is *yokoten*, which means "across everywhere." *Yokoten* is done through direct person-to-person transfer of knowledge, but that does not mean that the adopter of the practice should simply copy a best practice exactly. For those who are thoroughly practiced in *kaizen*, it is easy to think in terms of how a particular best practice can be improved and adjusted for better performance in a different context. Within *yokoten*, the responsibility lies with the adopter to understand her own situation and where a practice may be useful—and also how that practice can be improved. The adoption process itself follows the PDCA process, which prevents blind copying or, even worse, blind mandates from the top of the company.

A good example of how *yokoten* works is the process of adopting *minomi* that we discussed in Chapter 4: the Americans experimented and found a better way, which led to the Japanese learning from the Americans and finding a still better way, which spurred more *kaizen* by the Americans. The process kept getting better and better as *yokoten* went back and forth. This process wouldn't have happened if V.J. and his team had simply implemented the "best practice" of Central Motors uncritically. Unfortunately, traditional best practice sharing guided by the corporate office views an innovation as something that is static and fixed and must be copied exactly. It is often audited to be sure that is copied correctly. This greatly limits *kaizen*. In fact, Intel used to use the phrase "copy exactly" until it realized the limitations of that process and switched to "copy intelligently." A comparison of the more traditional corporate best practice sharing process and the *yokoten* process at Toyota is summarized in Table 5-1.

Setting KPIs, which allowed comparisons of the various shops across plants, quickly spurred a lot of learning and positive competition. Several of the shops at more mature plants were surprised to find that they were lagging younger plants, and vice versa, and teams were immediately dispatched to the high performers to learn from them. Perhaps the greatest impact was on new model launches.

TMMK was the first plant to launch a new model, a Camry, after the self-reliance *yokoten hoshin* had been set. The TMMK new model launch team spent months learning from the plant in Japan that had achieved the fastest model changeover: the plant had managed to switch models and get up to full line speed in just three days. This was astounding to the team from TMMK; on its previous new model

**Table 5.1.** Comparison of Spreading Best Practices and *Yokoten*

| Spread Best Practices (Pushed from Corporate Office) | Yokoten (Pulled by Each Individual Operation) |
|---|---|
| Find the best practices | Scan the environment for ideas |
| Document the best practices and expected results | *Genchi genbutsu* (go see actual place, actual part) |
| Standardize best practices | Identify your problems and understand root causes |
| Communicate the best practices | Share learnings with others through direct contact |
| Organizations apply best practices wherever possible | Each operation considers many ideas and implements best solutions to problems |
| Audit to check for compliance | Check own results and adjust |

Spreading Best Practices = Copy Mindlessly to Comply
*Yokoten* = Understand Your Problems and Consider Best Practices as Possible Solutions

launch, the plant had taken 59 days to get up to full line speed (which involves working out all the bugs). The team members knew that they could not jump to the level of the much more experienced Japanese mother plant in one step, so they set a target of cutting this to 15 days.

After several more months of preparation based on learning from the Japanese experts, the team members thought that they were ready. On the first line (TMMK has two lines), they managed to get the model changeover done and up to full line speed in 16 days. After making a few adjustments based on that experience, the team was able to hit the 15-day goal when it launched the new Camry on the second line. While this achievement was remarkable in its own right, it didn't help meet the self-reliance goal. North America was still learning from Japan. To support self-reliance, the Camry launch team thoroughly documented its process, what it had learned, and ideas for improvement—and then participated in training other North American plants. The next new model launch was a new Corolla at NUMMI. Based on what the NUMMI team had learned from TMMK, it was able to better the TMMK mark. Then the Toyota truck plant in San Antonio took the lessons from TMMK and NUMMI and succeeded in raising the bar still further. Overall, this process of *yokoten* on new model launches took several years, but it is measurable progress toward achieving the *hoshin* of self-reliance.

## Achieving One Toyota through Cross-Organizational *Hoshin Kanri*

The benchmarking process was one example of cross-organizational cooperation spurred by Global Vision 2010, but there were others that went beyond manufacturing to include all North American organizations. When the North American 2010 vision was developed, Gary, as executive vice president for manufacturing and managing officer, took responsibility for leading team member development and customer satisfaction. One major *hoshin* effort to support customer satisfaction involved Sales, Manufacturing, Engineering, and even the supply base in Japan, and after six years led to the reduction of warranty costs by 60 percent.

This North American project was led by Gary personally and challenged him to lead horizontally to a degree that he never had experienced before. The kicker was that TMC wanted North America to improve warranty returns in the first three months of ownership by 60 percent from the 2002 baseline. The target was given to Gary, by a member of the board who was responsible for quality, outside the board meeting in an almost off-handed way; it was now Gary's task to figure out how to achieve it. Fortunately, this was a six-year objective, so Gary could break it down to a 10 percent reduction per year, but even that was hard to imagine at the time. By most judgments, Toyota's vehicle warranty in North America was already the benchmark of the North American auto industry, so to improve that target by 60 percent was a real stretch objective. Small incremental improvements by each independent organization would never make this target. Gary was going to have to assemble a cross-cutting team to entirely rethink the process.

There were some opportunities for warranty reduction by tightening up quality processes within manufacturing, and Gary naturally worked on that, but the biggest gains would involve making engineering design changes to the product. Responsibility for vehicles that were North American–specific, like the Avalon, resided in the Michigan-based Toyota Technical Center (TTC). Working with the president of TTC was straightforward, but the responsibility for global cars like the Camry stayed in Japan and even involved suppliers in Japan. To coordinate this, Gary called together the heads of Sales, Engineering, and Manufacturing in North America and drew on his network of leaders in Japan.

Prior to this warranty initiative, each North American plant and sales and engineering organization had worked separately with TMC Engineering in Japan to resolve quality concerns, a process that was very inefficient and only marginally effective. Engineers in Japan were already stretched to the limit because of the rapid growth of new products globally, so they tended to push off these requests for changes into the next major model change, which could be several years out. Gary and his team realized that they needed to have one Toyota voice in America with one point of contact for engineering change requests. They also needed a way to clearly identify the root causes of problems and prioritize those problems before sending them to Japan. In Japan, they needed a single point of contact for receiving those requests who would take responsibility for getting them to the right party (internal or in the supply base) and following up on progress. They also needed enough data to get to the root cause; data from dealers were based on checking a box describing the problem in broad terms and some, often cryptic, descriptions.

For a North American point of contact, they established a new Customer Satisfaction Center at Toyota Motor Sales (TMS) headquarters in Torrance, California, where there were more than 1,200 TMS employees, all of whom drove Toyota cars and trucks under Toyota's vehicle lease program. They communicated the quality initiative to TMS employees, and said that they needed help to find the root cause of any and all quality issues they had on their vehicles. Employees agreed that if they had any warranty work done, they would bring in the defective parts that had been replaced for an investigation. Since warranty work was done on site at TMS using its own garage, engineers could speak directly with the mechanics about the problems with specific parts. This allowed the engineers to get reliable, hands-on information with enough detail to determine the root cause of the problem.

A team of TMC engineers in Japan became the key connection there, and the team set up a daily videoconference to cover the detailed issues that the North American team had found. Parts were sent overnight to engineers in Japan, who got them to the right people, including suppliers. A detailed visual tracking system was developed, with strict timelines for follow-up. TMC top management in Japan was aware of these programs, and in typical Toyota fashion, the managers personally visited the TMS Customer Satisfaction Center in California to understand the status, recognize people's efforts, and see how TMC might support them further. To see legendary members of the board of directors of TMC visit on a regular basis was inspiring to the entire team, and it sent a strong message that perfect quality and customer satisfaction was the most important focus of the company.

Of course, the warranty reduction efforts became a key annual *hoshin kanri* item for all those who were directly involved. Through these and other efforts across Toyota, the North American customer satisfaction team was able to achieve a 40 percent reduction in warranty claims in four years, and a 60 percent reduction by January 2009. The project saved Toyota hundreds of millions of dollars each year, and saved customers many headaches from bringing cars in for repair. Through the process, Gary and many other leaders developed their abilities to lead horizontally across the company.

## Conclusion

*Hoshin kanri* is the most powerful process in Toyota for aligning the direction of all the individuals doing *kaizen* throughout different parts of Toyota in different countries and regions so that "the numbers add up" to a huge positive business impact. *Hoshin kanri* and the Plan–Do–Check–Act problem-solving steps are completely intertwined. The problem-solving way of thinking prevents a simplistic view in which people at the top issue orders that get carried out in mindless ways. If each level starts by asking what its problems are—the gap between the current state and what it is trying to achieve—and what are the root causes of these problems, the people at that level will develop a plan that is right for their part of the company. The details of that plan will be different in every part of the company, even though these plans will align with common objectives. This leads to ownership of a plan that makes sense for each unit, given its situation and capability. It unleashes the creativity of people throughout the company to develop truly innovative solutions to problems.

*Hoshin kanri* and developing people are also intimately intertwined at Toyota. It is through the *hoshin kanri* system that challenging goals are set for leaders and progress in achieving those goals is reviewed. The performance appraisal process focuses on both the what and the how. As leaders are watched by their mentors regularly throughout the year, they are judged and coached on how they approach the challenges. The use of brute force to look good on the metrics is not rewarded at Toyota. The use of a good process that engages people is much more desirable, even if it does not initially achieve all the results.

There is an important lesson for others in the way in which Toyota approaches *hoshin kanri* in America. The company uses it as a tool for leadership development. Management by Objectives is mostly used by companies as a business tool to drive results from the top: "Get me a 10 percent cost reduction because the business environment demands it." The lieutenants then charge off to get the 10 percent, which often means across-the-board budget cuts, regardless of how critical a given activity is. To those who are trying to implement *hoshin kanri*, the most important advice we can give is to slow down. Use *hoshin kanri* very selectively, and carry out the process more fully as leaders mature. *Hoshin kanri* cannot be forced by ordering everyone to fill out forms. In the early stages, it may well look more like Management by Objectives, and it may be more top-down. Much of the catch-ball may be limited to the top three levels of the company. As *kaizen* capability within work groups matures, the plans will become more sophisticated, connecting the top-down goals to the group leaders and then the team leaders.

This brings us to the most important point about *hoshin kanri* at Toyota: it is intimately connected to the company's culture. *Hoshin kanri* by itself does not align people to work collaboratively toward a common goal. That is what a strong culture does. The culture has focused first and foremost on satisfying customers. Leaders at NUMMI and TMMK spent the early years emphasizing that quality is never sacrificed for cost or expediency. *Hoshin kanri* reinforces the cultural view that Toyota is one company that is working to satisfy customers with high quality, low cost, and on-time delivery. Unfortunately, a company that has a weak culture, with individuals out only for themselves, will not solve that problem with the tools of *hoshin kanri*.

# Chapter 6

# Toyota Leadership Turning Around Dana Corporation

*Rough waters are truer tests of leadership. In calm water, every ship has a good captain.*

—Swedish proverb

We believe that it is too easy for other companies to take away the wrong lessons from Toyota—by focusing on tools rather than on culture or on metrics rather than on leadership, for instance. But it's also easy to simply reject the Toyota approach on the grounds that it would "never work here." It's no doubt true that the Toyota culture is distinct from, and even foreign to, the standards and practices that have become the norm in most global companies. Taking the long view, patiently developing people and leaders, and treating employees as appreciating assets is not always within the power of even the most senior executives of a company, who must answer to shareholders and the board of directors.

So is there really anything that other companies can learn from Toyota? Clearly, we believe that the answer is yes, or we wouldn't have written this book. Our answer is built on more than just the hope of selling a few more books, though. We've seen lots of real-world examples of companies that have learned from Toyota and succeeded (in some cases for a few years, and in other cases for more than 15 years). This process can never be broken down into a simple checklist of steps—that's the recipe for failure that characterizes too much of the lean movement. We think it's far more helpful to provide a window into a company that is learning from the Toyota Way and Toyota's leadership model—Dana Holding Corporation, a major vehicular parts manufacturing company.

We believe that other companies can learn from Toyota leadership because Dana has done so, and it has done so in the worst possible scenario: while emerging from bankruptcy just as the Great Recession was starting. We can give you a front-row seat for the process of an existing company, with its own culture and practices, laying the groundwork for following in Toyota's footsteps because Gary has been a big part of the process at Dana, serving as CEO, then as vice chairman, and, as we write this, as a *sensei* on retainer to advise the firm's current leaders.

The process is not limited to *yamazumi* charts and TPS training. Nor is it a linear, step-by-step walk through the four-point Toyota leadership model. It also doesn't mean that a company can avoid painful choices and dramatic changes. It starts by building a stable financial and management foundation and a culture in which Toyota leadership can develop and thrive. At Dana, the introduction of true lean leadership involved both layoffs and management shake-ups, but it also involved long-term investment. The first steps understandably did not involve deep investments throughout the company—but neither did anyone think that the first steps were sufficient or worth celebrating. Introducing Toyota leadership will always take years of investment, and even as we finalize this book, three and a half years after the process began, the team at Dana believes that it is just getting started.

## Dana's Situation and Setting Priorities

Dana Holding Corporation, a global supplier of components for the vehicular market, has a long and proud heritage dating back to 1904. Like Toyota, Dana was founded on technical innovation: engineering student Clarence Spicer developed the first practical universal joint to power an automobile; he left Cornell University to start a company to produce his invention. Dana grew into a large automotive supplier, building chassis and drive-train components for trucks and other large vehicles in several distinct markets: light vehicles like pickup trucks and sport utility vehicles for automotive companies, heavy commercial trucks, and construction equipment. By 2011, Dana was selling to every major vehicle manufacturer in the world through 100 facilities in 26 countries.

Like most American parts suppliers, Dana was buffeted by the rapid change and increased competition in the automotive industry during the 1990s and 2000s; it also made some ill-advised acquisitions, and, as for many of its cohorts, the result was insolvency. In March 2006, Dana filed for Chapter 11 bankruptcy protection, emerging from Chapter 11 in February 2008.

After 20 years with GM and Ford and then almost 25 years with NUMMI and Toyota, Gary decided to retire in 2007. He used the usual Toyota approach of phasing out his retirement over three years as a half-time "senior advisor." Phasing into retirement at Toyota, Gary joined the board of several companies. He was invited to join the Dana board by John Devine, the acting CEO and chairman of the board. Devine was a former CFO at Ford and GM, and, given the industry's increasingly high standards for efficiency, quality, innovation, and on-time delivery, he recognized that in order for Dana to emerge from bankruptcy successfully, it needed a board member who had a track record in delivering operational excellence.

One of Gary's roles as a board member was serving on the committee to select a permanent CEO. Gary, thinking about the next phase of his post-Toyota career, suggested himself as a short-term option. He became CEO in April 2008, shortly after the company emerged from bankruptcy protection.

As if emerging from bankruptcy was not enough of a challenge, Dana was soon hit by a triple whammy: steel prices more than doubled (steel is the main raw material for Dana's products); fuel prices doubled, leading to plummeting sales of trucks; and then the Great Recession essentially shut down every segment of Dana's core markets, from construction equipment to passenger vehicles. Dana's carefully planned strategies, which had been approved by creditors and the bankruptcy court, essentially became works of fiction. Even the most pessimistic forecast in the company's pre-emergence planning had not allowed for this economic disaster.

The possible approaches to dealing with this catastrophe that Gary could take are simplified into three models in Figure 6-1, which summarizes the Toyota model of leadership development, the typical approach taken by companies in crisis, and the approach that Gary helped to lead, which combines Toyota-style leadership development with crisis management. We have seen how Toyota patiently developed American leaders over decades through increasingly severe challenges and ongoing coaching. Companies that are dealing with a life-or-death crisis do not have decades—they must act immediately and decisively to keep the company afloat. They typically shake up the executive level, bringing in new leaders from the outside who have no emotional connections to the people in the firm. Their job is to "restructure," which usually means that a lot of people lose their jobs. Through aggressive cost reduction, they may achieve a measure of financial stability, but all too often this is at the cost of the long-term stability of the business. The business culture changes radically, and many of the most valuable employees—valuable because of their experience—leave, either through layoffs or because they can easily find jobs elsewhere. Often the turnaround-specialist CEO is not the best at rebuilding this weakened organization to a high level of performance, so another CEO who supposedly has that skill set is brought in.

The challenge for Gary and Dana was to find a third alternative that would incorporate the necessary downsizing and restructuring to keep the company solvent in the short term, but, in parallel, would also begin to build the leadership and operational excellence that would be needed to succeed in the long term. The sad truth is that radical restructuring is sometimes necessary to correct the results of years of neglect and provide an opportunity to build a new winning team. Toyota's approach, building the company by investing in people via training and *kaizen* during downturns is not an option for some companies.[1] Gary had neither the business analysis knowledge nor the experience to be comfortable leading a major company through the actions needed for radical restructuring, such as closing plants, renegotiating contracts, and making massive reductions in force. In fact, being CEO was a new challenge in and of itself and required fast self-development on Gary's part.

Fortunately, he was working with John Devine, who had decades of experience as a CFO in the automotive industry and plenty of

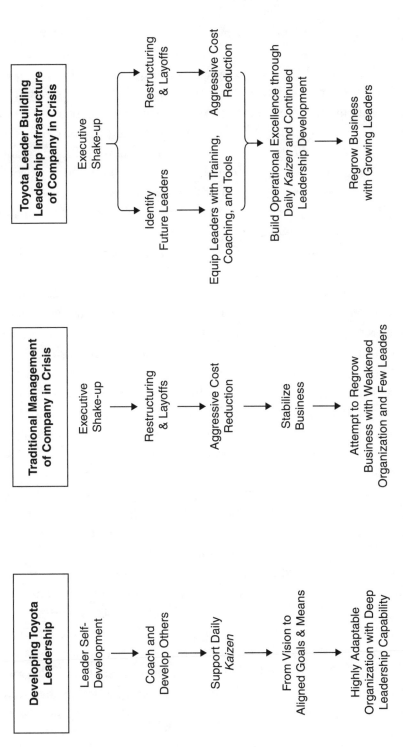

**Figure 6.1.** Leading a Company through a Crisis: The Traditional Way vs. the Toyota Way

189

experience in restructuring. Devine had also brought in a strong team to lead the traditional side of the restructuring of Dana. In fact, ultimately 11 of the 12 top Dana executives were replaced. For example, Devine brought in longtime Ford associate Bob Marcin as executive vice president and chief administration officer. Bob had many years of experience working with the United Auto Workers at Ford and took responsibility for renegotiating contracts, restructuring benefit plans, and making the hard decisions that Devine did not feel the existing Dana executives could make. James Yost was brought in as chief financial officer; he analyzed the major opportunities for cost reduction and managed new stock offerings when the company's situation had improved. Jacqui Dedo, as chief strategy and procurement officer, negotiated agreements with Dongfeng in China to expand Dana's position in a joint venture to serve Asian markets from 4 percent to 50 percent. Marc Levin, as head of Legal, was involved in every major business transaction and was the only long-term Dana senior executive who survived the bankruptcy and the transition to new leadership.

Having this deep bench of talent working on the transactional side of recovering from the bankruptcy freed up Gary to focus on getting cost reductions by eliminating waste through a lean approach and, at the same time, beginning the necessary long-term investment in leadership development and operational excellence based on what he had learned at Toyota.

Together, Gary and John set three priorities for Dana: survival, building a new culture of accountability, and building a foundation for future excellence. Obviously, these were not linear steps—actions had to be taken on all three fronts simultaneously.

Gary understood the need for restructuring and radical cost reduction so that the company could survive, but his main skill set and passion was in building operational excellence. To begin this process, Gary knew that he needed two things: (1) leaders who had the passion, knowledge, and capability to lead team members to eliminate waste and develop the capacity for continuous improvement, and (2) common metrics so that he and other leaders could see where they were going, what progress they were making, and where they needed to focus their attention.

The company needed daily *kaizen,* but of an aggressive variety in the near term. A vastly simplified version of *hoshin kanri* had to be started so that everyone at the company had an understanding of both the challenges that confronted Dana and their role in facing those challenges in concrete and specific terms.

But the need for rapid action just highlighted the need for capable leaders up and down the management chain. Identifying those leaders was a key part of Gary's agenda. He was looking for the same qualities that Toyota had seen in him when he was hired at NUMMI: a commitment to excellence and a willingness and desire to learn a new way of thinking and a new way of leading. There were some outstanding leaders at Dana who were open to learning and willing to adapt to a new culture, but unfortunately, there were also several leaders who weren't willing or able to change their perspective and approach and step up to the challenge of self-development. To jump-start the process of eliminating waste and improving productivity and quality, Gary needed leaders with knowledge and experience who could get quick wins the right way (without harming long-term prospects) and could act as internal *sensei* and coaches to bring others along.

## Priority 1: Survival

As would any leader who had been well trained at Toyota, Gary focused right away on getting a firsthand view of Dana by "going and seeing." The company had decades of history of continuous improvement programs, so lean was not a foreign concept to the management team. But, as Gary would learn, these programs had decayed during the bankruptcy because of a lack of senior management commitment, and the passion to achieve challenging business objectives that he had experienced at Toyota was lacking. It quickly became apparent to Gary that the company as it existed now could not survive. There were four major problems that had to be addressed immediately:

1. *Chimney organization.* Dana had seven product divisions that were run completely independently from one another under presidents with profit-and-loss accountability. As long as the

presidents "made the numbers," they were left alone to manage as they chose. Gary's experience working toward the vision of "one Toyota" showed him that such an approach severely hampered operational excellence and productivity: plants couldn't learn from one another, capacity couldn't be dynamically balanced, and different parts of the organization could easily be working at cross-purposes.

2. *Redundant functions.* Each division had its own staff support, engineering staff, offices, labs, and test facilities, leading to high fixed overhead, and also limiting learning across the company.

3. *Excess capacity/too many small plants.* Dana had 113 plants in 26 countries. Many of these plants were operating far below capacity, but excess capacity couldn't be reallocated to other product lines. Additionally, the fixed costs of plant operation made it virtually impossible to make many of the plants profitable with the reduced volume that was likely to continue for quite some time.

4. *No standard operating philosophy or key performance indicators.* Essentially, plant managers were operating without any clear vision, and there was no line of sight on performance visible to Gary at the top of the company. There were plenty of numbers, but they did not give Gary the picture he needed in order to know where to focus effort to achieve higher performance in terms of cost, quality, and delivery. Even the plant managers lacked insight into the daily performance of individual departments within their own plants because aggregated results obscured their understanding of the processes leading to those results.

The rapidly deteriorating financial situation meant that there wasn't time to patiently assess capabilities or to evaluate people, plants, and product lines one by one. Dana had to ratchet costs down as quickly as sales were falling. That meant layoffs in the hourly and salary ranks and plant closings (though this itself is very expensive). This traditional restructuring had started under the leadership of John Devine and his team before Gary became CEO, and they continued to take the lead, with Gary participating in decisions. One could say that the complementary strengths of John Devine and Gary made one super-CEO to get Dana through the crisis and prepare for the future.

Gary's primary contribution to the rapid cost-reduction process was leading radical *kaizen*, finding and eliminating waste in large chunks, while still building the leadership and lean processes needed for operational excellence. That included improving quality and safety, for instance. Every cost, from energy to real estate to scrapped parts and inventory, was scrutinized, not just via spreadsheet, but by careful analysis, for opportunities to cut costs quickly. Even existing sales contracts were examined; in many cases, it became clear that Dana couldn't make a profit under the existing terms of the deal. In each of these cases, Dana attempted to renegotiate or cancel the contract. The plant managers were put in a situation that was entirely new to most of them: zero-based budgeting. They started with no budget and had to justify every cost—and were told that only those costs that were absolutely essential to making product for the customer would be approved.

Despite these efforts to cut costs quickly, by December 2008, with the severe sales drought brought on by the recession, Dana could not meet the covenants it had negotiated with its lenders before the series of crises.[2] The lenders had to either agree to change the covenants or force Dana into liquidation. In this regard, the severity of the recession was probably a help: investors and lenders were loath to liquidate the company when there were no buyers for the assets. Eventually an agreement was reached to keep Dana operating, but only after John and Gary agreed to an additional set of aggressive cost-reduction targets. Dana's progress on covenants was checked every quarter, so there was an intense focus on making the numbers by the end of the quarter.

It certainly wasn't the ideal environment for thinking long term and investing in a culture of respect for people and continuous improvement, but Gary and John knew that just surviving wasn't enough. To escape the downward cycle of cost reduction followed by deteriorating capability followed by deteriorating offerings to customers, Dana needed a new culture and the capability to drive operational excellence in manufacturing and in engineering.

# Vision in a Turnaround: Long-Term versus Near-Term

We have emphasized that Toyota's planning process always starts with a vision. So it stands to reason that the first thing Gary would do as CEO of Dana would be to put together a 10-year vision. But he did not. Why?

First, all of the leaders at Dana had to be focused on stopping the bleeding—a 10-year vision wouldn't mean much if Dana did-n't exist in 12 months. Second, there were so many fundamental problems in manufacturing, organizational structure, and leadership that a 10-year vision would simply be an empty abstraction. The kind of vision needed for the short term was a clear operating philosophy and near-term financial indicators that would clearly communicate the direction for improvement. These need-ed to communicate that while cost reduction was essential to survival, there was an equal need to focus on other aspects of operational excellence, such as on-time delivery, quality, and safety. It was a return to the basics of building stable operations, which meant solving the immediate big problems. Only after those fundamental problems were on the way to being solved (what Toyota calls "clearing the clouds"[3]) would there be an opportunity to set a guiding vision for the future. Third, John and Gary were, in a sense, caretakers of Dana while they hired and trained a new generation of leaders who would be leading the company 10 years into the future. The next generation of leaders needed to play an active role in creating the vision—creating one before these leaders were on board would be a waste of time.

That's not to say that there was no plan or vision for the future at all. The shared vision of the board was the need for Dana to move toward operational excellence, and Gary quickly established the Dana Operating System and a vision for manufacturing. Dana, like Toyota, was at its heart a manufacturing company. It would succeed or fail based on the quality of its products and the product innovation that it delivered to its customers. This interim vision was ultimately stated this way:

> *Dana will become the best global driveline manufacturer by teaching and applying the Dana Operating System, and by motivating and engaging every employee to actively participate in and support these efforts, thereby creating a continuous improvement culture.*

You will recognize this as being very similar to the Toyota Way vision, which of course it is modeled after—just as the new Dana Operating System was adapted from TPS. For those laying the groundwork for Dana's future by building a new culture and a foundation for operational excellence, this statement served as a guide for short- and medium-term planning.

## Priority 2: Build a New Culture of Accountability

The ultimate source of many of the problems that Dana had to solve if it were to survive was the corporate culture. It was the existing corporate culture that tolerated a chimney organization. It was the existing corporate culture that valued autonomy over accountability. It was the existing corporate culture that led people to extend loyalty only to those in their own chimney and to distrust other parts of the organization.

It's impossible to impose a new culture on an organization by fiat—a new mode of operating takes years to really sink in and become second nature. Many leaders have learned this the hard way during mergers and acquisitions or in turnaround situations. An entrenched culture can easily defeat a charismatic, visionary leader. But even patient efforts to build a new culture will be defeated if the leaders and the metrics that the organization employs are not aligned with the desired new culture. This was the second priority for Gary and John: building a new culture at Dana by ensuring that the right leaders and the right metrics were in place.

Of course, figuring out who the "right" leaders were and what the "right" metrics should be was the hard part. Gary, of course, relied on his decades of experience at Toyota. The right leaders were ones who could self-develop and develop others, who could learn to lead daily *kaizen* and major change, and who could keep their teams pointed at True North. The right metrics were those that allowed for self-development and daily *kaizen* and that exposed progress toward True North. In other words, Gary pursued a quick and dirty version of the leadership development model, making a speedy first pass through all four phases in months instead of decades. We will describe the things that Dana did to achieve this, recognizing that it is not neatly sequential and that a great many things were all happening in parallel.

***New Matrix Organizational Structure***    It may seem odd, but one of the keys to developing accountability was a shift to a matrix structure. A matrix means that leaders have multiple bosses, which sometimes can confuse accountability, but at Dana it actually helped streamline the lines of responsibility and accountability. If you look closely, you will see matrix organizations throughout Toyota, whether in Manufacturing or in Product Development.[4] A key factor in making the matrix structure work, however, was combining and greatly simplifying the siloed business units that had been in place.

Dana had become a complex business, with many product families, many plants, and many global regions. The organization had six presidents running seven product-line businesses, with no single leader for Manufacturing, nobody responsible for R&D globally, and no regional leaders. There was no way the six presidents could keep track of what was going on in the plants; historically, the presidents had been focused not on manufacturing operations but on financials, and this focus was reflected in the skill sets of the existing presidents, which leaned heavily toward financial rather than operational management. Making rapid progress required that Dana have one person accountable for the profitability of each business unit; one person responsible for each major function, such as Manufacturing and R&D; and regional leaders, each of whom could drive operational excellence at all the plants within a given region, reporting to a global vice president of operational excellence. These three different needs led to a three-sided matrix organization.

In the initial reorganization, the six presidents were reduced to three running six different business units. Manufacturing plants began reporting to one global operational excellence president as well as to regional leaders for Asia Pacific, South America, and Europe. A chief technical officer was appointed to run R&D globally; similarly, one senior vice president for strategy and business development was given responsibility for all of global marketing. Some additional executive positions had to be created at first, but with the elimination of duplicated positions in plants and business units, there was a huge net savings to Dana. In addition, as time went on, some of the positions were collapsed. The three business unit presidents became two, one responsible for light vehicles and the other for heavy vehicles. One of these retained responsibility for global operational excellence in all the plants.

## Hard Driving to Results through Key Performance Indicators

As we've stressed, metrics are not a solution, but they are a tool—particularly in a life-or-death struggle for survival like the one that Dana faced. John and Gary needed to drive rapid cost reduction while increasing productivity; they also needed to set the tone for a new culture and find a way to evaluate quickly which leaders at Dana could and would adapt to the new culture. New metrics were a tool for accomplishing all of these goals simultaneously.

The first step was to create common key performance indicators (KPIs) across the company's manufacturing operations. Gary put together a team that came up with a set of metrics that emphasized operational excellence and piloted them in two plants in each of the business units. The team members then reflected and revised the metrics based on input from all involved, which helped in getting buy-in from all the regions. These KPIs clearly showed what mattered to the new Dana: cost reduction, quality, and safety were chief among them.

In the short term, there was a lot of low-hanging fruit. For example, under the old regime, the two greatest sins were stock-outs and shipping delays. Conversely, there were no inventory metrics. Obviously, this led to building large inventory stocks. Dana had lots of rented warehouses loaded with finished goods, even for very low-volume products where inventory would sit for months and sometimes more than a year. One of the new KPIs was limiting inventory; within one year of taking over, Dana's new leaders were able to drive $200 million in inventory savings—all money that immediately became available working capital for Dana. Of course, a set of inventory metrics didn't transform Dana into a model of just-in-time production, but it did indicate the need to scrutinize inventory-related decisions and reduce inventory wherever possible.

The single most powerful metric for Dana's short-term needs was "plant conversion cost," which included all of the controllable costs in the plant. This led to a broad view of costs beyond labor. Other short-term improvements focused on safety, reduction of quality defects, overhead ratios, and product complexity. (The KPIs are summarized in Figure 6-2.)

More important than the specific new metrics were new ways of reporting on and using the metrics. Gary and the operational excellence team set out to put a standard visual management system in place in every plant. Each plant implemented daily reviews of the KPIs relative to targets for the entire plant management team; the plant managers had to report on the metrics weekly to Gary and his team. With that structure in place, there was no question but that the new Dana would take these metrics—and accountability for them—seriously.

During plant visits, it became apparent that there was very little sharing of information about performance, even within an individual plant. Occasionally someone would print out a set of charts, but it was

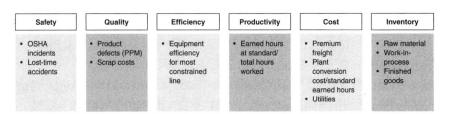

**Figure 6.2.** New Dana Global Key Performance Indicators

obvious that the data were updated infrequently and used for decision making even less frequently. Installing a visual management system was crucial for driving change at the speed that Dana's survival required.

The rollout of visual management was first piloted in two plants in each of the business units, and after reflection and modification, the company began the global implementation. The goal was to emulate the visual management systems that were commonly used at Toyota. The plant-level metrics area was dubbed the "diamond area," named after the Dana diamond-shaped logo, where progress on the KPIs was posted for all to see. This was a top-down directive, and every plant in the world developed a diamond area with the same design and the same metrics.

At the suggestion of a large shareholder, Brandt McKee, an executive with a background in lean at Danaher Corporation, was brought in to monitor and drive cost reduction. Gary quickly brought Brandt into the turnaround team and assigned him the job of handling weekly phone calls from every plant in the world to report on progress on KPIs. As Brandt described it:

> *We deployed common KPIs throughout the business. Then we started reporting of KPIs on a weekly basis through the regional operations leaders. On a weekly basis, I would have phone calls from all over the world for sixteen hours for two days and eight hours for the third day, talking with the individual plants and with the regional operations leaders.*

The goal of these efforts was to drive the accountability required for and reinforced by the Toyota approach to leadership. At Dana, many leaders had become unaccountable—as long as they didn't rock the boat with exceptionally bad performance, they were left to their own devices. A culture of mediocrity had developed; missing deadlines, people coming late to meetings, and people not finishing what they started were all tolerated.

To lead global operational excellence, Gary brought in Marty Bryant, who had worked for Gary earlier in his career at TMMK and then moved on to become an executive for a Toyota supplier. Marty had had experience outside Toyota, but he was still shocked by the lack of discipline and accountability at Dana:

> *Visual management illustrates accountability in its purest form in Toyota. I cannot recall a single incident in Toyota when someone would come to a KPI progress meeting late or without a well-thought-out plan to meet their targets. If your name is on an action item, you own it and take responsibility. The system forces clear expectations. Everyone knows the line should not stop, and you should meet all your targets on KPIs. The basic concept is simple. Here is your target—green is good, and red is no good.*

Over a one-year period, a sophisticated visual management system evolved that connected common KPIs from the senior executive level to each department of each plant. At first, the metrics were collected and posted manually, but this eventually evolved into a computer system to track the metrics so that they could be aggregated at the regional level and up to the company level (although the metrics were still posted on visual boards in the Dana diamond area and in each major department). Gary could view all the metrics at any level from his computer. This established a rigorous and standardized process for identifying and solving problems with a clear structure (see Figure 6-3).

## New Leaders Who Could Self-Develop and Develop Others

The KPIs, and their visibility, were important for driving the rapid change that Dana needed if it was to survive, but they also played another important role: they helped identify the leaders who were willing to take on a challenge, accept responsibility, and develop themselves. As Brandt McKee succinctly, and a bit starkly, put it, "The leaders who got you in trouble are rarely the leaders who bring you out." Building a new culture of operational excellence required a new approach to leadership. That didn't mean replacing all of the existing leaders at Dana or simply transplanting in a bunch of former Toyota leaders. It did mean rapidly identifying those leaders at Dana who were willing and able to learn and implement a new culture (which would

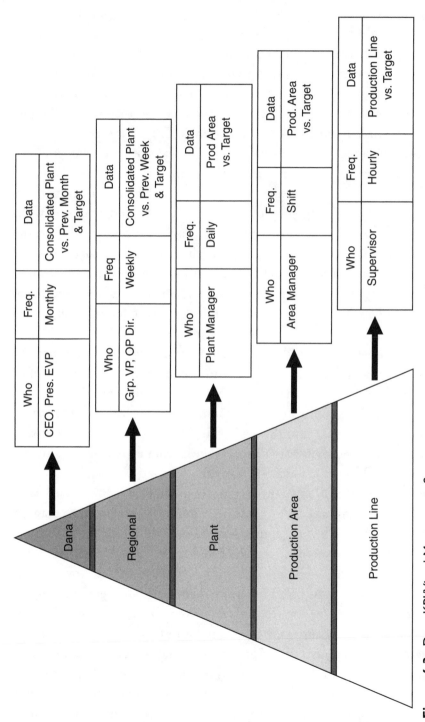

**Figure 6.3.** Dana KPI/Visual Management System

require not only self-development but rapid development of Dana team members)—and quickly replacing those who weren't.

Much of the assessment was done by Gary, Marty, and Brandt as they visited every Dana plant around the world and walked the floors with plant managers and other leaders. Gary and his team still believed in the Toyota principle of *genchi genbutsu*, and so they were willing to take the time to go and see for themselves. The KPIs served as indicators of where to look. This led to a rapid assessment of who was willing to step up and learn the new system and who needed to be replaced. It became immediately apparent whether any particular plant manager was making progress on improvement and what his weak points were. Those who survived were those who were open to learning and were willing to accept the challenges. The challenges for improvements in safety, quality, and cost in order to ensure Dana's survival were continual and relentless. In all, 50 percent of the plant managers in North America, where the most intensive focus began, either left voluntarily or were asked to leave in short order.

To shore up the leadership team, Gary brought in more than 20 executives and managers, digging into his network. Some were former Toyota or NUMMI leaders, others were from suppliers to Toyota, and still others had no direct Toyota connections but had the mindset to be open to learning and the leadership capability to deliver results. It should be noted that Gary did not take Toyota experience as a necessary or sufficient qualification for this new and challenging role. In fact, he believed that many Toyota managers who functioned very effectively within the Toyota culture would be ill equipped to manage the kind of transformation that was needed within Dana.

In fact, not everyone who was hired from Toyota succeeded. Even a successful leader who can drive improvement in a stable Toyota environment may not be able to drive change in the alien environment of a firm that is struggling to survive. Toyota-style consensus decision making and slow, nurturing development of people—regardless of the desire to emulate such practices over the long term—had to be scaled back, at least until the company was financially stabilized. Some of the new hires could make the "difficult decisions," like replacing people at breakneck speed, and still keep their eyes on the long-term vision of creating a continuous improvement culture. Not all could, and some had to leave.

Dana was evolving a hybrid culture that blended traditional, hard-driving American management, looking for results at all costs, with the more patient environment of developing leaders for long-term operational excellence. Many companies that are going through downsizing and restructuring are reluctant to add any people, even in positions where they are really needed. Gary understood that some key capabilities were missing in Dana and got board approval to do some new hiring. Specifically, Gary established and staffed an internal training and consulting group to teach TPS and a process engineering group to help redesign technical processes as part of building a foundation for operational excellence and Toyota-style leadership. As discussed later in the chapter, he also invested in creating the hourly team leader role, which in traditional terms meant adding "overhead."

## Priority 3: Build a Foundation for Operational Excellence and Toyota-Style Leadership

In tandem with the downsizing and cost cutting, setting new metrics, and finding new leaders, Gary was taking some immediate actions to build the foundation for operational excellence. Restructuring and standard KPIs that were visible at every level of the business from the CEO level to an individual department on the shop floor focused people's attention, but more was needed. Having metrics that are focused on the right things and presenting them visually is useless unless there is also the expertise required to achieve the metrics.

*Teaching TPS*    The tools for achieving the metrics come from TPS, and the only way to teach TPS is by doing. Taking charge of training on TPS, Marty's first principle was to emulate TPS to the letter. He had seen other suppliers try to develop their own watered-down versions without success. Where simplification was necessary was in the tools that were used. Marty knew that expertise in problem solving develops only over time, and so trying to teach too many tools would be counterproductive. He decided to focus on a subset of the TPS and problem-solving tools to drive quick wins and the results Dana needed, such as standardized work, *yamazumi* charts, and even basic cleanup and organization of the workplace (called 5S).

The training group developed a simplified version of Toyota's problem-solving process, and every leader was expected to learn it and use it religiously. The single-page "A3 report" quickly became the main tool for communicating the current status of processes and the problem-solving efforts that were used to make improvements. Single-page reports are a double-edged sword. Oversimplifying is a real danger—indeed, a number of experts point to the "bullet-point" format of PowerPoint as a cause of mistakes ranging from poor risk management in the financial crisis to the crash of one of NASA's Mars robots. This happens when the focus is on meeting the requirement of keeping the report to a single page rather than on the quality of what is on that page. The reason the rapid rollout of A3 reports at Dana worked was that there were enough new leaders who had experience with the tool and knew the difference between a "good" A3 and a bad one—and they could coach team members and other leaders on how to use them.

In addition to visual management, the Lima, Ohio, plant was also chosen to pilot a crash course in applying *kaizen*. A cross-functional group of 28 people was pulled together from around the world. The larger group was broken down into smaller *kaizen* teams assigned to specific areas. The workshop was quite similar to those that we've described Toyota using in earlier chapters, although instead of the team's being sent to a supplier, it was performing *kaizen* in the Lima plant. The first two days focused on identifying problems. Then the teams went to work finding solutions to the problems they had identified and implementing their ideas. The *kaizen* workshops were by no means casual. When Marty kicked off the workshop, he announced an unusual rule: no one on the team could leave until the problems the team was focusing on were solved and the new process was working. As it turned out, about 40 percent of the 28-person group were not allowed to leave after the first week because their *kaizen* projects had not been implemented; some stayed as long as five additional weeks.

This rule was another object lesson in the accountability and discipline required for operational excellence. Historically, workshops at

Dana had consisted of a few classes, some brainstorming, and then business as usual as all the participants dispersed to their "real" jobs. Marty wanted to model the commitment to excellence required of a new generation of Dana leaders. Soon this rule would become part of the new culture: "At Dana, you don't go home until the problem is fixed." Such focus achieved remarkable results: these initial *kaizen* projects often generated productivity improvements of 100 percent or more.

From Lima, the *kaizen* workshops were expanded to other plants. Marty and Brandt frequently led the workshops as they staffed up the training and lean consulting groups. As 2008 progressed, most Dana plants throughout the world were running workshops and reporting back on results. The workshops also provided an opportunity to identify the potential future leaders of operational excellence. As a result of the *kaizen* workshops, many of the plants met their cost-reduction targets early and were able to expand the scope of their *kaizen* efforts.

Brandt McKee also used the weekly KPI reporting phone conversations as an opportunity to train more and more people on TPS and problem solving. He explained:

> *I taught them how to ask questions about their KPIs, and I was effectively acting as a mentor on problem solving, e.g., why is your productivity the way that it is this week? What happened? So the press shut down. Why did the press shut down? "We were out of materials." Well, why were we out of materials? I was trying to drive the Five Whys thought process.*

By the end of 2008, most Dana plants had experience in the *kaizen* process, had formed a baseline, and could look ahead to 2009. The next step was to establish specific targets for further improvement, but the plant leadership was still not mature enough for a lot of catch-ball. The plant leaders still did not know what they or their teams were really capable of. The senior executive team established three or four fundamental improvement targets and rolled them out worldwide; the chief one focused on a target for reducing conversion costs. Operations managers who ran several plants and their plant managers were responsible for developing a plan in A3 format to meet the improvement targets, including methods and interim targets. These plans were presented to Gary, Marty, and Brandt for approval. Starting on December 17, 2008, Gary, Marty, and Brandt spent three days in Lima, Ohio, on the phone from 7:00 in the morning until 11:00 at night with plant managers all over the world who were reporting on their data and getting agreement on the 2009 targets and the plans for achieving them.

The initial plans for how the goals were to be accomplished showed how far Dana still had to go. The plans of each of the 112 plant managers worldwide were graded, using the standard visual management green/yellow/red rubric. After the first review, more than half the plants were red. Gary and his team wrote down the weaknesses they heard as they were listening and immediately e-mailed the plant manager about what they felt were areas of weakness. The plant managers were required to use this feedback to create new plans by January 5. Then they set up a cadence of monthly reports to senior executives and weekly reports to regional managers and started measuring how they were doing in moving toward the targets.

This approach should not be viewed as a pure form of *hoshin kanri*. This was a very top-down, directive approach to driving results, much more like traditional Management by Objectives. The key difference was that the focus was not just on achieving results. Equally important was teaching Dana leaders how to focus their improvement efforts on clear business objectives and how to develop a well-thought-out plan for achieving those objectives. We should note that in preparation for 2010, a process closer to *hoshin kanri* that allowed a degree of catch-ball with the regional operations began to be used. This was a maturation process that started fast and aggressive, and then, as the company stabilized, slowed down to focus on the long term.

**Building Trust**    An underappreciated, yet critical, part of operational excellence and Toyota-style leadership is trust. To drive the kind of no-holds-barred commitment to operational excellence that is required, everyone in a plant has to believe in the process and that she won't be "rewarded" for driving progress toward lean by having her job cut. Without trust, *kaizen* projects quickly devolve from finding and fixing critical problems to battles to shift blame and accountability to others.

Equally, the Toyota leadership model depends heavily on trust. If a potential leader or leader in training doesn't trust that self-development will be rewarded, he won't take the necessary steps to master his current tasks and seek new challenges.

Trust is built into the Toyota system, and it grew during the three successive crises (the global recession, the U.S. recalls, and the Japan earthquake) as team members experienced firsthand that Toyota treats people as assets, not as costs to be slashed. No regular employee was laid off in Manufacturing, even when plants were shut down because of oversupply during the recession or because they were missing key parts as a result of the 2011 earthquake.[5] But Dana was in a different situation. How do you reduce costs by at least one-third using aggressive top-down management and build trust at the same time? It takes a great deal of effort and communication, but if you do the best you can under the circumstances to treat people with respect, the seeds for future trust can be sown.

Part of trust building was making sure that *kaizen* did not get confused with head-count reduction. In the *kaizen* workshops, one of Marty's rules, in addition to "stay until the job is done," was that there had to be hourly workers on every team. Additionally, before a *kaizen* team could present an idea to the operations excellence team for approval, it had to get the approval of the relevant group of hourly workers. In unionized plants, the union leaders also had to give their approval. Engaging the entire organization in *kaizen* was a key step in building not only capability but trust as well.

Marty also insisted that the workshops focus on waste elimination, not head-count reduction. There is a subtle, but critical difference. Often lean consultants will sell their services as a means of head-count reduction. To protect against falling into the trap of seeing *kaizen* as a head-count-reduction exercise, Marty would not accept any head-count reductions from the first two workshops that were held at a plant. Instead, he wanted the teams to focus on identifying the most efficient, waste-free process and put that in place. Of course, eliminating waste often leads to reducing the number of people needed on the line. In the initial rounds of *kaizen*, hourly workers who were displaced by reducing waste and rebalancing lines were redeployed to other parts of the plant or used on *kaizen* teams. If the financial situation dictated further layoffs, that process would be handled entirely separately from the *kaizen* projects. We realize that this is a subtle difference, and it may seem that there is no difference. If you lose your job, you lose your job. However, the difference, although subtle, is critical. The reality was that nobody lost her job because of *kaizen*. The individual lost her job because the company determined that it needed to cut costs if it was to stay alive, and that could be clearly explained and understood.

This perspective of waste reduction rather than head-count reduction was drilled into the heads of the managers in the first week of training: "If you focus on head count, you will miss opportunities for waste reduction." If managers think they need to take two people out of a process to make their financials look good, they will try to take two people out of a ten-person line and get a 20 percent improvement. But if they engage the team, get a 25 percent improvement in output, and still have ten people, they will come out better in the long run. Using this technique, the *kaizen* workshops were frequently finding 50 to 100 percent productivity improvements.

While there was in fact an intense focus on cost reduction, and labor budgets were being slashed month after month, another aspect of building a foundation of trust and operational excellence was creating a team leader role at Dana plants. This was actually an additional set of positions, which, remarkably, was added while radically cutting head count to keep the company afloat. Gary and his team understood the criticality of that role for *kaizen* and kept enough head count to implement team leaders, taking the short-term hit for the long-term benefit. None of the team leaders were new hires. All were hourly workers who had been freed up through *kaizen*.

**The Road to Trust Sometimes Runs through Conflict**   We certainly do not want to give the impression that building trust was easy, but rather that Gary and his associates tried to practice respect for people as much as possible while doing what it took to keep Dana alive as a company. There were many tense conflicts, but even some of these evolved into bright spots. One example is the manufacturing plant in Fort Wayne, Indiana.

As we saw in Chapter 1, the traditional union-management relationship in the auto industry is based on a conflict model. Management focuses on cost reduction and profitability, while labor focuses on preserving jobs and protecting the safety and welfare of the workforce. As this win-lose relationship between labor and management developed, a key battleground was formal work regulations and job classifications.

You can judge the quality of the relationship by the flexibility, or lack thereof, in the work rules and job classifications written into operating agreements negotiated between the company and its unions. When management and labor build trust, operating agreements give management the flexibility to organize teams, cross-train, and reassign workers for maximum productivity. When relationships break down, when labor doesn't trust management, the work rules and job classifications are used to resist every management initiative and protect every privilege of unionized labor.

Gary, as vice chairman of Dana, realized that he needed a lot of flexibility, as well as the union's participation in productivity improvement, if Dana were to have any chance to survive. Management's goal was to have each local union agree to a new union contract, similar to the operating agreements that were already in existence at some Dana plants, that allowed flexibility and to create an environment in which the union would work proactively with management to implement the Dana Operating System and reduce waste. The carrot that Gary and his team were offering the unions was that by embracing the Dana Operating System, the company would become more competitive, thus bringing in new business and creating more jobs for union members. As is often the case, the union did not always view favorably these new ideas, and some rough negotiations were necessary to make these changes.

The important thing after difficult negotiations is the mending process. Do the management and the union continue as adversaries, or do they begin to work cooperatively for the good of the company and its employees? At Dana, some of the most adversarial relations became positive as the union began to see that the operational excellence program generally made jobs easier and safer for the team members. In the plant at Fort Wayne, the plant manager, Bob Flynn, was an exceptional leader who knew how to build a cooperative spirit. There had been some rough negotiations while Gary was still vice chairman, but when he returned 18 months later after retiring from Dana and taking a senior advisor role, Gary visited the plant and was delighted to see the level of cooperation.

One of the ideas that Bob Flynn, the plant manager, had for building trust was having management and union leaders participate together in 5S cleanup exercises once a month. Leaders from both sides formed a team that spent two hours between shifts cleaning up a part of the plant. Often these were areas that hadn't been cleaned in 20 years. The leadership teams, wearing their oldest, dirtiest clothes, would emerge from these cleaning sessions covered in dirt, grease, and gunk. On one visit to the plant, Gary was able to participate in one of these exercises. By chance he found himself next to the vice president of the union. Soon Denny Leazier, the union president, joined them, and the three men were working side by side mopping and scrubbing—truly an unprecedented experience at the plant.

The process of working together—doing the truly dirty work of restoring the plant—accomplished its goal. Not only did it serve as a platform for building trust, but it began to affect the culture of the plant. Team members could see firsthand that management was committed to making things better and wasn't afraid to work hard and make sacrifices. A lot of positive buzz was created around the plant: you can imagine the effect on a longtime union member of coming to his shift to find his area of the plant spick-and-span and the most senior member of management standing there with a bucket and a mop, covered in gunk.

Mutual respect built during these sessions began paying off in negotiations between plant management and the union. Every time Gary visited the plant, he stopped in to meet with the bargaining committee. The changes in the union's perspective were striking. On one visit, the topic under discussion in the bargaining committee was union members who had been laid off as volume fell. Denny was pressing for some of these workers to be recalled: "I have to get my guys back," he told Gary. Gary responded, "Denny, you can't do that, and I can't do that." Denny, a bit riled up, asked, "What do you mean I can't?" Gary said, "Denny, the only people who can bring back your laid-off workers are our customers, because they and their orders decide how much work we have. If we keep going down this path and getting more efficient, we can win business, and then we can get those guys back. We want to bring those guys back as much as you do."

On another visit, Gary found that the team was hitting a sticking point on what was required of team leaders. Under the old job classification system, a team leader was barred from actually working on the line; his role was restricted to overseeing the line workers. In the Toyota system, as we discussed in Chapter 2, the team leaders frequently step in to help or coach line workers and can cover any of the jobs in their team if needed. Gary worked with Denny to help the union team see that having flexible team leaders made things better for all the line workers: it gave everyone more flexibility for vacations, sick days, jury duty, or family emergencies.

This kind of back-and-forth, and evidence that the changes that Gary and his team were putting in place would make life better for everyone rather than just being standard management attempts to extract more from union members for less, changed the whole environment in the plant. A big part of that was the management team's efforts to do the right thing for workers. For instance, on one of Marty's visits to the plant when he was president of the light vehicle division, he overheard a conversation between team members about how terrible the bathrooms were. He immediately went to take a look at the bathrooms. Terrible was probably an understatement. The bathrooms were all located on the second tier, above the equipment, and so were inconvenient to get to. But worse, because they were generally beyond the reach of the plant's climate control system, they were sweltering in the summer and freezing in the winter. And, of course, they had been at the bottom of the maintenance list for decades. Marty quickly authorized spending to refurbish the bathrooms.

As bids for refurbishing the upstairs bathrooms were coming in, Gary pointed out that the plumbing was all accessible on the first floor, and that since all of the *kaizen* work to eliminate waste and inventory had freed up a lot of space, there was now plenty of room to put the bathrooms on the main floor. He suggested to Bob Flynn that they get bids to compare the cost of refurbishing the old bathrooms to the cost of building brand-new ones on the first floor, where team members really wanted them to be. It turned out that the cost was comparable. There are now seven new bathrooms on the ground floor.

This small act created a huge amount of goodwill. Workers had tangible proof that management wasn't trying to cut costs at the expense of workers. As the union contract was coming up for renewal, the union and management were working more cooperatively, the workforce was happier, and the work environment was becoming much more positive and productive. Denny Leazier was now a leader in helping to implement the Dana Operating System. Gary got a Christmas card that year from Denny and the bargaining team. It was the first time in his life that Gary had ever gotten any kind of holiday card from a union organization—an indication of how far the relationship had come. Because of the success of plant management and the union working together, Dana began reinvesting in the plant, buying new equipment, and increasing production and employment.

## Formalizing Implementation of the Dana Operating System

The initial wave of *kaizen* and intensive leadership development was successful at helping to save the company from ruin. The traditional restructuring (that is, layoffs, plant closings, and eliminating benefits for salaried workers) definitely had the greatest short-term effects. But in addition to this, DOS and other operational excellence efforts enabled Dana plants to reduce conversion costs by $200 million in 2009 alone.

Much of these early operational improvements that led to greatly reduced manufacturing costs can be credited to the executive leadership of Marty and an associate whom he recommended, Mark Wallace. Marty was hired by Gary as the vice president of global operational excellence. Marty's success led to a quick series of promotions; he recommended his former boss, Mark, to fill his old position. Eventually, as the presidential positions were consolidated to two,

Marty became president of the light truck division, which served the automotive truck market, and Mark Wallace became president of heavy commercial trucks. They recognized the need to continue to develop the formal operational excellence structure to support the company's transformation and organized it with two vice presidents as leaders. One of them, Dave Gibson, was a veteran of TPS who had worked with Gary at NUMMI and TMMK. Dave took responsibility for all the hands-on *kaizen* support teams. Ed Kopkowski, who was already an executive at Dana, became the vice president responsible for all of the formal training, planning, auditing, and high-level coaching.

Dave Gibson was one of the most important people that Gary hired in terms of actually driving DOS throughout the plants. Dave's history illustrates that leadership in TPS depends more on aptitude and the drive to learn than on someone's formal position in the organization hierarchy. He started his career as an electrician and was hired by NUMMI as an hourly employee. Over the years, his leadership abilities allowed him to move up to be manager of maintenance in truck assembly at NUMMI. From there, he also took on leadership of all *kaizen* teams in the assembly operation. Dave then followed Gary to TMMK, where he had similar responsibilities. When Gary became CEO at Dana, Dave followed him again, eventually rising to the position of vice president overseeing all the operations excellence teams.

Ed, on the other hand, didn't have any direct experience with TPS. He did have a long career in Operations, with experience in a variety of approaches to process improvement. He had started his career at AlliedSignal, which was one of the pioneers of Six Sigma; he led the operational excellence initiative using Six Sigma for the brake division. Ed had also had exposure to a more "lean"-centric approach after Bosch bought the brake division, and then with several other automotive industry firms; in all those companies, he had held operations management and operational excellence roles. Ed joined Dana in 2006 as a vice president of operations, and then in 2008 became vice president for operational excellence for Dana globally.

Despite all his experience, Ed's first time seeing TPS and Toyota's approach up close was when Gary and Marty arrived at Dana. He immediately noticed that their approach was different from the tool-based approach he had seen and led before:

> *The management style is the part that is very different—the true commitment to go and see and being on the shop floor. The focus on problem solving and leadership development. The leaders have to be teaching the rest of the organization. Those are the things that I really felt were unique in style with Gary and his team.*

Ed had a steep learning curve ahead to self-develop in the Toyota approach. But learning wasn't the only challenge. He also had to simultaneously develop and deploy a formal plan for continuous improvement at more than 90 plants around the world, as well as the support operations. How did he meet the challenge? According to Ed:

> *We at first were very focused on day-to-day, week-to-week, month-to-month operational results to survive. At the same time, we laid out our five-year Dana Operating System deployment plan and began executing that. So while we were watching every dollar we spent, we remained committed and diligent about developing the people and conducting workshops. But every time we would do a lean event to create learning and progress the Dana Operating System, we always did it with the intent of delivering dramatic results.*

The Dana Operating System was represented as a house, very similar to the Toyota Production System house (see Figure 6-4).[6] As in TPS, there are twin pillars. The first is just-in-time (JIT), which has the True North vision of building exactly what the customer wants, in the right amount, when the customer wants it. This pillar is supported by tools such as standard work, one-piece flow cells, eliminating changeovers between products, and having equipment that functions flawlessly. The second pillar is *jidoka*, or building in quality without errors. *Jidoka* requires stopping and immediately fixing every problem as it is found, as facilitated by tools like the *andon* system, visual management, and mistake-proofing devices.

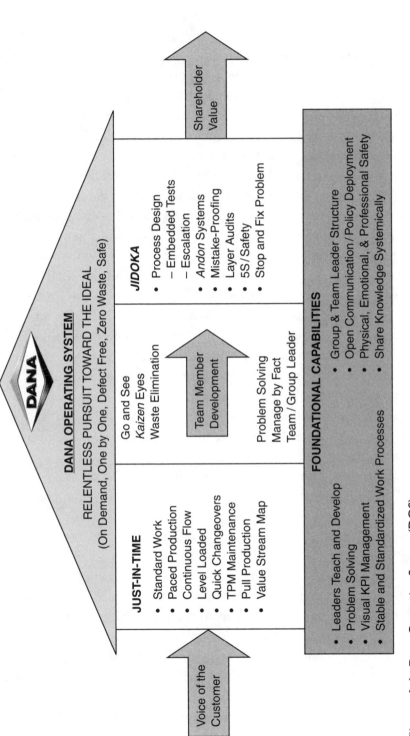

**Figure 6.4.** Dana Operating System (DOS)

215

The DOS road map was designed as a five-year plan. At a high level, it is a series of seven steps that looks quite mechanistic (see Figure 6.5). The first step, discussed in detail previously, was to focus on radical improvement through developing KPIs that clearly displayed the difference between target and actual, then using structured problem solving to close the gaps. The second step was to define DOS in greater detail, deploy more formal training, and develop local subject-matter experts in all of the DOS tools globally for each plant.

The seven steps were not just high-level generalizations. Each step had a set of extremely detailed actions and plans. For example, Step 3, "Implement Flow," and Step 4, "Stabilize Cells" (which are very interrelated), were broken down into 11 discrete activities, as shown in Figure 6.5. The earlier steps were somewhat destabilizing, as they were necessarily a rapid push to fix the big problems quickly: a lot was changed in the plants all at once to achieve the cost-reduction and productivity targets needed to keep the company solvent. The 11 steps were focused on going back over all the processes at a more refined and detailed level to find additional waste, remove it, standardize the improved processes, and implement monitoring to track progress and implement continuous improvement. Of course, daily audits at the *gemba* mean that management has further opportunities for self-development and for developing others.

A detailed road map like this will look familiar to many readers and could appear to be a highly structured, tool-driven approach to change. But there are several important aspects built in that ensure the proper balance between deploying tools, getting results, and developing people.

First, the focus was as much on leadership development as it was on driving change and getting results. This began with Gary, Brandt, Marty, and others teaching leaders to achieve challenging objectives on KPIs. Standardizing A3 reports was an important part of this process so that executives and coaches could clearly understand the thinking processes of managers—and coach them on improving those processes.

This first stage provided the key elements for self-development of leaders: challenging goals, clear targets on meaningful metrics, education on the right processes, and coaches providing frequent support and

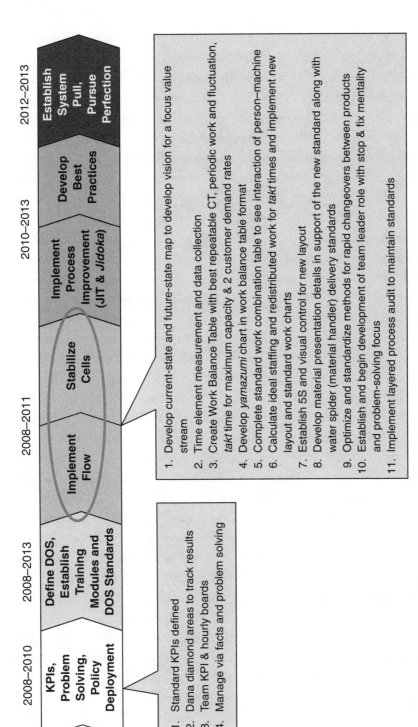

**Figure 6.5.** Dana Operating System Five-Year Implementation Road Map

feedback. The plant managers also had the opportunity to self-develop through the process of coaching those below them. Each plant manager was expected to raise the level of his teams. The important point here is that the tools were a means to an end, not the end in and of themselves. They provided a very tangible framework for getting feedback and for seeing strengths, weaknesses, and opportunities to improve for the new leaders as much as for the processes they were trying to improve. An approach focused on the tools, rather than on the leaders, might have reaped some short-term gains, but it could not have achieved the sustained improvement that Dana needed if it was to survive.

Second, even though the road map appears sequential, in reality, you can see by the ranges of dates in Figure 6-5 that there was considerable overlap in the stages. Ed and his team didn't have rigid rules on the sequence of implementation of the tools. The road map that they created was a set of guidelines for the plant managers, who were at the *gemba* and had a better sense of what was needed in their particular context. Different plants applied different tools in different sequences, although all needed the foundation of the first phase.

Third, in the first three years, there was a very conscious effort to keep everything, especially the tools, simple. In Gary's view, the most critical tools needed for achieving the early results that were essential to Dana's survival were basic problem solving driven by the KPIs, *yamazumi* charts to visualize the balance of value-added work and waste across processes, and value stream mapping to visualize waste in the current state and develop the future state for the process. Implementing more refined pull systems and leveling of the schedule were pushed out to later years. But all along, the team's eyes were on the long term. For instance, even in the early phase, Gary brought in TSSC, Toyota's externally focused not-for-profit TPS training arm, to begin a pilot of a complete pull system.[7] TSSC sent one of its top experts to work side by side with the Dana team to implement a pull system using *kanban* in Dana's Gordonsville, Tennessee, plant. Gordonsville later became the model for teaching and supporting expanding pull systems in the rest of the Dana plants globally.

Fourth, every plant was required to have a model line so that there was an opportunity to experiment and to learn tools and supporting approaches before they were expanded across the plant. For instance, the new team leaders needed training to understand their role, and this was carried out on the model line. This approach allowed everyone involved to iron out the kinks and gain trust in the approach and the tools before the changes were expanded to the whole plant. The alternative, going broad without this deep learning, often leads to superficial tool deployment, as there are no strong champions, and even the advocates are not well practiced in the tools.[8]

Fifth, subject-matter experts were developed along with the tools. Ed and his team knew that there was a lot to learn about each of the many tools that they were trying to deploy. Local experts had to be in place in each plant so that they could provide the rapid response and immediate coaching needed to keep the momentum going. So the operations excellence team focused on developing these local experts for each tool (they reported to operations managers) in every plant. The commitment to local expertise was evident in the fact that local resources were committed even though plant managers had to meet aggressive cost KPI targets. Ed described how the training of local experts was done in Europe, as an example:

> We would do the workshops focusing on different tools. In the first one we did, we brought in people from about half of the plants in Europe, and we asked them to identify a subject-matter expert— someone who had technical capability and was good on the shop floor and good working with people. We set an expectation that they would participate actively in three full workshops—first as a participant, second on a different value stream taking more responsibility, and third co-facilitating. At that point, our intent was that the fourth time they could do it on their own.

The results of the DOS efforts speak for themselves. We have already noted an example of the conversion cost savings in 2009, but the overall cost reductions, productivity improvements, quality improvements, and inventory reductions were stunning. Much of this was achieved through daily *kaizen* activities, but formal workshops also generated tremendous returns on all the KPIs (from before to after each workshop), as summarized in Table 6-1 for 2009 and 2010. The much larger number of workshops completed in 2010 was because DOS implementation, which had initially focused mainly on North America, continued to spread globally in 2010, with even broader impact. These results don't include the tremendous learning by plant leaders and team members from each of these learning cycles, learning that is a huge investment in future improvement.

It is important to recognize that Ed, who was leading the education and training of this deployment globally, did not meet the standards of a Toyota leader when Gary first arrived. Ed needed to shift his thinking from Lean Six Sigma as a tool set led by process improvement experts to lean as continuous improvement led by those who were directly responsible for operations. To his credit, Ed gained Gary's trust (no small feat). As Ed put it:

*Going back to 1994, deploying Six Sigma at AlliedSignal, it was a structure where at a business-unit level, the resources, the Black Belts back at that time in every plant in AlliedSignal, were reporting to the [Black Belt] champions. I have learned since working for Gary that the resources need to be owned by the plant managers and the people running the business. The expectation, the reason you'd set it up the way AlliedSignal did, is so that you could make sure everyone followed directives, a command-and-control kind of approach. But it doesn't lend itself to sustainability long term.*

**Table 6.1.** Dana Operating System 2009 and 2010 Workshop Global Summary (Average KPI Improvement vs. Prior State)

| Year | Workshops Completed | Safety Burden (kg × m) | Quality (internal PPM) | WIP | Floor Space | Productivity (parts/ labor hour) |
|---|---|---|---|---|---|---|
| 2009 | 75 | 58% | 62% | 64% | 36% | 76% |
| 2010 | 467 | 52% | 51% | 57% | 34% | 52% |

WIP: Work-in-progress (inventory)

PPM: Parts per million defective

Safety Burden (kg × m of material moved)

*I learned that you need to keep the resources, where they're being paid and where they work, accountable to the plant manager who is accountable for the implementation and the culture shift that we're trying to achieve.*

## Conclusion

Unfortunately, there is no magic in the Toyota bag of tricks that can bring a company that is on its deathbed back to life without any pain. Dana had to close plants and lay off a lot of people. There were, frankly, people at Dana who were not qualified for their jobs—at least, not by the high standards that Gary and John Devine wanted Dana to reach. On the other hand, simply getting through the recession with a financially viable business was not of great value unless at the other end of the tunnel there were strong leaders and team leaders who could make Dana a world-class company. Surviving without developing leaders would simply be delaying the inevitable.

As of September 2011, it was becoming clearer that Dana was over the hump and was on the road to a healthy, long-term future. The short-term turnaround resulting from the work of Gary, John, Brandt, Marty, Ed, and the whole Dana team down to the shop floor was stunning. In 2007, Dana's sales were $8.7 billion; they fell to $8.1 billion in 2008. In the first quarter of 2009, sales had dropped to an annualized level of $5.6 billion. Yet profits went from a loss of $122 million in 2008 to an annualized profit of $93 million (exclusive of interest, taxes, depreciation, amortization, and restructuring costs). Essentially, that means that the expenses required to run the business were cut by one-third, including a 51 percent reduction in direct labor cost. Dana could break even at $6.5 billion in sales, when in the past it would have lost money even at $9 billion. The largest portion of the cost reduction was in restructuring, which meant that 13,500 out of 35,500 people lost their livelihood. But the company was still alive, and more than 20,000 jobs had been saved.

At the low point in March 2009, Dana stock traded for just 19 cents. Over the course of the year, the stock price skyrocketed by 68 times to a little over $13 per share, the largest improvement in stock value of any automotive company in the world. In September 2009, Dana held an exceptionally successful capital offering. It sold 36 million shares of stock, demand far exceeding what the company was willing to sell, so the price far exceeded expectations. This was enough to reduce Dana's debt by $100 million and still have more than $600 million in available cash to run the business. Moreover, Dana had obtained contracts for new business exceeding $1 billion over the next four years.

By 2010, revenues had reached $6.1 billion, from $5.6 billion in 2009, and Dana was forecasting revenue increases of another 50 percent over the next five years. And in early 2011, the company reported an annualized one-year return on equity (ROE) of 17.6 percent. The strong results meant that in early 2011, Dana was able to refinance its debt and eliminate the covenants that had been imposed by creditors when it emerged from bankruptcy and during the crisis immediately thereafter. That meant that the company was no longer living quarter to quarter, wondering whether the banks would liquidate the company. It also meant that the company's cost of capital fell dramatically, making investing in the future much easier.

Dana was able to shift from short-term survival mode to a more aggressive growth strategy, particularly in emerging markets like China and India. For example, it entered into an agreement with Indian company Axles India, LTC, to acquire selected assets of its commercial truck axle business for $13 million. India's commercial vehicle market is growing at a compound annual rate of 8 percent. The transaction is expected to generate about $50 million in annual revenue. In China, it broke ground on a technical center in Wuxi, Jiangsu province, which was to be fully operational by the end of 2011. The center joined seven other facilities in China in which the company has an interest. The company was also able to invest further in Brazil. As a result of its operations in Brazil, annual sales in South America rose to more than $1 billion.

There is some similarity between the way Dana used this near-death experience to transform the company and the way Toyota used the Great Recession to reduce costs, increase quality, and further develop its people, but there are also large differences. Toyota had spent decades developing leaders who had the Toyota Way ingrained, and because of 50 years of consecutive profits and a conservative approach to financing, it had a war chest of cash and the ability to borrow at low interest rates. The recession was an opportunity to activate the best of those capabilities, and it used the crisis as a catalyst to accelerate the development of people down to the production associate level and move the company toward self-reliance in each region. The leadership style and philosophy did not change; in fact, it was amplified and accelerated.

Dana could not simply activate the leadership capabilities that already existed at the company, because for the most part they were not there. Yet what Gary did to lead this struggling company was very Toyota-like. In essence, he brought a simplified version of the Toyota leadership development model to Dana. The first pass through the cycle had to be done very quickly and in a simplified way, but it also had to be done in a way that would allow for future passes through the cycle.

Dana needed to start building the foundation for Toyota leadership and operational excellence right from the beginning. It needed to begin setting its eyes on True North—what true leadership and operational excellence would look like. Of course, it couldn't reach True North on the first attempt; after all, Toyota hasn't reached True North after more than half a century. Gary and his team realized that quick and dirty identification of those who could self-develop and develop others, jump-start daily *kaizen,* and drive goals and common metrics was necessary to bring Dana to a point at which it could make the big changes that were needed if it was to survive without permanently damaging the core capabilities of a strong manufacturing company. The result was the foundation that would put Dana in a position to think seriously about longer-term strategic plans to become the best in its business.

There was help from outside consultants, but Gary quickly hired the best of them as full-time employees so that they could lead from within. From the very beginning, though, Gary made it clear that the responsibility for achieving the challenging metrics, such as reductions in transformation costs, fell squarely on the shoulders of the plant managers and their reports. Gary did not want responsibility for improvement to be in the hands of consultants or continuous improvement departments.

Even after Ed began to formalize the Dana Operating System training and develop a five-year road map for change, flexibility was built in so that each plant could adapt the plan to its own context and needs. Overall, the focus was the same, however: drive DOS to the shop floor and develop work groups capable of daily *kaizen*. Even while radically cutting costs, Gary and the executives he brought into Dana insisted on investing in leadership for the future, both by rapidly developing people inside Dana and by hiring people from outside.

A particular focus was on creating the team leader role, mostly using production workers who had been freed up through *kaizen*. The executive team also insisted that plant managers, even though they were struggling to meet the challenging cost-reduction targets with reduced staff, free up people to take on the role of subject-matter experts to learn the lean tools. While the effort was extremely results-oriented, the executive team had a very strong vision of the future organization and its culture and made investments to put the building blocks for that organization in place. The culture was being steadily changed from the ground up. Improvement was becoming an accepted part of the daily work instead of a sporadic response to a crisis.

We have focused on the efforts to improve the plants, but similar efforts were taking place throughout the company, including in R&D, back-office operations, and strategic planning. In all cases, lead times were slashed, cross-functional teamwork was greatly enhanced, problem solving became much more transparent and systematic using A3 formats, visual management became commonplace, KPIs were identified, and processes began operating at levels of efficiency that had never before been seen at Dana. George Constand, whom Gary selected from within Dana for the new position of chief technical officer, began to develop lean leaders and use lean methods in product development to generate new technologies more quickly in order to keep ahead of the competition, while still driving down cost. He also took on the job of combining and right-sizing all global engineering, combining light and heavy axles into one unit and light and heavy drive shafts into a second unit. In addition, he developed a 24/7 engineering process by building a design center in India, allowing him to support every business with around-the-clock design capability. By right-sizing and sharing resources, he was also able to open an engineering support office in China for customer support as Dana was growing in China.

We would like to say that this is just another day in the life of a lean leader and that Dana is typical of what companies are achieving everywhere simply by applying the lean tools and philosophy. But Dana's turnaround was anything but typical. Unfortunately, lean tools can be used to brutally cut costs, restructure, downsize, and leave a company in a weakened state. That, tragically, is the typical story that we've seen. Rather than creating strong companies with the capability to build in quality, carry out daily *kaizen*, respond to increasing challenges from customers and the environment, and create a continual flow of innovative new products, many lean consultants hollow out companies and declare victory based on a set of very short-term metrics. It's probably appropriate that the general term for this approach is *leaning out* a company—because it truly does leave a company weakened and often leaning over the precipice.

The key difference at Dana was the investment in hiring and developing leaders (an investment of both time and extremely scarce capital), even during the darkest days, when survival was very much in question. While the short-term metrics had to be hit, Gary and the team made sure that the long-term metrics for leadership development were also being hit. That's why the Dana story is positive today. In the final chapter, we will reflect on lean leadership and the challenges for organizations that wish to truly make the journey toward a culture of continuous improvement.

# Chapter 7

# Learning from Toyota Leadership

*Go to the people. Live with them. Learn from them. Start with what they know. Build with what they have. But with the best leaders, when the work is done, the task accomplished, the people will say "We have done this ourselves."*

—Lao-Tsu, founder of Daoism

Our purpose in this book has been to present and explore a model of lean leadership based on the Toyota Way in order to teach others how they too can become leaders in operational excellence in their business segment. We have argued that for long-term operational excellence, this or a similar leadership approach is essential; this is illustrated by Toyota's long-term success, despite dramatic environmental change. Of course Toyota stumbled between 2008 and 2011, taking severe blows from the Great Recession, the recall crisis in the United States, and the earthquake and tsunami in Japan, but in each case it used the downtime for training and *kaizen*, and through deep reflection and countermeasures recovered quickly and came out stronger. Dana's dramatic turnaround after bankruptcy illustrates that lean leadership that adheres to the Toyota Way can help companies outside Toyota build a path to true operational excellence, even in the worst of circumstances.

The Toyota Way is both a technical and a social system. It requires leaders who are capable in both areas—able to use tools expertly and to engage and develop people in order to make continuous improvement a daily reality. With an effective leader as a teacher and a daily coach, process improvement and people development go hand in hand.

No one doubts the importance of strong leadership. Ask practically anyone about exemplars of great leadership, and he will easily name four, five, or perhaps even ten examples. Yet if you ask Westerners what it was about those leaders that made them great, the conversation will quickly devolve into abstractions. Abraham Lincoln had "conviction"; Dr. King's dream offered an inspiring "vision"; Jack Welch acted "decisively"; Michael Jordan had "intensity." These statements, while true, offer a rather fuzzy template for anyone who is trying to cultivate leadership within an organization. Can a company really teach conviction, or vision, or decisiveness, or intensity?

Obviously this does not happen in some course or off-site. But can a company create an environment in which people are empowered through concrete experiences to develop conviction, trust in a vision, face challenges and come out stronger, and act decisively in response to rapid change? Yes. It largely comes down to creating a culture and then constantly reinforcing consistent practices that enable *true* leadership to develop. Culture and leadership are two sides of the same coin, and both must be constantly—literally every day—recreated and reinforced through deliberate attention and action. Continuous improvement of processes requires continuous leadership.

Westerners most often think of Japanese culture as being mild-mannered and averse to conflict. Yet while Toyota leaders are accountable for living the value of respect for people, a leader's engagement is not always mild-mannered, not when it comes to solving problems for customers. When Gary was asked to reduce warranty costs by 60 percent, this was both direct and challenging. It was not simply a pleasant suggestion; rather, it was a startling challenge that would demand all the leadership skills he had developed to that point and more.

Toyota shows that developing leaders within new cultures can be done, but it is not easy, and it does not come fast. Where should a company—or even an individual—begin?

In this book, we have described the developmental path of Toyota leaders, derived from the experiences of Gary and others. The lean leadership development model that we designed based on our experiences at NUMMI and Toyota begins with the really tough job of self-development. Even proven leaders have to look themselves in the mirror and reflect, "Despite my success, I have many weaknesses and a great deal to learn." A developing lean leader can then begin to develop others; in fact, teaching others is one of the best ways to improve yourself. When a critical mass of leaders down to the working level has been developed, the leader can coach a steady diet of daily *kaizen* and continuous improvement and ultimately create *hoshin kanri*, which aligns actions in all parts of the company to face even the most daunting environmental challenges. But, like Dana, many companies find themselves in what we might call a pre-lean leadership world.

These companies may be in a state of crisis. Or their culture may be too reactive and short-term focused, often driven solely by transactions such as mergers and acquisitions or by short-term cost reductions to drive quarterly earnings and the stock price. And, having been promoted many times already and viewed as "successful," some existing leaders are not committed to self-development and do not value developing others. Some perhaps see the environment as being more combative than cooperative—survival of the fittest. It can be difficult for aspiring leaders hoping to take their cue from Toyota's excellence to know where to even begin.

# Do You Really Want to Be Excellent?

Gary's most vivid impression when he first went to Toyota was that it was like a fine symphony orchestra of skilled musicians making beautiful music. How could hourly employees doing short, repetitive jobs on an assembly line be anything like skilled musicians? This is what Toyota calls *monozukuri*—an all-encompassing passion for innovating and doing things well. Toyota is a manufacturing company, first and foremost. Its value resides in the products that it engineers and produces, so it must be able to build and sell its products with pride.

Whether you are a hospital servicing patients, a law firm representing clients, or a utility powering the city, you need to have a passion for delivering value. Only from a place of committed passion can a leader or a company create a vision that actually fosters and inspires leadership, whether it is a long-term "Global Vision 2020" type plan or a shorter-term compass for recovery like the one that Dana needed if it was to survive.

If you want to start on the path to true lean leadership, the most important question to ask yourself is: "Do I really want to be excellent?" If getting by is good enough for you, you do not need Toyota as a model. There are many ways to get the job done, get enough results to make money, and survive long enough to retire. We hope you desire more than that. We hope you are willing to pursue mastery.

Martial arts offer a strong metaphor for the role of mastery at Toyota. Author Mike Rother uses the Japanese term *kata* to explain how to master the skills of process improvement and coaching improvement at a deep level.[1] *Kata* literally means "form," but more broadly, it refers to the precisely choreographed patterns of movement that are seen in kabuki theater, karate, and the tea ceremony. In all of these disciplines, there is a logic and a sequence that is followed in pursuit of mastery, under the watchful eye of a *sensei*. Perfection, of course, is elusive and is not really attainable. Nonetheless, it should be the goal—compromising the pursuit of perfection leads to a downward spiral.

As modern multinational companies and formal business disciplines have evolved, it seems as if we've lost the challenge and thrill of personal mastery. While there are plenty of books and consultants that advise companies on competitive advantage and differentiation as a concept, we seem to have lost the goal of encouraging people to be the best they can be. George Leonard, a skilled practitioner of *aikido*, writes critically of "American's war against mastery," citing the television age, in which "consumerism has achieved unprecedented dominance over our value system," with life being portrayed as an endless series of "climactic moments," with no work or disciplined practice in between being required to achieve these outcomes.[2]

Robert Thomas conducted research on what makes highly effective leaders and found that such leaders uniformly went through defining moments that challenged them to their core.[3] It is how they personally processed these "crucible events" and learned from them that differentiates them from less effective leaders. Like accomplished athletes or artists, they practice as strenuously as they perform. They have developed "personal learning strategies" that provide a disciplined practice regimen to enable them to achieve their aspirations. Thomas finds that the most essential capability of successful leaders is "adaptive capacity: your ability to observe and be open to learning." And it is an "ongoing process of challenge, adaptation, and learning that prepares [leaders] for the next crucible, where the process is repeated." Toyota has developed deliberate methods for providing those key learning opportunities and the coaching necessary to help leaders and hourly team members to achieve mastery. Yet the enabling environment is not enough—it still depends on "self-development," a passion to learn and grow in pursuit of mastery that is woefully lacking in many people who aspire to leadership.

## Is Lean Leadership in the Toyota Way Really That Different?

There is a fundamental difference between the way of developing leaders that is deeply rooted in Toyota's DNA and that practiced by traditional Western companies. And just as *The Machine That Changed the World* identified "lean production" as a new paradigm of manufacturing, this book has presented a new paradigm of developing leadership. We summarize the main differences in Table 7-1. We sort the differences that we have observed into two categories: (1) those related to how leaders make business decisions and solve problems, and (2) those related to leadership style and motives. Toyota starts with a clear understanding of "True North" and works to perfect processes. A good process will repeatedly produce good results, but a leader who forces a bad process to get the results that she wants is relying on luck or temporary measures, like trying to inspect in quality, neither of which can be sustained in the long term. While many people we speak with easily understand the conceptual difference between a good process and a bad process that produces results in the short term, we find that few really grasp the Toyota concept of a "good process." Most Western managers immediately assume that a good process is one that is free of errors. In contrast, Toyota's concept of a good process is one that

**Table 7.1.** Summary of Traditional Western Leadership Compared to Toyota Leadership

| Traditional Western Leader | Toyota Leader |
|---|---|
| *Business Decision Making and Problem Solving* | |
| Work to a financial business plan | Reach for True North vision |
| Results at all costs | The right process and well-defined targets will lead to the right results |
| Manage by the numbers | Deeply understand the process at the *gemba* |
| Quick results, short-term thinking | Take time to plan and prepare the people and processes for the long term |
| Overcome barriers | Deeply understand problems and the root cause before acting |
| *Leadership Style and Personal Motives* | |
| Proud and conquering hero | Humble and learning |
| Advancement focus: climb ladder rapidly to achieve increasing rewards and recognition | Mastery focus: learn deeply and broadly, then take on increasing responsibility for development of self and others |
| Use metrics plus rewards and punishments to control people | Metrics are targets to align people and teams and motivate them to achieve goals that they help set |
| Accomplish objectives through people | Develop people to work effectively in teams to solve problems |
| Transactional relationship to company: what is in it for me? | Commitment relationship to company: how can we build something great? |

expects and reveals problems, without blame, not one that is problem-free. People at Toyota learn from being repetitively immersed in real problems, not through contrived exercises or classroom learning.

This naturally leads to differences in the roles and motives of leaders. In the traditional Western model, there seems to be an underlying assumption that most employees are interested only in themselves and are not very capable. The leaders have to take on the burden of thinking for the masses and manipulating people into doing the right things through metrics, incentives, and punishments. We're often asked about Toyota's system of incentives. This question assumes that everyone, hourly workers and managers alike, must be bribed if they are to achieve excellence. This tends to be a self-fulfilling prophecy, as studies have shown that once extrinsic motivators dominate, people will cease to get enjoyment out of the activity itself unless they see some tangible and immediate reward.[4]

The Toyota model, by contrast, assumes that people will be motivated in many ways if they have a clear vision of success, are taught the tools of problem solving, and participate in setting goals and improving how they do their work. This assumption has been proven by decades of continuous improvement and through extensive research on the motivating power of goal setting.[5]

Toyota uses metrics not primarily as a way for managers to coerce desired behavior, but so that individuals and teams have the tools to judge their own performance. Metrics are designed for self-improvement rather than primarily for oversight and managerial control. They support conscious daily management of quality, cost, and delivery goals. The real difference isn't in the metrics; it is in the dedicated, short, speedy, and repetitive execution cycles of Plan–Do–Check–Act (PDCA), for which leaders provide both accountability and support. In contrast, many companies that we work with establish layers of metrics as a way for managers to enforce control when they do not truly understand the work that is being done by the teams they supervise, let alone have any systematic method for improving that work.

## It Is Not So Different from the Best Leadership Books

We have emphasized the differences between Toyota leadership and what we commonly see in Western companies, but we also see many similarities between Toyota and the prescriptions of the best Western leadership literature. In Chapter 3, we noted how Barry was referred to contemporary books on "servant leadership" to help him understand what Toyota leadership is really about. You may have found yourself thinking about Level 5 leadership from Jim Collins's *Good to Great*[6] while you were reading about Toyota leadership—there are plenty of places where the concepts overlap, from humility to passion to having the right people "on the bus."

Other readers may have recalled Stephen Covey's *Seven Habits of Highly Effective People*.[7] If you show Covey's seven habits to any Toyota leader, you are likely to hear: "Those habits all make sense, and I agree that this is what we at Toyota strive for." Among the Toyota-like habits that Covey identifies are setting long-term goals based on a vision of True North, using visualization, empathetically listening to others before giving advice, and applying effective problem solving to cooperate with others.

We could go on and on. Ken Blanchard's "situational leadership,"[8] which emphasizes using the right way of leading in the right situation, is frequently taught within Toyota in North America to emphasize that people need the right level of support and structure, one that fits their current development stage. Toyota strives to be a learning organization of system thinkers that fits Peter Senge's model in his seminal work *The Fifth Discipline*[9] well. Senge's learning organization has five parts: personal mastery, developing clear mental models of success, shared vision, team learning, and system thinking. These are very similar to what Toyota strives to develop at every level of the company.

## The Difference Is in the Cultural Value Placed on Capability versus Charisma

Toyota is not so much unique in its leadership formula as in its execution of that formula. Two things stand out to us. The first is the remarkable consistency with which, year by year, level by level, the company develops leaders who live the Toyota Way. We could randomly select a group of Toyota leaders from different levels and different countries, and we would see a set of strong common values in action (though there would certainly be some variation in level of competency in the Toyota Way).

Second, and partly as a result of this, Toyota leadership has been evolving and developing as a system. Just as Senge preaches becoming a learning organization, Toyota as a learning organization assimilates these various leadership methods and concepts into a coherent whole that is continually evolving. The totality of this learning is considered the Toyota DNA. This, of course, begs the question: how has Toyota succeeded at getting its DNA ingrained so consistently across so many different leaders for so long?

Most companies have some very effective leaders, but the variation across different leaders and different points in the company's history is dramatic. The norm is not for great companies to stay great, but rather for them to revert to ordinary. In statistics, this is called "regression toward the mean," and without True North leadership, a degree of "snap-back" from lean changes is a given. For instance, the S&P 500 is incredibly dynamic: only 86 companies maintained a place in the index over its first 50 years (an anniversary that was reached in 2007).

The leadership development model that we've explored in this book is the mechanism that Toyota has evolved (and is continuing to evolve) to ingrain the Toyota DNA in all its leaders. It starts with careful selection of new hires; these are then grown from within and selected for more challenging opportunities based on demonstrated leadership in action and how they learn from these opportunities.

One thing that Toyota does not select for is charisma. Many of the best Toyota leaders appear to outsiders to be very ordinary. They would not win elections or popularity contests. When Toyota leaders, including Akio Toyoda, were called before the U.S. Congress as part of the unintended acceleration hearings in February 2010, they did not get high marks for their charisma in handling the hostile questions that were fired at them. Toyota does not particularly value charisma. The more understated person, who is humble, accepts responsibility, is willing to work as part of a team, and is open to learning, is much preferred. Toyota values highly competent leaders who repeatedly demonstrate their capability by showing it on the job. It is only by proving that they have high levels of competence that Toyota team members have the opportunity to advance into a leadership position. What is it that they must show?

First, they must deeply understand the work itself. A common complaint heard in many companies is that the boss does not really understand the work and does not deserve to be the boss. The office gossip suggests that he got there because of political connections, or because he was a smooth talker, or because he was loyal and stayed around long enough. The person who is complaining may not realize that she herself is far from being highly competent, but she can sense that something is wrong. When Toyota leaders, like Gary and Marty, go into other companies, as we saw in Dana, it is typical for them to see managers who seem less than fully competent by Toyota standards. Yet these are the majority of leaders in most companies—dedicated to a degree, competent to a degree, but falling short of excellence or mastery. They have never had the support or the structure to learn to be anything more. A company like Toyota, with a True North vision of *monozukuri*, needs excellent leaders who are highly competent at understanding the work, so it puts remarkable amounts of time and resources into developing such leaders, resources that go far beyond a measurable ROI.

Second, they must go beyond surface-level understanding to deep mastery of lean thinking. To gain and maintain competence in the Toyota Way of leading, even senior executives need to be immersed in the *gemba*. Even for people who have been trained in the Toyota Way, it can be hard to know what immersion in the *gemba* means and what the leader is supposed to do when he is there. Gary himself had a lot of trouble in his first years at NUMMI. At GM and Ford, he was accustomed to going to the source of a problem in order to *directly* assess it and solve it himself, but that is not what immersion in the *gemba* means at Toyota. Executives do not go to the *gemba* so that they can do the problem solving themselves; that would be counterproductive to people development. Going to the *gemba* instead means that the aspiring leader goes firsthand to the place where the work is done in order to gain a deep understanding of it. Once there, she provides challenge, coaching, and support.

In contrast, Western leadership culture often provides subtle incentives to shy away from tough problems. The rewards for taking on a tough problem materialize only if the manager is successful; the risk and consequences of failure are substantial. And if the company culture is to "shoot the messenger," leaders may hide problems for years.

Drilling down to the root causes of problems can be gut-wrenching, requiring patient dialogue with involved employees while building enough trust so that the employees are willing to be honest even when they feel vulnerable. That doesn't mean that such conversations are abstract or mealymouthed. Any leader at Toyota can tell stories of having his mistakes and failures critiqued in excruciating detail by a *sensei*.

The Japanese custom of avoiding any embarrassing situation so that others can "save face" (*mentsu*) is very strong in dealing with outsiders to the organization, but there is a very different set of rules for dealing internally with subordinates or associates. We have observed within Toyota that when an issue is "in the family," especially in private meetings, discussions can be very direct, particularly when a higher-ranking manager is addressing a subordinate. In such situations, pointing to weaknesses in the performance of a subordinate is regarded by those involved not as conflict, but as caring attempts to help the individual improve, like "tough love."[10]

Third is the passion for True North. It is an important concept in everything that Toyota does. True North gives the aspiring leader the faith to go right into the unknown of a new challenge, without a ready-made answer. It takes years of training, coaching by *sensei*, and experience to have a deep understanding of Toyota's vision of perfection. It takes even more time to learn to assess the current situation compared to True North—the gap—skillfully. The gap is always there because perfection is unattainable, but a well-coached and well-led team using an effective problem-solving process can get closer and closer to this vision.

## Toyota Leadership Is Management by Means and Results

Another key aspect of Toyota leadership that we explored in Chapter 5 is the *hoshin kanri* system. In fact, we described this as the final stage of linking together the capable leaders developed at all levels and the ever-shifting business objectives for the company in response to the environment.

*Hoshin kanri* is often compared favorably to the roundly criticized management practice of Management by Objectives (MBO).[11] The ideal of MBO is to empower everyone in the enterprise by articulating clear goals and objectives and allowing managers and workers, through delegation, to figure out how best to achieve them. Concrete measures of actual results compared with the planned results are used for employee evaluation. The theory is that this approach empowers people, limits micromanagement, and encourages accountability—all recognizable positive goals of enlightened management, and indeed goals to aspire to.

But as good as the intentions are, MBO can have negative consequences. By essentially ignoring the ways in which managers and workers achieve the objectives that are laid out, MBO creates ample space for unintended consequences. There are many cases in which MBO leads to people cutting corners to meet their targets. In many companies that employ MBO, the targets clearly matter more than the methods—and everyone, up and down the chain of management, reacts accordingly. (See the sidebar, "Why a Short-Term Focus on Cost Reduction Will Kill Real Lean Transformation.")

Many in the lean community have noted that MBO ignores the ways in which objectives are achieved. As a counterbalance to this unbalanced focus on results only, this has led to the development of a new trend called "Management by Means" (MBM), built on the theory that if managers pursue their jobs in the right way, positive outcomes will necessarily follow.[12] Some of the advocates of MBM go so far as to develop "management standardized work," a set of prescribed practices for managers (such as daily walks to the *gemba* on a standard path through jobs to ask a prescribed list of questions and provide coaching) in order to ensure that the proper "means" of management are being employed.[13]

MBM is a noble idea, and it correctly recognizes that most executives are far too focused on results, without having a real understanding of the means to get there, but in practice its limitations are as serious as those of MBO. Why? Because, quite simply, if you don't have targets for results, there is no way to know whether you're pursuing those targets in the right way. MBM seeks to redress the imbalance caused by focusing on results only, but it goes too far to the other extreme. We are not trying to justify a "results at any cost" mentality, but rather arguing that objectives and means are inextricably linked.

Not hitting his metrics is a source of deep shame for a Toyota leader. You'll never hear a Toyota leader say: "It's OK that we didn't hit our results targets because we worked on them in the right way." One Toyota general manager who had been given the task of cutting the time to develop a stamping die in half was asked by Jeff how he would feel if he achieved 49 percent lead time reduction. His response: "I would lose a lot of sleep at night." It's not about means versus objectives but about both. A true Toyota Way leader pursues his objectives for results with every ounce of his energy, but he does so in ways that are consistent with the Toyota Way.

It's obviously true that you could have the wrong targets, or that circumstances could change, leading to an inability to meet the targets the right way. But that reflects on the target-setting process. True lean management recognizes that the target-setting process and the pursuit of targets cannot be independent. If you don't set targets in the right way, and if people do not have the skills or motivation to develop a good plan, it's irrelevant whether your management approach is "by means" or "by objectives."

As we saw in Chapter 5, Global Vision 2010 had an aspirational goal based on its values: "To be the most admired auto company in the world." That's a hard goal to measure, and so it was translated into specific targets, including, among others, 15 percent global market share. The targets in Toyota's *hoshin kanri* system always start with results and break these down level by level to specific plans (means), with metrics to track progress on the means, thus integrating objectives and means. The translation of Global Vision 2010 in North America was to set targets in four areas: supplier development, cost reduction, people development, and customer satisfaction. We went into detail about how Gary approached one key objective of the customer satisfaction goal: to reduce warranty claims by 60 percent. That goal was achieved by the end of the decade. There was nothing wrong with any of these goals, and they were pursued in a way that was consistent with the values of the company.

We do believe that management by means is in some ways a useful counterbalance to the decades of focusing only on results, and that management standardized work has some value, but it is not sufficient. It is only the first very small step toward being a lean leader. We argued in Chapter 2 that every Toyota team member goes through a basic set of development steps at each stage of her development, following the process of basic learning by copying exactly (*shu*), mastering the basics so that they become second nature (*ha*), and becoming so masterful at the basics that she can go beyond these and improvise (*ri*).

Management standardized work is only the *shu* stage of learning. Management by means is only a small piece of the *ha* stage. You don't get to the *ri* stage as a leader until you can consistently use the right means *and* achieve the results that you signed up for.

## Why a Short-Term Focus on Cost Reduction Will Kill Real Lean Transformation

Unfortunately, top executives in most companies have viewed lean management as a cost-reduction program, pure and simple. At first, those who are assigned to the lean effort are given some latitude to develop a vision, develop training modules, think about what operational excellence looks like for the long term, and even perhaps begin with a model line project. Then comes the shift— where are the dollars? We have seen this shift happen as early as a few months into the effort, after the first *kaizen* event is run or the first training program is held. The CEO makes it clear that he expects a dollar return on the lean effort by the end of the year.

As we have mentioned, doing lean the right way and saving money are not antithetical. They can be achieved simultaneously. The operative word is *can*. Too often, when the orders to save money come down from the top, the lean leaders panic. They fire the *sensei* and stop focusing on the long-term development of people—it's all hands on deck to find cost savings. And cost savings means "hard dollars," which almost always focuses on head count—do lean events to take out heads. Throughout this book, we have emphasized the challenge and resources required to create a true culture of continuous improvement. Commands from the top for quick cost savings generally kill this investment in the culture for the future and ruin employee trust, and lean becomes a tool-based program to cut costs.

In Chapter 2 we used the analogy of management standardized work[13] as the functional equivalent of using training wheels to learn to ride a bicycle. Management by means, which focuses on monitoring people to see that they follow the right process, and management standardized work fit this metaphor. They are the very basics that you need if you are to get started. Getting started is, of course, necessary, and therefore these tools can be helpful and perhaps can start to shift the balance away from pure management for results. Unfortunately, too many managers do not realize that they are still in the early *shu* stage of learning, and they too quickly stop developing their skills. Then they wonder why they aren't seeing the transformative and breakthrough results that are achieved by Toyota and other companies that have spent years developing true lean leaders.

## Lean Leadership Is the Force That Allows Toyota to Adapt to Major Environmental Change

Liker and Ogden analyzed Toyota's response to the recent crises in detail in *Toyota under Fire*,[14] and we summarized Toyota's response to the recall crisis in the prologue to this book. But *Toyota under Fire* also talks about the Great Recession, and it is worth summarizing Toyota's unusual and almost unique approach to dealing with economic cycles like the financial collapse.

During the two most recent economic booms, stories in the news media about companies providing their employees with lavish perks became commonplace. Whether those perks were cash bonuses, stock grants, or free gourmet food, the pattern was consistent: flush with cash and facing a tight labor market, many companies preached the value of investing in and rewarding employees. Many CEOs were the subject of glowing profiles in business magazines that noted their commitment to people and "out-of-the-box" leadership.

Then tough times hit. Employees who had been told that they were the company's most valuable asset found themselves being laid off in droves. Many "out-of-the-box" leaders found themselves out of the box on the organizational chart. Those who held on to their jobs were the ones who quickly transformed themselves into in-the-box cost cutters. There's every reason to be skeptical of laudatory pronouncements about leadership in a company that's riding high on a decade of profitability. It's easy to talk about treating employees as your most valuable asset and about leadership styles that value consensus, teamwork, and patient investment in developing new leaders when a company is making money hand over fist.

There's an old axiom that a person's character is revealed by how she acts when no one is looking. For leaders and companies, in some ways, the opposite is true. Leadership character is revealed when everyone is looking—at the bottom line. Psychologists tell us that our most permanent personality traits are revealed when we are under stress. What a company really believes about leadership is revealed when it is under stress. The Great Recession, then, is a perfect lens through which to view Toyota's approach to leadership. This is particularly true because Toyota had more than 50 consecutive years of profits under its belt before it posted an annual loss for fiscal year 2008. Does the Toyota leadership model stand up when the company is under stress? How does Toyota approach leadership in a crisis? The short answer: when times are tough, Toyota doesn't just stick by its approach to leadership; Toyota punches the accelerator.

The Great Recession wasn't Toyota's first experience of operating in a challenging environment. Toyota has used challenge repeatedly as an opportunity to grow leaders. Challenge is the first of the five foundational values of the Toyota Way. That's no accident.

When he invented an automated loom in impoverished rural Japan, Sakichi Toyoda founded Toyota in an environment that was far more challenging than the one that Toyota faced in the modern recession. Only a few years after Sakichi asked his son, Kiichiro, to start a car company, the fledging operation was forced to confront the devastation of World War II. Toyota, like all Japanese companies, was severely hit by the oil embargo in 1973; Japan was entirely dependent on oil imports. From each of these challenges, the company rose stronger.

As we've noted repeatedly, the Toyota Production System (TPS) purposely creates challenges every day. These daily challenges help the company fight complacency and provide training opportunities for growing leaders. In other words, Toyota is serious about facing challenges with a creative spirit and with courage—only leaders who frame challenges as opportunities (and because of TPS, they have many chances to do so) move up the ladder. An old saying in Japan is, "An error is a treasure." The point of this is that breakdowns and errors yield opportunities to identify the root causes and then to improve the system, so as to prevent that problem in the future.

Internally generated challenges, whether they are the result of TPS and leading *kaizen* or the stretch goals delineated by the board, such as doubling market share to 15 percent, are quite different from major environmental shifts like global recessions. For the last two decades, Toyota has had a margin of safety in the challenges that it faced. If the company didn't quite reach its targets, it was still ahead of the game, gaining market share, earning significant profits, and besting its competitors in quality and productivity. Toyota's record of meeting its goals and constantly raising the bar is certainly impressive, given the human temptation to complacency. But there is no such margin of safety when steel and oil prices double in six months, and then every developed country in the world enters a deep recession at essentially the same time.

Surviving and thriving during such rapid change requires more than strong leaders at the top of the company. There are simply too many moving parts in a global company even one-tenth Toyota's size to rely on leadership that comes only from the top. Every leader throughout the company has to be ready to respond rapidly to major change and participate in mobilizing the organization to adapt to a changing environment.

In one sense, it is difficult to write about how Toyota leadership adapts to the challenges of a major crisis simply because Toyota doesn't respond to major change by asking leaders to do things differently. Like a champion athlete responding to a loss, Toyota responds to a setback by doing more of the good things that it was already doing—only better, with an even more intense focus. Responding rapidly to major change means more self-development, not less; demanding more development of others, not just employee sacrifice; providing more support for daily *kaizen*, not canceling *kaizen* activities; and driving *hoshin kanri* faster and further to look to the future, not the current crisis. In fact,

Toyota Engineering and Manufacturing did not close any of its plants, did not lay off any regular employees (although temporary employees were let go), continued to significantly outspend its competitors in R&D (although there was some reduction in spending), and used the opportunity to build a stronger foundation for the future.

Toyota's manufacturing plants were hit the hardest during the recession because there was simply much less work to do. In the United States, plants that made large vehicles that consumed a lot of gas were particularly hard hit, since a large gas price increase in the summer of 2008 preceded the recession.

Toyota's plant in Princeton, Indiana, TMMI, was launched in 1996 and soon became the crown jewel of profitability for North America. TMMI built the large Sequoia SUV, the Sienna minivan, and the Tundra trucks. Between 2000 and 2008, TMMI won J.D. Power awards for initial quality every year except 2003. Production peaked in 2005, when the plant built 370,000 vehicles. When the gas price hike hit in the late spring of 2008, the number of large vehicles sold plummeted faster than anyone had ever seen. By the summer, it was clear that Tundra and Sequoia inventories were building up drastically, so a decision was made (too late by Toyota standards) to stop production of these vehicles completely for three months and to shut down one of the two assembly lines at the plant (the Sienna minivan line kept running). Even after that assembly line started up again, when the full weight of the recession hit, annualized production late in 2008 declined by 48 percent from the prior year.

But even while the assembly line was shut down, Toyota didn't lay off any of its regular team members (temporary labor and overtime were eliminated). During that three-month period, 1,800 team members were coming to work at the Indiana plant with essentially no production work to do on one of the two assembly lines. Instead, they were participating in intense training and *kaizen*. After the shutdown, with the recession reducing sales volume to 50 to 60 percent of earlier levels for more than eight months, the plant was split into two groups that alternated time on the line and additional time for training and *kaizen*.

Anyone who has sat through any amount of corporate training, let alone three months' worth, may rightly ask how Toyota knew that investing in training would produce any kind of return. After all, training exercises that have no concrete goals attached quickly devolve into training for training's sake—an opportunity for employees to catch a nap and goof off, not necessarily to learn anything that they can put to use.

To combat this tendency, TMMI matched classroom training with hands-on *kaizen* on projects run by hourly team members with support from trainers, and pulled ahead its *hoshin kanri* objectives by one year. The plant used a full-size mock-up of an assembly line that ran on a continuous loop so that teams could get hands-on experience even while the real lines were not running. More than 120 group leaders and managers were trained as trainers in the Toyota Way, all the basic tools of TPS, and problem solving. Team members were encouraged to apply the classroom training immediately and to follow the processes that they were practicing rigidly. They were revisiting the *shu* stage of learning, in which strict adherence to the standard process should be carried out. Concrete goals were set for improved safety, quality, and productivity at the end of the three months, to provide team members with a goal to measure themselves against.

One discovery in Indiana was that *hoshin kanri* had not traveled down to the work group level effectively. Group leaders and team leaders had not been formally trained in TBP before the recession, and while team members had done a lot of *kaizen*, it was not linked to the *hoshin* objectives of upper management. So a major focus in this period was on developing a "floor management development system" for each work group (based on a visual metrics board) that would be operational throughout the plant and would link objectives at all levels.

All the investment in developing people paid off in the short term. The plant found many millions of dollars of cost savings; launched a new product (the Highlander), doing itself a lot of the work that would ordinarily have been contracted out; and brought quality, safety, and morale to a whole new level. TMMI set a new standard for fewest defects per hundred vehicles built in a North American plant. Of course, the investment is likely to have an even greater payoff over the long term.

When the recall crisis hit and demand was temporarily reduced, and later when Japan's worst earthquake of the century shuttered the production of suppliers making about 500 parts for Toyota, the same recipe was followed—*kaizen* and training as well as volunteer work on community projects. Protecting jobs through bad times and contributing to the community seem natural to Toyota leaders, who have deeply internalized the philosophies of contributing to society and protecting the well-being of the company's team members.

## Starting the Journey

It is all well and good that over many decades, Toyota has developed a strong culture driven by a distinctive philosophy of leadership, but what does that mean for other companies with very different cultures? We have seen that Toyota has been able to teach and adapt its leadership models to the American culture, and indeed to cultures all over the world where Toyota has factories, R&D, and sales operations. It may also be comforting to know that Toyota is far from perfect, and in fact that is the starting point for all *kaizen*. We have given examples of weaknesses throughout this book, including at TMMK, where Gary had to begin to rebuild the leadership and culture at a time when the plant externally had the reputation of being a benchmark facility. Nobody at Toyota believes that Toyota was perfect in responding to the recall crisis. Deep reflection during and since the crisis exposed serious weaknesses that would have led to major future problems. Toyota has set out to solve these weaknesses and their root causes through many countermeasures. If Toyota, which we have argued has an exceptional system for developing leaders and a strong culture of continuous improvement, has had serious weaknesses at various times and locations, then it's likely that every company will encounter similar, if not greater, challenges. Toyota's ability to overcome weakness when they surface is why we believe its leadership is a model worth learning from.

So how can someone not at Toyota start on the road to a systematic approach to becoming a true leader and developing others? In many ways, you have already started. The fact that you've read this book indicates a penchant for self-development and for identifying gaps between where you are and where you want to be. Now you need to determine what challenge to take on next.

Identifying the right challenges can start only when you have a vision of uncompromising excellence and a brutally honest assessment of your firm's current condition. The gap between the ideal vision and the current state helps in identifying the problem around which you and other leaders can focus your efforts to self-develop, develop others, and promote continuous improvement by both small and large changes. This process of identifying the gap between the current and the ideal will repeat itself many times in the life of a company and the career of an aspiring leader.

You can then turn our diamond model of leadership development around and treat it as a diagnostic for your organization:

1. *Is there a shared vision of True North in your organization?*
   We believe that in most companies, the answer is no. There is a mission statement or some other document floating around, but it is so general that it quickly loses meaning. The vision needs to be believable, actionable, and reinforced in concrete terms as the work is done. As we noted in the case of Dana, the vision should fit the level of maturity of the organization. When the organization does not have the leadership maturity to handle bold ten-year visions, a shorter-term set of operating principles with clear targets for key performance indicators may be a good starting point.
2. *Do we have leaders in place who are willing to take on challenges with a positive mindset and develop themselves?*
   The long-term goal is to have all leaders, up, down, and across the organization, busy self-developing. As we have noted, self-development does not mean that you do this alone; there is a critical role for a *sensei* to teach and coach. Unfortunately, few medium to large companies have enough *sensei* around to handle the mentoring that would be needed to get started everywhere all at once. In this case, a more targeted approach is needed. Some companies have started with mentoring senior leaders by engaging them in *kaizen* on the floor. The model that Gary used at TMMK, taking upper-middle-level leaders to suppliers to lead *kaizen* events and then holding them accountable for applying what they learned back in their home departments, is

another approach. Yet other companies have developed a "model line," which involves transforming one significant part of one value stream, or even a model site that leads the way for other sites. Wherever you are starting from, the key point is to realize that it is only a start on the path to a cycle of learning that deepens and spreads.[15]

3. *Are leaders at all levels embracing their roles as teachers, developing others to lead the way in the future?*

Starting the process of self-development is a challenge, but in some ways it's simple compared to the process of transforming leaders who have learned over decades to be decision makers into teachers who are developing others. Learning to hold back from offering solutions was perhaps the most difficult lesson for Gary, and it is something that he continues to work on even today. What Barry was really learning from "servant leadership" was that he needed to focus on developing others, instead of using his power to give orders. This requires remarkable maturity and discipline. The starting point is to make clear the expectation that leaders will develop others and to make that part of their ongoing performance assessment and feedback.

4. *Are leaders at all levels using a rigorous process to solve the right problems step by step?*

We are talking about more than an intellectual process of knowing the steps. Root-cause problem solving involves fundamental behavioral tendencies. It's natural to want to jump in with "solutions" so that you can see the "results" quickly. The Plan–Do–Check–Act process focuses the majority of the effort on the planning and then stresses that the job is not complete until we Check and start planning for further action. "Doing" is at best one step out of eight. Unfortunately, doing to get results is what excites many leaders. Teaching problem solving that keeps "doing" in proper perspective must become the center of the ongoing training and development in any company that wishes to learn from Toyota.[16]

5. *Does the company have an environment in which aligned targets for improvement are developed and good ideas for achieving those targets are shared across the organization?*

We have emphasized that the nature of *hoshin kanri* will evolve as the organization evolves. At first, as we saw in the Dana case, the emphasis often needs to be on how we can set the right goals at the top and then measure and reward the achievement of those goals. The most important point about *hoshin kanri* is the importance of having good plans for achieving the goals at each level in the organization. Gary and his team did this at Dana by insisting on A3 reports of plans from each plant manager and then critically evaluating those plans. *Hoshin kanri* is a leadership development tool, not just a tool for achieving business objectives. As leaders develop and follow good problem-solving processes, achieving the business objectives will come more naturally.

6. *Do we use major challenges from the environment to further strengthen our leadership and our company to work toward a long-term vision?*

Unfortunately, most of the companies we have studied recently have "wasted a good crisis," in Rahm Emanuel's phrase.[17] They panicked and started to tear apart their organizations, leaving them in a weakened state for growing the business as the economy heals. The challenge is that a crisis tends to bring out existing tendencies, so it is hard for a company to start to build a culture of excellence in the midst of a recession. Toyota used the recession and earthquake recall crisis as opportunities to further develop its people and the company. Dana brought in leaders who were already quite developed in the Toyota Way to turn what could have been mostly negative into a positive start at building a foundation for excellence. Other companies have an opportunity now to start to build the capability to deal with the next great tsunami that will hit the world economy.

## The Need for a *Sensei*

We would love to give you a road map to lean leadership. Leadership standardized work appears to be a nice road map, and that is comforting. How do we train leaders? How long does it take? What is the optimal mix between classroom training and floor walking? How many *kaizen* events should the CEO personally participate in? We could go on and on with questions we can answer only with the unsatisfying statement: It depends!

There is no cookbook for developing Toyota-style lean leadership, but we suggest that the six questions in the last section will have to be answered over and over as you progress on the leadership development journey. It would be great if *sensei* weren't required, but Toyota-like management culture, beliefs, and habits run in opposition to the core values and routine behaviors of companies that follow the Toyota Way, so coaching is required if you are to succeed in building a new culture. Fortunately, at Toyota, there are guides to help new and aspiring leaders learn how to walk through this process. They are veterans who have been living Toyota leadership principles for 20 to 30 years. At Dana, the ranks of people who were capable of this level of thinking was thin at best, so Gary had to recruit from outside and play a strong *sensei* role himself. For many companies, getting senior leadership trained in this style of leading will require contracting with an advisor as a *sensei*, or even with more than one.

This may sound like self-serving advice to hire lean consultants. We are not suggesting that at all. At Dana, Gary deliberately limited the number of consultants as much as possible and focused on bringing experts in as managers and executives. Using consultants was mainly a way of testing their capability before they were hired.

Traditionally, the role of consultants is to run a project and deliver an action plan. In essence, the consultant is doing the thinking for the client. Many "lean consultants" follow this practice. They claim to have expertise in lean methods and guarantee that they can eliminate waste. They can deliver quick financial benefits and even a degree of learning with this approach. But invariably, the majority of the learning stays with the consultants, and what they leave behind is fragile at best. Beware of slick consultants with cool confidence that they can deliver on an aggressive "value proposition." Delivering on the value proposition in a short period of time usually means that the consultants have to act fast—the antithesis of good lean practice, which is based on finding the root causes and the best solutions and sharing lessons for continued improvement. The quick-fix consultant doesn't have time to let internal staff members struggle with a challenge and learn good practices. We have been in many companies that have had external consultants lead blitzes that delivered great short-term results, but the processes that they put in place were not sustained. When the emphasis is on Do, the Plan–Do–Check–Act cycle will always break down.

A good *sensei*, in contrast, will function much as the internal coaches in Toyota do. She will challenge, walk through the process with the leaders, question them, make suggestions, and let them struggle. She will refuse to take over and do the thinking for the company. She will seed the internal leadership development process to find enough people who can self-develop, encourage them to learn from one another, and then expect them to develop others, who in turn will keep the cycle going. The *sensei's* measure of value is how much your organization is learning and how it is developing internal leaders who can become teachers. If senior executives hire the *sensei* and stand back, waiting for the organization to change, the process will surely fail. It is impossible to delegate self-improvement. We are often asked how a company can "sustain the gains" from lean. A good *sensei* knows that it is not the gains that you want to sustain; it is the interconnected processes of people development and process improvement that need to be sustained.

## You Do Not Need to Wait for the Perfect CEO

So what if you are in the middle of the company? Or what if your CEO believes that the key to motivating employees is to cultivate a culture of survival of the fittest, not mutual development? This is in fact the situation in many large organizations.

Our answer is that you can still get started. We mean that: we've seen many directors and managers become passionate about the Toyota Way and apply its values within their purview. In *The Toyota Way to Continuous Improvement*,[18] there are examples of two leaders at the executive vice president level who delivered successful cultural transformations of their own portions of the business without strong support from the CEO or the rest of the business. Remember that good problem solving always recognizes the current constraints, and there are many, many countermeasures that are possible within your purview, whatever your situation. We suggest that you work on what you control and become a role model for others.

Try. Then reflect. Then try some more. If you have an opportunity to engage a *sensei*, seize it. There is always more to learn. And success generally leads to positive attention and interest. Even if you eventually leave your current company for a place that is more compatible with your values (as Gary did when he left Ford for Toyota), you will be better equipped because you have worked on yourself as a leader.

Using Toyota as a model requires a leadership commitment beyond what most companies have experienced. It is not a program with a defined starting point and finish line. Self-development and developing others is a lifelong journey, and it never ends.

Are you up for the challenge?

# Notes

## Prologue

1. A thorough analysis of Toyota's response to the Great Recession and the recall crisis can be found in Jeffrey Liker and Timothy Ogden, *Toyota under Fire* (New York: McGraw-Hill, 2011).
2. It is not accurate to say there were no layoffs in any part of Toyota. At Toyota Motor Sales, there were some layoffs of dock workers during the recession. And NUMMI was closed, though it was an affiliate, not a Toyota plant.
3. Andrea Tse, "2010 U.S. Auto Recalls," The Street, June 28, 2010.
4. The vision can be found at http://www.toyota-global.com/company/vision_philosophy/toyota_global_vision_2020.html.

## Introduction

1. Jesse Snyder, "Ford Scores Tumble, Toyota Rebounds in Initial Quality Survey," *Automotive News*, June 23, 2011; http://www.autoweek.com/article/20110623/CARNEWS/110629937.
2. Jeffrey Liker and James Franz, *The Toyota Way to Continuous Improvement* (New York: McGraw-Hill, 2011).
3. Geert Hofstede, Gert Jan Hofstede, and Michael Minkov, *Culture and Organizations: Software for the Mind*, 3d ed. (New York: McGraw-Hill, 2010).

4. Samuel Smiles, *Self Help* (1859; West Valley City, Utah: Waking Lion Press, 2006).

5. The Toyoda family name is spelled with a *d*. Toyota Motor Company is spelled with a *t* for several reasons: when you write out the Japanese symbols for Toyota, the version with a *t* takes eight brushstrokes, which is a lucky number; it is visually simpler; and it includes a voiceless consonant rather than a voiced one, which seemed more pleasant to the ear. And the Toyoda family wanted to keep some distance between the family and the auto company.

6. Back in 1971, psychologist E. L. Deci summarized research demonstrating this counterintuitive negative effect of explicit rewards [E. L. Deci, "Effects of Externally Mediated Rewards on Intrinsic Motivation," *Journal of Personality and Social Psychology* 18 (1971): 105–115]. A more recent study looked at computer games. People in a control group just played the games and had fun, so they kept playing them. People in the experimental group were paid to play the games, and as soon as the payment stopped, they stopped playing the games [Brian Tietje, "When Do Rewards Have Enhancement Effects?" *Journal of Consumer Psychology* 12, no. 4 (2002): 363–373].

7. Jeffrey Liker and Michael Hoseus, *Toyota Culture* (New York: McGraw-Hill, 2008).

# Chapter 1

1. This story is abstracted from Akira Yokoi's unpublished memoirs, written several years before he passed away, entitled "Fighting the Three River Kings: Project Files of Indonesia, Australia, and Europe."

2. C. K. Prahalad, *The Fortune at the Bottom of the Pyramid* (New York: Pearson Prentice Hall, 2009).

3. Jeffrey Liker and Timothy Ogden, *Toyota under Fire* (New York: McGraw-Hill, 2011).

4. The concepts in this section come from an internal Toyota document titled *The Toyota Way 2001*. It was created under the auspices of Fujio Cho and was the first document to lay out explicitly and in print the principles of the Toyota Way.

5. Jeffrey Liker and Michael Hoseus, *Toyota Culture* (New York: McGraw-Hill, 2008).
6. Liker and Ogden, *Toyota under Fire*.
7. Toyota had already successfully introduced TPS to TABC, a plant in southern California that made truck beds, but that was a much smaller and simpler operation.

## Chapter 2

1. This and the opening quote are from *The Doctrine of the Mean*, written by the grandson of Confucius, Zisi. The translation is from William Theodore De Bary et al., *Sources of Chinese Tradition*, vol. 1 2nd ed. (New York: Columbia University Press, 2000).
2. John H. Berthrong and Evelyn Nagai Berthrong, *Confucianism: A Short Introduction* (Oxford, U.K.: Oneworld Publications, 2000).
3. Malcolm Gladwell, *Outliers: The Story of Success* (New York: Little Brown, 2008).
4. Jeffrey Liker and Michael Hoseus, *Toyota Culture* (New York: McGraw-Hill, 2008).
5. Geoff Calvin, *Talent Is Overrated: What Really Separates World-Class Performers from Everybody Else* (New York: Portfolio, 2008).
6. Jeffrey Liker and David Meier, *Toyota Talent* (New York: McGraw-Hill, 2007).
7. Dori Digenti, *Zen Learning: A New Approach to Creating Multiskilled Workers*, Center for International Studies, Massachusetts Institute of Technology working paper MIT JP 96-29, 1996. Digenti analyzed the Zen approach to teaching in the context of Japanese culture and refers to it as "Zen learning."
8. Mike Rother, *Toyota Kata: Managing People for Improvement, Adaptiveness and Superior Results* (New York: McGraw-Hill, 2009).
9. A detailed description of the process of job instruction training can be found in Liker and Meier, *Toyota Talent*, and Calvin, *Talent Is Overrated*.
10. See, for example, Gladwell, *Outliers*, and Calvin, *Talent Is Overrated*.
11. H. Dreyfus and S. Dreyfus, *Mind Over Machine* (New York: Free Press, 1982).

12. We'll quickly note that those who think they can make suggestion systems work better by offering bigger and bigger payments for suggestions have it exactly wrong. From a Toyota perspective, larger payments take the focus away from self-development and put it on gaming the system for personal financial gain. Large payments are a way of making those who are self-serving rather than self-developing stand out.

13. Jeffrey Liker, *The Toyota Way* (New York: McGraw-Hill, 2004).

14. In a few cases, top government officials, such as from the Ministry of International Trade and Industry (MITI), have joined Toyota and the board of directors. Otherwise, the board members are executive vice presidents or above of Toyota who have spent their entire career with the company.

15. Liker and Meier, *Toyota Talent*.

16. James Morgan and Jeffrey Liker, T*he Toyota Product Development System* (New York: Productivity Press, 2006).

# Chapter 3

1. For an excellent treatment of the right way to use A3 reports to coach and develop people, see John Shook, *Managing to Learn* (Cambridge, Mass.: Lean Enterprise Institute, 2009).

2. Now it is the Toyota Production System Support Center, and in 2011 it became a not-for-profit center with half its efforts going to private companies, most with no business relationship with Toyota, and half to other not-for-profit institutions in health care, education, and charitable outreach.

3. In fact, even at the point of the recall crisis, Americans were not completely self-reliant—almost 25 years after NUMMI was established. One result of the recall crisis was the decision to speed up the process of regional self-reliance and place more Americans into the most senior leadership roles.

4. Robert Greenleaf, *The Power of Servant Leadership* (San Francisco: Berrett-Koehler, 1998).

# Chapter 4

1. Rensis Likert, *The Human Organization: Its Management and Value* (New York: McGraw-Hill, 1967).
2. Jeffrey Liker, *The Toyota Way* (New York: McGraw-Hill, 2004), pp. 188–191.
3. This service parts warehouse and most of Toyota in North America has become familiar with the concept of "situational leadership" as taught by Ken Blanchard [Ken Blanchard, Eunice Parisi-Carew, and Donald Carew, *The One Minute Manager Builds High Performing Teams* (New York: William Morrow, 2009)]. The right type of leadership needs to be used for the right situation. In the early stages of a new group, directive leadership is needed; as the group evolves, leadership becomes more supportive; and finally, mature groups can operate relatively autonomously.

# Chapter 5

1. Examples of forms that can be used for this purpose can be found in Thomas L. Jackson, Hoshin Kanri *for the Lean Enterprise* (New York: Productivity Press, 2006) and Pascale Dennis, *Getting the Right Things Done: A Leader's Guide for Planning and Execution* (Cambridge, Mass.: Lean Enterprise Institute, 2006).
2. And, of course, historically the board was almost entirely composed of Japanese men, something we expect to change in the future.
3. When Gary was executive vice president for North American manufacturing, he was the first American manufacturing executive to be a managing officer of Toyota Motor Corporation (TMC). Jim Press, the former president of Toyota Motor Sales North America, was the first American to become a member of the board of directors of TMC.
4. A detailed description of FMDS and how this is linked to *hoshin* planning at TMMK is contained in Chapter 15 of Jeffrey Liker and Michael Hoseus, *Toyota Culture* (New York: McGraw-Hill, 2008).
5. See for example, http://www.resourcesystemsconsulting.com/blog/archives/102.

# Chapter 6

1. Jeffrey Liker and Timothy Ogden, *Toyota under Fire* (New York: McGraw-Hill, 2011).
2. Covenants are typically financial indicators that are negotiated with lenders during bankruptcy. In Dana's case, for instance, one of the covenants stipulated that Dana would generate cash flow at least two times greater than interest payments on its outstanding debt. It was quickly apparent that with the recession, this would not be possible as quickly as the covenants required.
3. Jeffrey Liker and David Meier, *The Toyota Way Fieldbook* (New York: McGraw-Hill, 2006), Chapter 4.
4. The matrix organization in manufacturing is described in Jeffrey Liker and Michael Hoseus, *Toyota Culture* (New York: McGraw-Hill, 2008), and in product development in James Morgan and Jeffrey Liker, *The Toyota Product Development System* (New York: Productivity Press, 2006).
5. Liker and Ogden, *Toyota under Fire.*
6. Jeffrey Liker, *The Toyota Way* (New York: McGraw-Hill, 2004).
7. TSSC is the Toyota Production System Support Center, which was a spin-off from the Operations Management Consulting Division of Toyota in Japan. This was the group that helped Gary train TMMK managers, as we discussed in Chapter 3. The consultant that TSSC sent was Jamie Bonini, assistant general manager of TEMA, whom Gary had hired into TMMK while he was president there.
8. For a discussion of the role of the model line and the advantages of depth versus breadth in implementation, see Section Three of Jeffrey Liker and James Franz, T*he Toyota Way to Continuous Improvement* (New York: McGraw-Hill, 2011).

# Chapter 7

1. Mike Rother, *Toyota Kata: Managing People for Improvement, Adaptiveness and Superior Results* (New York: McGraw-Hill, 2009).

2. George Leonard, *Mastery: The Keys to Success and Long-Term Fulfillment* (New York: Penguin Books, 1991).
3. Robert J. Thomas, *Crucibles of Leadership: How to Learn from Experience to Become a Great Leader* (Cambridge, Mass.: Harvard Business School Press, 2008).
4. Daniel Pink, *Drive: The Surprising Truth about What Motivates Us* (New York: Riverhead Trade, 2011).
5. Edwin A. Locke and Gary P. Latham, *Goal Setting: A Motivational Technique That Works* (Englewood Cliffs, N.J.: Prentice-Hall Trade, 1984).
6. Jim Collins, *Good to Great: Why Some Companies Make the Leap . . . and Others Don't* (New York: HarperBusiness, 2001).
7. Stephen Covey, *The 7 Habits of Highly Effective People*, rev. ed. (Boston: Free Press, 2004).
8. Ken Blanchard, Eunice Parisi-Carew, and Donald Carew, *The One Minute Manager Builds High Performing Teams* (New York: William Morrow, 1991).
9. Peter Senge, *The Fifth Discipline: The Art and Practice of the Learning Organization*, rev. ed. (New York: Crown Business, 2006).
10. Chun-Chi Lin and Susumu Yamaguchi, "Japanese Folk Concept of *Mentsu*: An Indigenous Approach from Psychological Perspectives," in G. Zheng, K. Leung, and J. Adair (eds.), *Perspectives and Progress in Contemporary Cross-Cultural Psychology*, Selected Papers from the Seventeenth International Congress of the International Association for Cross-Cultural Psychology, online edition, 2004; http://ebooks.iaccp.org/xian/TOC.htm.
11. George S. Odiorne, *Management by Objectives: A System of Managerial Leadership* (New York: Pitman Pub., 1965).
12. H. Thomas Johnson, *Profit beyond Measure* (New York: Free Press, 2008).
13. Joe Murli, "Integrating Leader Standard Work with Visual Management Tools," pdf download from Lean Enterprise Institute, 2011; www.lean.org/downloads/lei_dec_9_visual_managment.pdf.
14. Jeffrey Liker and Timothy Ogden, *Toyota under Fire* (New York: McGraw-Hill, 2011).

15. This process of deepening and spreading is discussed at length in Chapter 18 of Jeffrey Liker and Michael Hoseus, *Toyota Culture* (New York: McGraw-Hill, 2008).

16. Rother, *Toyota Kata.*

17. Former chief of staff for President Obama; http://online.wsj.com/article/SB122721278056345271.html.

18. Jeffrey Liker and James Franz, *The Toyota Way to Continuous Improvement* (New York: McGraw-Hill, 2011). See Chapter 8 for an example of a vice president transforming pathology and laboratory medicine at Henry Ford Health System and Chapter 11 for an example of a vice president transforming an engineering organization at an automotive supplier.

# Acknowledgments

The genesis of this book began when Jeff presented a summary of *The Toyota Way* in 2004 at Toyota headquarters in Erlanger, Kentucky, with Gary in attendance. Gary came up to Jeff after the session, praised Jeff for the book, and said: "I will be retiring in three years and would like to write a book about what I have learned in my career at NUMMI and Toyota. Would you consider writing it with me?" Jeff was honored, but skeptical, given how many great ideas lead to no action, but almost to the day three years later, Gary contacted Jeff to say: "I am starting my three-year retirement as senior advisor on a partial appointment. Do you still want to do the book?" And here we are.

Of course, the big question was: What should the book be about? Should it be like an autobiography and chronicle how Gary learned to become a Toyota leader over time, telling his story like that of some retired CEOs, filled with wise observations? Should it be a sociohistorical analysis of Toyota over a 25-year period starting with the launch of NUMMI? Should it be a combination? To be honest, it was Jeff's son Jesse who tipped the scales. He had read the first draft of the introductory chapter, making detailed (mostly negative) comments, and about 20 pages into the book wrote: "Hallelujah! I can't believe it. Finally something about leadership! I am so excited! I am actually learning something besides the history of Toyota. I want more of this!" Following Jesse's gentle suggestion that the book should "teach something useful" (fun kid to live with), we decided to focus the book on leadership.

When we asked a lot of whys, it was clear to both of us that leadership, or the lack thereof, was the main root cause of the failure of so many companies that have tried to copy Toyota's management system, and the reason that Toyota has been so resilient and adaptable over so many decades. This shifted our thinking about the book and the interviews we needed to conduct. Leadership and leadership development became the focus of interviews in Toyota plants and offices. Then Gary, a board member, became the CEO of Dana, a struggling American auto supplier emerging from Chapter 11. The experience of working with a team who turned around the company through their leadership, the exceptional people they recruited, and some very painful decisions about who could and could not develop into effective leaders provided a totally different view on developing people who can lead a company, plant, or work group to operational excellence.

Our focus on operational excellence comes from a simple idea that seems to fly in the face of most stock market analysts: a valuable company should be great at what it does at every level and across the organization! Simply making transactional decisions about what businesses to buy or sell, what product lines to invest in, how many people should be hired or fired, what part of operations should be outsourced to low-wage countries, and who should be the next superstar CEO is not enough for greatness. Excellence has to permeate every part of the organization, penetrating the very culture of the organization.

However, operational excellence needs to be linked to a strategy. How to do this is what Gary learned from Toyota and what we want to share. In doing so, we are drawing on the collective wisdom of countless people who have taught and mentored us, been examples to learn from, challenged us to think at the very times we believed we were quite expert, and more than anything inspired us. We will list some of those people here to thank them for all of their life lessons, but unfortunately, we will miss so many more. For every example we give in the book of someone doing a remarkable job of leading, there are thousands of other examples we could have used.

First, there are those people who had a profound influence on the training of Gary to think in the Toyota Way, many of whom also taught Jeff about the deep philosophy underlying Toyota's management system, are

- Dr. Shoichiro Toyoda, former president and at this time honorary chairman of TMC. His vision and confidence in Toyota's future was the driving force behind Toyota's exceptionally successful global expansion, starting with NUMMI in 1984. Dr. Toyoda's leadership over the last 30 years has had the greatest influence of any one single leader in the company and continues to ensure that future leaders deeply understand and manage the Toyota Way.
- Eiji Toyoda, former president and honorary chairman. It can be honestly said that the NUMMI joint venture with GM would never have been possible without Ejii's full support and commitment. The success of NUMMI gave Toyota the understanding and confidence to move forward in North America on its own. Toyota invested billions of dollars in America and Canada, providing local people with thousands of excellent jobs, and becoming true partners with local communities.
- Tatsuro Toyoda, former Toyota Motor Corporation (TMC) president and senior advisor. Tatsuro personally led the NUMMI team as its first president, illustrating the importance Toyota placed on the success of NUMMI. Coming from a man of such high stature, his personal charisma and warm-heartedness won the support from everyone involved at NUMMI.
- Fujio Cho, former president and later chairman of TMC. A disciple of Taiichi Ono and a Toyota Production System expert, his warm and patient leadership won over thousands of Kentucky people as Toyota began its expansion into North America at Georgetown, Kentucky.
- Kaneyoshi Kusunoki, former TMC EVP in charge of global engineering and manufacturing. His deep technical knowledge of Toyota's manufacturing processes and equipment, combined

with remarkable vision, guided Toyota's strategic investments as it expanded outside Japan.

- Kosuke Ikebuchi, former TMC EVP of global manufacturing and logistics and vice chairman and leader of the NUMMI start-up team (another disciple of Taiichi Ono). He taught Gary the true meaning of Toyota Way leadership.

- Toshiaki "Tag" Taguchi, former president and CEO of Toyota North America. Tag's sincere, polished, and likable personality provided the kind of leadership in North America where hundreds of supporters inside and outside the company embraced Toyota's joining the American mainstream.

- Takeshi Uchiyamada, TMC EVP and the chief engineer of the original Prius. He demonstrated how Toyota engineers continuously strive to improve transportation technology for the future. Through his leadership, the Prius hybrid technology has become the most important environmentally friendly drive system of this century.

- Atsushi "Art" Niimi, TMC EVP in charge of global manufacturing and purchasing. Art taught Gary the importance of global strategic planning and alignment of all related functions to achieve Toyota's Global Vision 2010 in North America.

- Yoshimi "Yoshi" Inaba, president of Toyota North America and chairman and CEO of Toyota Motor Sales. While providing great leadership to Toyota Motor Sales in North America, Yoshi earned the respect and admiration of Toyota dealers, and later, in New York and Washington, D.C., became the face of Toyota to investors, analysts, and Washington politicians.

- Réal "Ray" Tanguay, EVP of Toyota Motor Engineering and Manufacturing America, SVP of Toyota Motor North America, and the first Canadian to become senior managing director of TMC. A strong leader who applied innovative social and technical solutions to manufacturing, Ray partnered with Gary for more than 20 years to help grow Toyota's North American manufacturing capacity to produce over 2 million high-quality vehicles per year. As head of Toyota Motor Manufacturing Canada (TMMC), Ray's leadership was critical to Toyota's decision to produce the Lexus in TMMC (the only place Lexus is produced today outside Japan).

- Steve St. Angelo, EVP of Toyota Motor Engineering and Manufacturing, and chief quality officer for the North American Quality Task Force. More than any of the hundreds of General Motors executives who worked in NUMMI, Steve internalized the Toyota Way and went on to become the senior American manufacturing leader and quality chief in North America.
- Bill Childs, former NUMMI VP of administration and human resources. Bill skillfully applied the Toyota Way to successfully manage human resources with all employees and truly partner with UAW representatives, which smoothed the way for NUMMI to become a leader in General Motors in productivity and quality soon after its launch.
- Dennis Cuneo, former senior VP, Toyota Motor North America (a lawyer who learned TPS deeply). Dennis shared his fount of experience at NUMMI and beyond, and he was instrumental in hiring Gary as general manager of NUMMI.
- Jesse Wingard, former NUMMI president and director of manufacturing. Gary's first recruit to join him at NUMMI, Jesse continuously demonstrated his extraordinary leadership and personally set the example for so many to follow.
- Gary Twisselman, former NUMMI director of manufacturing. As an outstanding ex-Ford engineer with deep experience in process engineering and maintenance, Gary was the inspirational leader who set the standard for NUMMI engineers, and whose hands-on involvement with the maintenance staff kept NUMMI's complex equipment running at a level rare in North America.
- Beth Nunez, former NUMMI administrative support for Gary and Jesse. As every executive in business knows, you cannot underestimate how important it is to have great support so you can focus on the job at hand; thankfully, for 14 years Beth was that indispensable person.
- Masamoto "Matt" Amezawa, former president and chairman of Toyota Motor Manufacturing Kentucky (TMMK). Matt mentored Gary during his first few years at TMMK after he left

NUMMI to become EVP there, and later president. Through his deep personal knowledge of the Toyota Production System, Gary was immersed in hands-on learning as they developed the managers' capabilities on the shop floor of many Toyota suppliers and within TMMK.

- Pete Gritton, former TMMK VP of administration and human resources. Pete demonstrated through daily actions how important good two-way communications, fairness, and transparency are in earning the trust of the workforce.

- Cheryl Jones, former TMMK VP of manufacturing. Cheryl never met a challenge she could not overcome. Less than 100 pounds soaking wet, Cheryl joined Toyota following several years working in a local grocery. Through her amazing capability and leadership, she mastered every challenge given her, and ultimately became the top female executive in Toyota Manufacturing North America.

- Don Jackson, former TMMK VP of manufacturing. Having developed strong problem-solving and project management skills in Quality Control, Don's leadership in managing some of Toyota's most challenging projects in TMMK was indispensable.

- Wil James, president of TMMK. Through more than 20 years of challenging roles and responsibilities, Wil's wonderful character and strong leadership made him an easy choice to become Toyota's first African American plant president.

- Pat D'Eramo, former TMMK VP of manufacturing. Pat, who joined Toyota following a very successful carrier in General Motors, met resistance as an "outsider" from many of the team members. His boundless energy, strong communication skills, honesty, and dedicated follow-up to fix problems quickly won their respect.

- Barry Sharpe, former general manager at TMMK. Ben, like Pat, came to Toyota from Ford and earned his way into the community through serious self-development, leading to his defining a standard for "servant leadership" at TMMK.

- Mark Reich, former general manager of TSSC. Mark provided key insights on *hoshin kanri*.

- Latondra Newton, vice president of strategic planning and diversity, Toyota Motor North America, provided great insight on on-the-job development at Toyota.
- Vahid Javid (V.J.), engineering technical specialist at TMMK. V.J. demonstrated the power of self-development and developing others as he shifted from a "technical specialist" to a leader of work groups, bringing world-class levels of innovation to the body shop at TMMK.
- Yuri Rodriguez, former manager of quality at TMMK. Yuri progressively built up his abilities to lead *kaizen* to one of the highest levels in the plant.
- Jacky Ammerman, former assistant to the president of TMMK. A "down home" country girl who started as a production team member on the shop floor, Jacky developed her skills to become one of Gary's valued supporters. Gary feels so fortunate she picked him to work with!

Second, there is a long list of people from Dana Corporation who have played critical roles in helping that great American company turn around from a near-death experience to a company on the road to a healthy future built on a foundation of operational excellence. Gary would like to thank everyone personally, but here are a few of the key individuals:

- John Devine, former chairman, Dana Holding Corp. As an ex-Ford CFO and vice chairman of GM, with a strong network of industry top management and deep business savvy, John was the perfect partner to provide Gary the flexibility as CEO to focus on rebuilding Dana's global manufacturing foundation based on his experience with Toyota.
- Robert Marcin, former Dana chief administration officer and head of human relations. Bob provided the seasoned leadership needed as the Great Recession forced significant restructuring and downsizing at a pace never anticipated.

- James Yost, Dana EVP and CFO. James led the challenge of rebuilding the global finance organization, renegotiating Dana's covenants, and building positive relations with financial investors and analysts to help them to understand the true value of Dana.

- Jacqui Dedo, Dana VP of purchasing, strategic planning, and business development. Jacqui's leadership in quickly organizing Dana's complex global organizations in purchasing and business development was essential to support the urgent improvements needed. In addition, she frequently reached out to communicate and build support for Dana through her vast network in the auto industry.

- Martin Bryant, former Dana president of light business. Marty was Gary's most important recruit into Dana. A former Toyota executive, his brilliance as a leader grew brighter with the ever-expanding businesses he was asked to run. As president of the frame business, he improved performance so well that it added millions of valuation when it was sold. Dana consolidated six businesses into two, and at each step, when John Devine asked who could run them, the answer was the same: Marty Bryant.

- Mark Wallace, Dana president of drive line, after market, and global operations. When Marty Bryant recommended hiring Mark Wallace (Marty's ex-boss) to run global operations, saying, "Mark is twice as capable as me," Gary was skeptical. However, as this dynamic duo frequently proved, they were *both* extraordinary leaders who were comfortable from the shop floor to the boardroom.

- George Constand, Dana chief technical officer. When looking for the leader who could take on the difficult job of consolidating and streamlining Dana's various design and engineering centers, while also developing new technology to meet customers needs, Dana was so fortunate to have George already in the company.

- Marc Levin, Dana general counsel. As the only leader on the executive committee with extensive years of experience working for Dana, Marc's deep understanding and sound judgment made him an invaluable asset as Dana navigated through the churning waters while exiting Chapter 11 and beyond.

- Brandt McKee, Centerbridge executive. Centerbridge's large financial investment in Dana was significantly strengthened when it "loaned" Brandt to work full time with the Dana operations team. His exceptional leadership to assist operational excellence development and implementation throughout 113 plants in 26 countries was vital to rebuilding Dana.

- Dave Gibson, VP of operational excellence, an ex-Toyota executive and expert at applying TPS on the shop floor. David's method of teaching Dana's global operations leaders to "learn by doing" was so effective that the team saved hundreds of millions of dollars in operating costs and inventory.

- Ed Kopkowski, VP of operational excellence. After decades of experience in traditional American companies leading Lean Six Sigma programs and various operations, Ed continued his self-development to lead the structuring and training of the Dana Operating System in the Toyota Way.

- Sandy Miller, Dana administrative assistant to the CEO. Gary never met a more competent, personable, and efficient assistant. Everyone in Dana asked Sandy to take on more and more work, and she always handled it like the true professional she is.

There are certain individuals who had a special relationship to each of us and to this book. Akio Toyoda, president of Toyota Motor Corporation, has continuously demonstrated his commitment to developing leaders to manage the Toyota Way. When they were at NUMMI together, he taught Gary that the most important people are always those at the *gemba* (where the work is done). He graciously agreed to write the foreword to this book. Most important, he has taken Toyota through some of the most difficult times in its history with humbleness and a deep commitment to the basics of the Toyota Way. It runs in his blood!

Tim Ogden and Laura Starita were our editors, but they were much more than that. Like the expression, "taking a tiger by the tail," we had no idea what we were getting when Sona Partners were recommended to us. We thought we were hiring editors to do our bidding and make sentences flow, and they became our harshest critics, questioning every assumption, and ultimately turning complex writing that hindered the message to smooth prose, adding their own concepts to explain "what we really meant to say." Michael Balle and Karen Marten, both authors of books on lean, also provided invaluable editorial help.

We must thank all the people who ever worked at NUMMI. This is where Gary cut his teeth and learned the fundamentals of Toyota leadership and where Toyota learned to develop its unique culture in America. They set the standard for thousands of organizations that toured the plant with wide eyes, seeing a truly engaged workforce, and helped General Motors transform its own operations to ever higher levels of excellence. As we were writing the book, in the midst of the Great Recession, General Motors pulled out of NUMMI, and then Toyota decided to stop producing vehicles at the plant. It was a tragic day in the history of lean manufacturing. Fortunately, like a great oak tree that produces a seedling, NUMMI was occupied by Tesla as it took over the site and will hopefully bring new levels of environmentally friendly vehicles to the world.

Last but not least, we were both blessed to have great families who love us, support us, inspire us, and put up with us. Deborah, Emma, and Jesse were always there to support Jeff. Deborah, Kolisa, Chad, Kevin, David, and Alicia were constantly supporting Gary as he juggled more than a full-time job and working on this book. Behind every book writer there is a family that is compensating for the loss of attention and contributions to daily living and helping to keep the writer sane.

# Index

# About the Authors

**Jeffrey K. Liker, Ph.D.** is Professor of Industrial and Operations Engineering at the University of Michigan and president of Liker Lean Advisors. He is author of the international best-seller, *The Toyota Way: 14 Management Principles from the World's Greatest Manufacturer* (McGraw-Hill, 2004; 26 languages, about 700,000 copies sold), and six other books about Toyota: with David Meier, *The Toyota Way Fieldbook*, McGraw-Hill, 2005; with Jim Morgan, *The Toyota Product Development System*, Productivity Press, 2006; with David Meier, *Toyota Talent: Developing Exceptional People the Toyota Way* (McGraw-Hill, 2007); and with Michael Hoseus, *Toyota Culture: The Heart and Soul of the Toyota Way* (McGraw-Hill, 2008).

His two most recent books, published by McGraw-Hill in 2011, are *The Toyota Way to Continuous Improvement* (with detailed case studies of transformation in different industries) and *Toyota under Fire: Lessons for Turning Crisis into Opportunity* (about how Toyota has adapted and is remaking itself through the recession and recall crisis). His articles and books have won nine Shingo Prizes for Research Excellence, and *The Toyota Way* also won the 2005 Institute of Industrial Engineers Book of the Year Award and 2007 Sloan Industry Studies Book of the Year.

Jeffrey Liker is a frequent keynote speaker and consultant. He has a B.S. in industrial engineering from Northeastern University and a Ph.D. in sociology from the University of Massachusetts.

**Gary L. Convis** is the former chief executive officer and board member of Dana Holding Corporation, a supplier to the global automotive, commercial vehicle, and off-highway markets. He later became special advisor to the CEO of Dana and speaks and consults to executives committed to transformation to operational excellence.

Mr. Convis spent more than four decades at Toyota, General Motors Corporation, and Ford Motor Company. In 1984 he was selected to manage the start-up of NUMMI. He became the first American president of Toyota's largest plant outside Japan, Toyota Motor Manufacturing, Kentucky (TMMK), in 2001. In 2003, he was the first American manufacturing executive appointed by Toyota Motor Corporation (TMC) to be a managing officer of TMC, as well as executive vice president of Toyota Motor Engineering and Manufacturing North America, Inc. Previously, he spent more than 20 years in various roles with GM and Ford Motor Company.

Mr. Convis is a board member of Cooper-Standard Automotive, Inc. and Compass Automotive Group, Inc. He holds a bachelor's degree in mathematics with a minor in physics from Michigan State University.

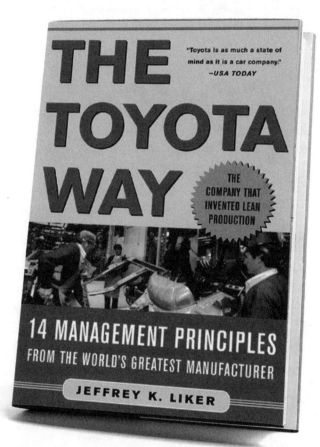

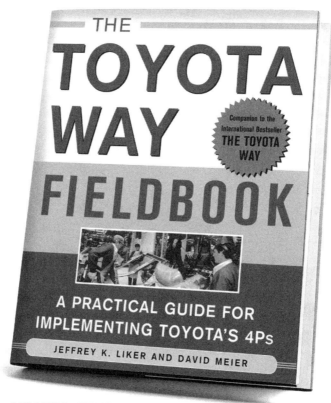

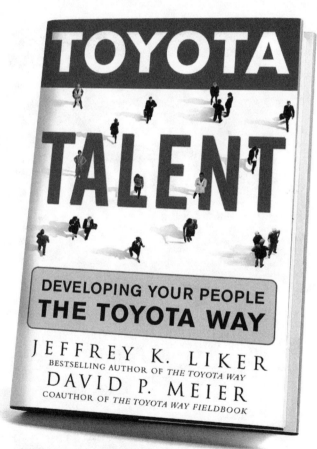

"I have found inspiration and lessons in these real stories from real people who find creative ways to succeed in adapting the principles of Deming and Toyota. You won't be able to put this book down."

—RICHARD ZARBO, MD, DMD, Senior Vice President and Chairman of Pathology and Laboratory Medicine, Henry Ford Health System

0071477462 • 9780071477468
e-Book: 0071762159 • 9780071762151
$28

www.mhprofessional.com
www.learnmore.mcgraw-hill.com

TOYOTA
LIKER

## Winner of the Shingo Prize for Research and Professional Publication, 2009

Make your business's culture the foundation for a total commitment to quality.

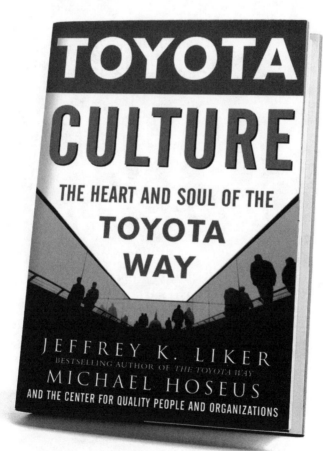

0071492178 • 9780071492171
e-book: 0071712577 • 9780071712576
$27.95

# Create a resilient organization that's engineered to overcome adversity.

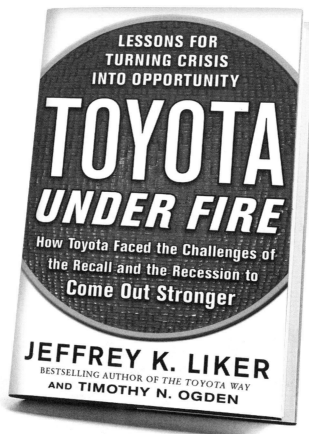

LESSONS FOR TURNING CRISIS INTO OPPORTUNITY

# TOYOTA UNDER FIRE

How Toyota Faced the Challenges of the Recall and the Recession to Come Out Stronger

JEFFREY K. LIKER
BESTSELLING AUTHOR OF *THE TOYOTA WAY*
AND TIMOTHY N. OGDEN

007176299X • 9780071762991
e-Book: 0071763074 • 9780071763073
$20